Shared Beliefs
in a Society

To all my close friends,
who are the source of my vitality.

Daniel Bar-Tal

Shared Beliefs
in a Society

Social

Psychological

Analysis

 Sage Publications, Inc.
International Educational and Professional Publisher
Thousand Oaks ▪ London ▪ New Delhi

For information:

Sage Publications, Inc.
2455 Teller Road
Thousand Oaks, California 91320
E-mail: order@sagepub.com

Sage Publications Ltd.
6 Bonhill Street
London EC2A 4PU
United Kingdom

Sage Publications India Pvt. Ltd.
M-32 Market
Greater Kailash I
New Delhi 110 048 India

Printed in the United States of America

Library of Congress Cataloging-in-Publication Data

Bar-Tal, Daniel.
     Shared beliefs in a society: Social psychological analysis /
by Daniel Bar-Tal.
          p.   cm.
     Includes bibliographical references and index.
     ISBN 0-7619-0658-4 (cloth: alk. paper)
     ISBN 0-7619-0659-2 (pbk.: alk. paper)
     1. Social perception.   2. Social perception—Israel.   3. Social
psychology.   4. Ethnopsychology.   5. National characteristics.
6. Social values.   7. Attitude (Psychology)   I. Title.
HM1041 .B37 2000
303.3'72—dc21   00-008359

This book is printed on acid-free paper.

00   01   02   03   04   05   06   7   6   5   4   3   2   1

Acquisition Editor:	Rolf Janke
Editorial Assistant:	Heidi Van Middlesworth
Production Editor:	Sanford Robinson
Editorial Assistant:	Victoria Cheng
Typesetter:	Lynn Miyata
Indexer:	Will Ragsdale
Cover Designer:	Michelle Lee

Contents

Preface

My work on the type of beliefs that are shared by societies began in the early 1980s, as I was changing my research interest from the study of helping behavior and attributions to the study of societal-political issues. This change came about because I, as a member of Israeli society, noticed what an effect commonly held beliefs had on all of us, on our own behaviors, and on the policies of our leaders. Specifically, it seemed to me that a society like the Israeli one, which is engaged in protracted and violent conflict, comes to be dominated by relatively stable beliefs that feed the continuation of the conflict and serve at the same time as obstacles to conflict resolution. This is what led me to start and elucidate some of the beliefs in the Israeli repertoire. The first paper that came out as a result of this new interest was on the beliefs encapsulated in the so-called Masada complex, which later I relabeled as beliefs about siege. Next, I moved on to conceptualize ideas about other widely shared beliefs concerning patriotism, conflict, delegitimization, and security. In my work on each of these beliefs, I tried to make the analyses relevant to a context beyond the particular Israeli experience. It seemed obvious to me that the beliefs I was studying were not unique to Israeli society but characterize and considerably affect other societies as well.

In the late 1980s, my preoccupation with shared beliefs led me to write the book, *Group Beliefs* (Bar-Tal, 1990a), which focused on those beliefs that define the identity of groups. The conceptual framework I developed there enabled the analysis of voluntary organizations or religious denominations but was less appropriate if I wanted to describe societies and nations. This was the case because the former have distinct beliefs that *define* their groupness, whereas it is frequently impossible to circumscribe whole societies or nations by reference to a number of particular beliefs. In the 1990s, in an attempt to find a solution to the difficulty of identifying beliefs held in common by entire societies/nations, I began to develop the concepts of societal beliefs and ethos. Having worked out this conception, I decided to summarize my work of the last 15 years about shared beliefs in societies under one conceptual framework. And so I found myself working on the present book.

This book can be seen as a contribution to societal psychology, a new emerging subfield of social psychology, which studies societies from a social psychological perspective. I would like the book to suggest, on the one hand, that social psychology has the potential of providing a unique perspective that can illuminate society's structures, its institutions, and its processes and functioning. On the other hand, I would also like to claim that social psychology can benefit greatly by integrating contributions of other social sciences into its own theorizing effort. Indeed, the book draws much from various disciplines of the social sciences and provides numerous historical, political, sociological, cultural, and educational examples taken from the lives of different societies. Nevertheless, as an Israeli, I could not but devote much space to examples drawn from my own society, a dynamic and conflict-torn society that does not provide the option of being an apathetic or passive observer. My writings, therefore, reflect a strong desire to try to make sense of the beliefs that underlie Israel's social-political course of action.

The theoretical chapters of the book (Chapters 1 to 4, 9, and 10) were originally written for the book. Chapters 5 to 8, which offer examples to illustrate the presented conceptual framework, were extensively rewritten on the basis of previously published articles, which I list below, together with my thanks to their publishers for allowing me to rewrite them:

Bar-Tal, D. (1990). Causes and consequences of delegitimization. *Journal of Social Issues, 46*(1), 65-81.

Bar-Tal, D. (1991). Contents and origins of the Israelis' beliefs about security. *International Journal of Group Tensions, 21,* 237-261.

Bar-Tal, D. (1993). Patriotism as fundamental beliefs of group members. *Politics and the Individual, 3,* 45-62.

Bar-Tal, D., & Antebi, D. (1992). Siege mentality in Israel. *International Journal of Intercultural Relations, 16,* 251-275.

The writing of this book was greatly facilitated by an invitation to spend 2 months as a Visiting Professor at the Department of Psychology of the University of Maryland in the United States during the summer of 1995, as well as 2 months as a Visiting Professor at the Department of Psychology of the University of Muenster, Germany, during the summer of 1997.

First, I would like to thank greatly the three reviewers of the first version of the book. Their thoughtful comments helped me to prepare the final draft of the book. Also, my heartfelt indebtedness goes to Alice Zilcha for her considerable help in the endless typing of the various versions of the manuscript, with the help of Annette Weil, and especially to Mirjam Hadar for her excellent editing, which helped me to clarify various ideas. Without their dedication, it would have been difficult for me to finish this book.

—Daniel Bar-Tal

Introduction

*There's a common Serb expression that could be the national motto—
"well, at least one of my neighbor's cows is dead." It's heard often
these days in this context: NATO may be bombing us and methodi-
cally destroying our bridges, our army, our fuel supplies, our minis-
tries. Our economy is ruined. We're forever shunned by Europe. Our
only friends are the Iraqis, the Chinese, the Greeks, the Russians. But
at least we put it to the Albanians, their cows are all dead. . . . What
accounts for the bile? First is a highly developed sense of victimization. Throughout the wars in Croatia and Bosnia, the Serbs, backed
by the powerful Yugoslav Army, insisted they were the underdog. . . .
The other critical element of the Serb psyche: inat, which means
"spite" but also includes the idea of revenge no matter what the cost.*

—Nordland, 1999, pp. 35-36

*Across China, people are struggling to redefine notions of success
and failure, right and wrong, good and evil. The quest for something
to believe in has become so universal and profound that it is one of
the unifying characteristics of life in China.*

—Pomfret, 1999, p. 1

These two excerpts illustrate a well-known social observation
that members of all human groups share beliefs. Sharing beliefs is an integral
part of group membership. Individuals, as members of different groups, hold
shared beliefs in their cognitive repertoire. Some of the shared beliefs serve
as a basis for group formation, provide meaning to their group membership,
and direct or justify many group actions. The present book focuses on the particular category of shared beliefs that are held in societies. I call these societal

beliefs and discuss them in detail throughout the chapters of the book. First, however, I would like to introduce the concept of *beliefs,* which is used as an object of sharing.

▨ BELIEFS

Beliefs, which are defined as propositions that express thoughts, are formed by human beings; their contents are of unlimited scope. Beliefs are basic units of knowledge categories such as ideology, values, norms, decisions, inferences, goals, expectations, religious dogmas, or justifications. They are stored in individuals' minds and are also expressed in various human products, such as books, newspapers, films, or even paintings. Although belief is not a popular concept for social psychologists, who prefer the term *cognition,* a number of psychologists use the word *belief* to represent a cognitive unit of the human repertoire (e.g., Bem, 1970; Fishbein & Ajzen, 1975; Kruglanski, 1989).

It is possible to differentiate between two types of beliefs, personal and common beliefs. The first type pertains to beliefs that are formed by individuals and are uniquely stored in their minds, constituting their private repertoire not shared with other people. The latter type is shared, and, as such, these beliefs are of interest for the present conceptual framework. But, even the first type of belief is not wholly unrelated to the social nature of beliefs, as individuals may share their personal beliefs with other people through, for instance, interpersonal communication or the various channels of mass communication. In these cases, personal beliefs may be adopted by other people and shared by them, becoming common beliefs.

Common beliefs can be shared by a few individuals, a small group, the members of a society, or even the majority of human beings. Common beliefs are usually acquired from external sources, except in cases when individuals form a belief or beliefs (personal beliefs) and subsequently communicate and disseminate it or them among other people. The dissemination of beliefs takes place through interpersonal communication networks or via societal mechanisms of communication. Moreover, certain societal institutions, such as the mass media or schools, are established to propagate common beliefs. Among the most salient categories of disseminated common beliefs are news information, religious dogmas, and scientific knowledge, which are types of common beliefs that are spread widely among people in different parts of the world.

The study of beliefs is carried out from micro and macro perspectives. The micro perspective focuses mostly on those beliefs, personal and common, that are stored by individuals; it elucidates their cognitive processes of formation and change, their structure and organization in the human mind, and the personal implications of their contents. Social psychology, being dominated by a social cognitive orientation, has played a major role in this endeavor, because it predominantly focuses on the individual's mental processes, structures, and products (Jones, 1985; Ostrom, 1984; Taylor, 1998). This orientation is based on the assumption that "constructs relevant to cognitive representation and process are fundamental to understanding all human responses, regardless of whether those responses are social or nonsocial in nature" (Ostrom, 1994, p. ix).

The macro perspective analyzes social units such as groups, societies, or nations, focusing on the beliefs shared by their members. It recognizes that common beliefs shared by members of the same group or society are prerequisites for the formation of the social system (see, e.g., Mannheim, 1952; Parsons, 1951) and common culture (see, e.g., Dougherty, 1985; Shweder & LeVine, 1984). Sociologists, anthropologists, and political scientists frequently use the concept *beliefs* or *belief system* in their political and social theory (e.g., Borhek & Curtis, 1975; Converse, 1964; Dougherty, 1985; Fiske, 1991; Harris, 1968; Lane, 1973; Merton, 1957; Parsons, 1951). These social scientists discuss those beliefs that are shared by society members and play a determining role in the explanation of societal structure and action. Sharing beliefs is a social necessity, because individuals who live in groups and societies must form a "shared communicative environment" to be able to communicate comprehensibly (Krauss & Fussell, 1991). Only in such an environment can the social functions of planning, coordination, influence, goal setting, and so on go forward.

Greenfeld (1992), the sociological historian, noted the importance of shared social reality by societies and nations. She suggested that

> Social reality is intrinsically cultural; it is necessarily a symbolic reality, created by the subjective meanings and perceptions of social actors. Every social order (that is, the overall *structure* of a society) represents a materialization, or objectivization, of its image shared by those who participate in it. It exists as much in the minds of people as in the outside world, and if it loses its grip on the minds of a sufficient power to impose it on others, it cannot be sustained and is bound to vanish from the outside world as well. (p. 18)

SOCIETAL BELIEFS AND ETHOS

The present book aims to deepen our understanding of the meaning of sharing beliefs by society members, taking the macro perspective within the social psychological framework. In trying to do this, the book focuses on particular types of shared beliefs, *societal beliefs,* defined as enduring beliefs shared by society members, with contents that are perceived by society members as characterizing their society. These beliefs allow a common view of the society and its concerns, facilitate communication among the society's members, and guide many societal behaviors. Of special importance are those societal beliefs that constitute the *ethos* of a society. *Ethos,* denoting the configuration of central societal beliefs, provides central characterization to the society and gives it a particular orientation. The present book suggests that the concepts of societal beliefs and ethos can contribute to the understanding of the basis that underlies society members' uniqueness and their functioning.

Societal Beliefs

Societal beliefs are collective ideas shared by society members. Their contents reflect concerns of society members with regard to life in a societal framework. Societal beliefs represent the social reality of society members regarding their societal life. They are the lenses through which society members look at their own society. These beliefs contribute to the sense of uniqueness of one society's members as distinct from members of other societies, and they allow a psychological connection between society members and their own society. They make an important contribution to the formation of social identity among society members by providing knowledge that society members share and to which they relate. Societal beliefs characterize the society as a whole, have meaning only on a societal level, and should be viewed as societal phenomenon.

Many members of the society hold a substantial number of societal beliefs in their cognitive repertoire. But, it is not important whether a given society member holds a particular societal belief, or even a set of societal beliefs. Each society member does not necessarily have to hold all the societal beliefs. Society members, or at least a significant majority of them, have to recognize the importance of societal beliefs, relate to them easily, and view them as the society's characteristics. In essence, societal beliefs exist independently of any particular society members, because not only are they stored in the cognitive repertoire of many society members, but they are also bound to appear in a variety of societal products. They are expressed through societal communication channels and are presented in societal institutions. They appear often on the societal agenda and in public debate, because they are related to many of the current issues with which the society copes. They thus exist as transcendent characteristics of the society, which are imparted to society members, who then again perpetuate them in their products.

The belief of Serbians in their victimhood, based on their collective memory of the Battle of Kosovo on June 28, 1389, is an example of a societal belief. This Serb societal belief refers to their defeat by Ottoman Turks, which led to the total occupation of Serbia by the Ottoman Empire. It implies to them their sacrifice on behalf of other European Christians, as the Serbs served as a buffer against the advancing Muslim Turks. These traumatized self-representations have sustained an identity of victimhood. To this day, Serbs use their belief about the battle as a way to express related beliefs about their helplessness and victimization (Volkan, 1996; Volkan & Itzkowitz, 1993).

Societal beliefs may concern relations with another country; thus, the Polish, Hungarian, and Czechoslovakian societies for several decades held a societal belief regarding their "occupation" by the Soviet Union (Dziewanowski, 1977; Krystufek, 1981; Shawcross, 1974). This was a central societal belief that deeply affected individual and collective life. There is little doubt that this societal belief shaped all the domains of life of Polish, Hungarian, and Czechoslovakian societies. It had potent affective and behavioral implications for many members of these societies.

Societal beliefs can also touch on particular concerns of a society. Thus, in Great Britain, a societal belief refers to the unemployment issue as characteristic of the British society (Metcalf & Richardson, 1986), whereas in the United States, there is a prevalent societal belief that the crime issue is typical of American society (Wilson & Hernstein, 1985). These beliefs preoccupy members of each society, are considered characteristic of a society, and have profound effects on societal life.

Ethos

In the present framework, as proposed, ethos reflects the totality of those societal beliefs that provide central features of a society. Ethos, thus, does not include all societal beliefs but only those that give the society its particular dominant characterization. Thus, no two societies have an identical ethos. The ethos of each society is unique, because the particular combination of central societal beliefs results in a particular whole. That is, although some societal beliefs may be found in a different societal ethos, the particular combination of central societal beliefs can be found only in one society. Potent factors such as a particular history and experiences, certain economic conditions and geographical characteristics, the population's composition, or the dominant political system of each society dictate the development of a unique set of societal beliefs that makes a society's ethos. Therefore, any attempt to understand the ethos of a society requires an analysis of the particular societal beliefs that compose it.

For example, the Irish ethos is based on at least three themes of societal beliefs—Catholicism, origin of Gaelic culture, and separatism, which refers to the goal of establishing a separate independent state over all Ireland (Boyce, 1995). The Cuban ethos is based on a combination of societal beliefs expressing Marxism-Leninism, together with societal beliefs of Cuban nationalism (Medin, 1990).

SOCIETY AS A UNIT OF ANALYSIS

The present book focuses on a society—a general concept that is used to denote a large stable social system, with boundaries that differentiate it from other societies. A society consists of a real collective of people who have a clear sense of common identity. These social collectives endure, evolving a tradition, culture, collective memory, belief systems, social structures, and institutions (Griswold, 1994). These binding and integrating elements unite differing groups into one society (Hoebel, 1960). Individuals who have a sense of being society members experience solidarity and a sense of unity. They establish, in essence, a common social identity. In Giddens's (1984) terms, societies are

> social systems which "stand out" in bas-relief from a background of a range of other systemic relationships in which they are embedded. They stand out because definite structural principles serve to produce a specifiable overall "clustering of institutions" across time and space. (p. 164)

In addition, Giddens suggested an association between social systems and a specific territory, with societies making claims to the legitimate occupation of the territory. In our times, the term *society* is often used to describe "national societies" that "embody a quality of nationality, with their own national culture, their own more self-contained than 'unself-contained' economic system, their own system of government, with their own genetic self-reproduction and their own sovereignty over a bounded territory" (Shils, 1972, p. 56).

National societies are very meaningful units of belonging in the modern age. Although individuals belong to various groups, their membership in a national society provides in many cases an important, if not the most important, basis for social identity. Moreover, much of individuals' beliefs and attitudes are acquired in their role as national society members. In this light, many examples provided in this book will focus on national societies.

However, although the national society is a central unit in our times, there are other societies as well, which may have their basis in ethnicity, ideological convictions, religion, regionality, socioeconomic status, or race. Thus, according to the present approach, a state may have many more than one national society. The boundaries of a society are determined by the criteria of forming a common identity, sense of solidarity, collective memory, social structure, institutions, and beliefs system.

Of special importance is the observation that "society is thus the creation of its members; the product of their construction of meaning, and of the action and relationships through which they attempt to impose meanings on their historical situation" (Dawe, 1970, p. 214). Society in its basic form is a collection of individuals who consider themselves to be society members. They provide the real meaning to the society by constructing beliefs that shape their reality as society members. This is the basic function of societal beliefs, which play a fundamental role in this construction. Societal beliefs supply the cognitive framing that serves as one of the essential foundations of a society. It is, thus, unfortunate that social psychology limits its scope of studies, restricting its boundaries to the examination of small groups only, with a few exceptional attempts to study societies (e.g., Billig, 1982; Himmelweit & Gaskell, 1990; McClelland, 1961; Reykowski, 1995; Staub, 1989). Social psychology, as part of the social sciences, has much to contribute to the understanding of large social systems by using the particular psychological perspective of analysis. The accumulated knowledge about beliefs, attitudes, and values, their formation, acquisition, dissemination, and change, could shed light on various societal processes and contents of societal beliefs. The present book attempts to achieve these goals. It uses social psychological knowledge, together with knowledge of other social sciences, to provide a conceptual framework for analyzing societies.

STRUCTURE OF THE BOOK

This book describes and analyzes in detail two key concepts—societal beliefs and ethos. However, before turning to them, two chapters provide a background for the focal discussions. Chapter 1 elaborates on the social meaning of sharing beliefs in groups, because sharing is a basic social phenomenon that underlies the essence of societal beliefs. This chapter presents a new model that delineates the consequences of sharing beliefs for individuals and groups alike. Chapter 2 reviews the past social psychological contribution to the study of sharing beliefs and its current state-of-the-art. First, works of the early social psychologists, Durkheim and McDougall, are reviewed. Then, seminal contributions of the founding fathers of modern social psychology are presented, and finally, present works on sharing beliefs are described.

Chapter 3 analyzes the nature of societal beliefs. It points to the uniqueness of the concept and its contribution to the understanding of societal functioning. Also, it analyzes the main characteristics of societal beliefs and their main functions for society members. After introducing the conceptual framework of societal beliefs and providing examples of their contents, Chapter 4 discusses the formation, dissemination, maintenance, and change of societal beliefs. Specifically, this chapter describes how societal beliefs are formed on the basis of meaningful collective experiences, which are relevant to the whole society. It, then, outlines how the formed beliefs are transmitted to society members via various channels of communication available in the society and acquired by them through negotiation. The chapter also describes methods of conservation, socialization, and acculturation, which all contribute to the maintenance of societal beliefs. Finally, it points to the factors that influence a change of their contents.

The next four chapters (Chapters 5, 6, 7, and 8) provide particular examples of themes in societal beliefs. Chapter 5 presents societal beliefs of patriotism; Chapter 6 describes societal beliefs of security; Chapter 7 depicts societal beliefs of a siege mentality; and Chapter 8 elucidates societal beliefs of delegitimization. Each chapter analyzes the contents of particular beliefs, their experiential origins, their functions, and their consequences for the society. Each analysis is accompanied by examples taken from different societies.

After comprehensive discussion of societal beliefs, the presentation of the ethos concept is expanded in Chapter 9. This chapter provides a conceptual framework for the ethos and presents two extensive illustrations. It analyzes the capitalistic and democratic American ethos and the conflictual ethos of the Jewish society in Israel. Both analyses also present methods for studying societal beliefs of ethos.

Finally, Chapter 10 summarizes the basic premises proposed by the present volume and locates them within the framework of the subdiscipline of societal psychology. It proposes that although the mainstream of social psychology, with its individualistic orientation, does not fulfill the promise of the founding fathers of social psychology, there is still promise in the development of societal psychology. Societal psychology, as an addition to social psychology, recognizes that individuals are society members, and their membership plays a determinative role in their lives: Societies are constructed by individuals who function in them and influence them, and these people themselves are products of the societal systems. Psychology, thus, cannot disregard this crucial interrelationship and, therefore, also has to study social behavior in a society.

1

Sharing Beliefs in Groups

THE SOCIAL NATURE OF BELIEFS

In contrast to the terms *cognitions* or *schemas,* which originally were formed by psychologists to describe individuals' mental structures, the concepts *belief* and *knowledge,* as used by social scientists, also denote ideas and opinions commonly held by communities, societies, or cultures (Bar-Tal & Kruglanski, 1988). In using the term beliefs, social scientists refer to their social nature.

The social nature of shared beliefs is well reflected in the way they are formed. Shared beliefs, which pertain to the realm of sociopolitical contents such as societal beliefs, may be viewed as socially constructed to a large extent. That means these beliefs are formed through social processes in social situations in which sociocultural meanings are established (see Berger & Luckmann, 1967; Burr, 1995; Gergen, 1994). These processes range from negotiation to unchallenged acceptance (Gergen, 1985; Resnick, 1991). The negotiation process indicates that society members, through interaction, come to construct knowledge on which they agree, whereas unchallenged acceptance indicates passive acquisition of beliefs from external sources, which are usually perceived as knowledge authorities. However, in both cases, individuals actively interpret the information. They process the acquired information and ascribe meaning to it on the basis of their own stored knowledge.

Once beliefs are formed, they are communicated. Individuals talk about them, write about them, or express them in other ways, such as paintings, sculptures, or even dance. Being communicated is an important feature of beliefs as social expression and social product. People spend many hours daily expressing their beliefs and absorbing the beliefs of others. Most individuals communicate their beliefs in an interpersonal context, usually to acquaintances. Whereas few have the opportunity to reach wide audiences by lecturing, giving speeches, or using the mass media such as television, radio, or newspapers, a much larger number "consume" beliefs via these various channels.

The fact that beliefs are communicated has at least three implications. First, beliefs are accumulated through years of human experience. Many beliefs are perpetualized via various means and are added to the vast repertoire of civilization. Second, beliefs are transmitted from generation to generation. Millennia ago, before human beings found ways to write down their ideas, beliefs were transmitted orally; later, handwriting, print, and electronic means allowed the consistent and continuous transmission of beliefs, especially in large groups. Third, many beliefs are shared by different populations and groups.

The last implication of sharing brings us back to the social characteristic of beliefs with which this analysis began. I propose that sharing beliefs is a social phenomenon with special social consequences. This phenomenon and especially its consequences are the focus of this chapter, which presents a conceptual model of sharing beliefs.

SHARING BELIEFS IN GROUPS

Beliefs are shared by people, a feature that plays a crucial role in their social meaning. Of special significance are those beliefs that are shared by a defined collective, such as a group, a society, or a nation. In fact, the sharing of beliefs by a group or a society, which differentiates it from other groups or societies, was considered by McGuire (1986) to be an important implication of the term *social,* added to cognition by social psychologists. In his view,

> If one was forced to choose the one meaning that best catches current polemical usages (of social), it would be the "shared" property, distinguishing representations shared within a culture from those of which there are pronounced individual differences among the members of a society. (p. 103)

Through these shared beliefs, collective members understand communications exchanged with others in interpersonal interaction, as well as the communications transmitted via societal channels. Shared beliefs also facilitate planning coordinated actions and carrying them out. The present work assumes that a group or society in which beliefs are shared serves as a positive reference group for its members. That is, the present conception of sharing applies to cases in which the society provides the desirable standards that society members use for evaluating themselves and others (Kelley, 1968). It means that they aspire to be members of this society and relate to it psychologically (Sherif & Sherif, 1964). The sharing of beliefs by members of such groups or societies has special social implications.

In one of the few psychological contributions to the understanding of shared cognitions, Cole (1991) identified two contrasting approaches. One approach, based on mainstream psychology, views cognition as unique to individuals, who process information in their mind. According to this approach, individuals may share cognitions, but what is important is their individual repertoire: Sharing beliefs does not have any special meaning. A very different approach regards cognition as being part of culture. Individuals who are members of the same culture share part of their knowledge, so that human cognition is a result of interaction among individuals and of social and cultural processes. The first approach, with its focus on individual processes in the study of cognition (i.e., beliefs), limits the picture of human cognition.

The second approach is also the view taken in this book: That is, the phenomenon of sharing beliefs cannot be studied merely as an individual's repertoire of beliefs. The observed existence of shared beliefs, and in our case, societal beliefs, implies the existence of a collective that shares the beliefs and of societal mechanisms that disseminate them, as well as the special functions and consequences that these beliefs have for the individuals as society members and for the whole society. It is thus essential to extend the study of beliefs to the nature of their sharing, because doing so not only sheds light on the nature of beliefs but also illuminates the nature of the collective and its functioning. If we want to consider the phenomenon of sharing beliefs, this requires knowledge of what kind of beliefs are shared, how many members of the group in question share the beliefs, and how these beliefs are held by them. The latter question refers to the confidence in a shared belief, its centrality for society members, and its interrelationship with other shared beliefs. We also ought to know how group members, as a collective, express their shared beliefs. Finally, sharing beliefs has important implications for the group. It is a powerful mechanism that has determining influences on the life of a group. Thus, an important part of studying sharing has to focus on its consequences.

The first question we should ask is what *sharing* actually entails. Sharing beliefs implies that at least some members of a group hold in their mental repertoire the same belief or beliefs and are aware of this sharing. Thus, if shared beliefs are identified only by an observer, this is not sufficient for considering these beliefs to be a meaningful social phenomenon; awareness of the sharing is important. In principle, group or society members can share a belief without being aware that they share it. In such a case, the belief in question has no special social significance. There is an important difference for the group or society between the cases when a belief is held by few members or even by all of them but they are not aware of sharing this belief and cases when a belief is held by all the members or a portion of them and they are aware of this sharing. The awareness of sharing beliefs turns sharing into a powerful psychological mechanism that has crucial effects on a group or a society. Shared beliefs are known to have important cognitive, affective, and behavioral consequences, both for group members as individuals and for the group as a whole, especially when their content concerns themes related to the group's life. Specifically, then, these shared beliefs may influence the nature of social reality that group members construct, the sense of solidarity and unity that they experience, the intensity and involvement of group members with these beliefs, the conformity expected from group members, the pressure exerted on leaders, and the direction of action taken by the group.

The awareness of sharing beliefs is derived from membership in a particular group (Krauss & Fussell, 1991): Members of a group are exposed to beliefs that are widespread, available, and disseminated to them (e.g., Clark & Marshall, 1981; Krauss & Fussell, 1991). Most group members can identify the shared beliefs, because they are public, and as such, they not only are stored in members' minds but are often communicated in channels of communication and perpetuated.

SOCIAL IDENTITY AND SHARING BELIEFS

A social psychological theory of self-categorization, proposed by Turner and his colleagues (Turner, 1991, 1999; Turner, Hogg, Oakes, Reicher, & Wetherell, 1987), is especially relevant for discussing the relationship between group members, social identity, and sharing beliefs in a group. The theory is based on Tajfel's social identity theory, which proposed that individuals form social identity by being psychologically connected to social groups through their self-definition as members of social categories. According to Tajfel, this categorization process, with its emotional and psychological implications, is meaningful for intergroup relations because he assumed that people are motivated to maintain positive self-evaluation through differentiation between ingroups and outgroups (Tajfel, 1978, 1981; Tajfel & Turner, 1986). Self-categorization theory extends this elaboration and provides further explanation of individuals' self-definition as group members and of the antecedents and consequences of psychological group formation.

The theory postulates that through the basic cognitive process of self-categorization, people define themselves in terms of a shared social category, for example, men, Moslems, Italians, or lawyers. This self-categorization leads to perceptual accentuation of intragroup similarities and intergroup differences on relevant correlated dimensions. That is, when people stereotype themselves and others in terms of salient social categorization, they enhance perceptual identity between self and ingroup members, on the one hand, and enhance perceptual contrast between ingroup and outgroup members, on the other hand. For example, when Palestinians focus on their group, they perceive themselves as being similar to their group members and different from other groups, such as Israeli Jews, Syrians, or Egyptians. In this process, individuals transform themselves into a collective, which is based on shared conceptions of social identity. The more accessible the particular shared conception of social identity, the more individuals depersonalize their self-perception and view themselves as group members.

The fundamental principle that follows from self-categorization theory is that psychological group formation is the basis for sharing beliefs. Sharing beliefs is one of the basic elements for the expression of common social identity, because beliefs with particular contents prototypically define a group. Defining themselves as group members, individuals adopt these beliefs as part of their social identity. Sharing these beliefs provides group members with validated information about reality. Group members, therefore, engage in rational cognitive activity in a quest for social validation of their beliefs, as part of their attempt to share beliefs with other members of their group. This is a process of depersonalization in which group members transform their beliefs so they are governed by ingroup prototype and not by their distinct biographical experiences. Furthermore, the theory posits that shared social identity produces shared expectation of agreement between ingroup members. When there is disagreement within the group about beliefs that are supposed to be consensual, subjective uncertainty arises. In this situation, group members exert social influence and, through persuasion and negotiation, try to establish consensus.

The theory instigated much experimental research in laboratories, which validated its premises (see, e.g., reviews by Haslam, Oakes, Turner, & McGarty, 1996; Haslam, Turner, Oakes, McGarty, & Reynolds, 1998; Hogg & Mullin, 1999; Terry, Hogg, & Duck, 1999). The studies provide unequivocal evidence affirming the importance of shared beliefs for group members in the construction of their social identity. But, going beyond social identity, shared beliefs also have special significance for group members functioning as individuals and for the group as a whole. Unfortunately, there is little conceptual empirical work on the effects of sharing beliefs. Thus, to describe systematically the possible impacts of sharing beliefs, a conceptual model is presented.

▓ CONSEQUENCES OF SHARING BELIEFS IN A GROUP: A MODEL

The awareness of sharing beliefs related to a group's life has serious consequences for group members and for the group itself. The delineated model in Figure 1.1 specifies these consequences, as well as antecedent variables. It provides a conceptual framework for analyzing the phenomenon of sharing beliefs in a group. This model is supported by empirical evidence from studies that examined some of the variables presented. Not all the studies were directly involved with the effects of sharing beliefs. Some had other objectives but manipulated the sharing of beliefs, and this allowed the author to observe its effects on individuals and groups (including societies).

The model suggests that awareness of the fact that a group shares beliefs evokes two immediate reactions: confidence in these beliefs and a sense of similarity. These reactions, viewed as mediating variables, lead to various consequences on an individual and group level. Also, these consequences, as mediated by senses of confidence and similarity, are influenced by an array of factors that the present model refers to as antecedent factors. This model will now be described in detail.

Mediating Variables

Confidence. Social psychologists have long understood that the awareness of shared beliefs is fundamental in the construction of social reality (e.g., Asch, 1952; Festinger, 1954; Mead, 1956; Sherif, 1936). Individuals feel more confidence in knowledge that they know is shared by their group members. Awareness of the sharedness of beliefs validates their contents and increases the sense of knowing. Festinger (1950) called this process *consensual validation,* suggesting that "an opinion, a belief, an attitude is 'correct,' 'valid,' and 'proper' to the extent that it is anchored in a group of people with similar beliefs, opinions, and attitudes" (pp. 272-273). Moreover, according to Festinger (1954), individuals actively try to compare their beliefs with the beliefs of their group members to establish their own social reality: "Those who discover that most others in the group agree with them become highly confident in their opinion and it is extremely rare to find one of them changing his opinion" (p. 122). Recently, Hardin and Higgins (1996), in a substantial survey of the literature, indicated that once beliefs are found to be shared, they achieve the phenomenological status of objective reality. A recent study by Wittenbrink and Henly (1996) showed that awareness of sharing beliefs validated and strengthened beliefs. Students were shown ostensibly prevalent beliefs in the society. When these beliefs corresponded to the negative stereotypes

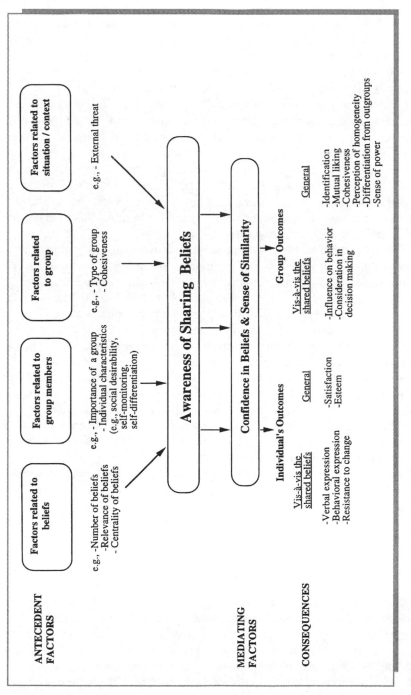

FIGURE 1.1. Model of sharing beliefs in a group

7

that the students held, they reported more of their own negative stereotypes and more of their own negative evaluation of a black person than when provided with information about others' beliefs that did not correspond to their own negative stereotypes. The authors suggested that shared beliefs "offer standards for potential meaning of the world around us" (p. 608).

Similarly, in addition to raising confidence in the shared beliefs, awareness of sharing beliefs increases the sense of similarity among group members. Indeed, the sharing of beliefs is one basis of the sense of similarity (Byrne, 1961). One way for individuals to realize that they are similar is when they discover that other individuals share their beliefs. Such discovery may even lead to group formation (e.g., Bar-Tal, 1990a; Campbell, 1958; Merton, 1957; Tajfel & Turner, 1979). In existing societies or groups, awareness of sharing beliefs strengthens the feeling of similarity, which in turn helps to maintain the group (Cartwright & Zander, 1968).

The presented theory of self-categorization also has an implication for the place of the confidence and similarity variables. According to the motivational group model of Hogg and Abrams (1993), through self-categorization as group members, individuals become aware of sharing beliefs. This focuses attention on the feeling of similarity with other group members and on differences with outgroups. At the same time, self-categorization and awareness of consensus reduce subjective uncertainty, because confidence in beliefs, or correctness and validity, are products of social agreement—not just an agreement with anyone, but agreement with those who are categorized as group members and as a result viewed as similar (see also Haslam, McGarty, & Turner, 1996; Turner, 1991; Turner et al., 1987). Thus, this conception implies that the awareness of sharing beliefs, which is an immanent consequence of self-categorization as group members, necessarily leads to a sense of similarity and confidence in beliefs.

The described mediating effects of sharing beliefs have a number of consequences that can be classified in two categories: individual and group consequences of being aware of shared beliefs.

Consequences

Individual consequences. The first category of individual consequences is divided into outcomes vis-à-vis the shared beliefs and general outcomes. The former refers to the effects that awareness of sharing has on the particular stored beliefs. Awareness of sharing beliefs influences the way these beliefs are held by group members. Such awareness, it can be assumed, makes these beliefs more resistant to change. In addition, the awareness of sharing beliefs increases the likelihood that they will be expressed verbally in communications and reflected in behavior.

The resistance to change of shared beliefs is mediated by the confidence these beliefs carry. As indicated, awareness of sharing beliefs raises their validity in the eyes of the beholder, and therefore, these beliefs, held as valid, are not easily changed (Kruglanski, 1989). Indeed, as McGuire (1964) demonstrated, beliefs that are widely shared within the person's social milieu are resistant to persuasion, and it is difficult to change them. Similar findings were obtained by Greenberg (1963). In his experiment, half of the participants received information making them aware that they shared beliefs with their group, whereas the others did not receive such information. Subsequently, a persuasive communication designed to change these beliefs was presented to the participants. The results clearly showed that persuasive communication was less effective in changing beliefs when individuals were aware that other group members shared their beliefs. The present model also suggests that group members express often-validated, shared beliefs rather than unvalidated, apparently unshared ones. Often-validated, shared beliefs become accessible and facilitate communication among group members, which requires mutual understanding, cooperative orientation, mutual perspective taking, and common agreement about rules (Cushman & Whiting, 1972; Rommetveit, 1974). Also, being held with great confidence and being used in communications, shared beliefs are considered when individual decision making about behavior is made.

The second subcategory of individual outcomes refers to general effects that awareness of sharing has on the group members. It is proposed that the awareness of sharing beliefs indicates to group members that they hold valid beliefs and that they are part of a society. This recognition leads to general feelings of self-satisfaction and self-esteem. As indicated before, individuals are motivated to validate their beliefs. Invalidated beliefs cause ambiguity and uncertainty—feelings that are unpleasant and uncomfortable. Finding, or knowing, that beliefs are validated produces satisfaction and esteem. These feelings are also based on the validated recognition of being part of the group.

Group consequences. The second category of consequences of sharing beliefs is divided into group outcomes vis-à-vis the shared beliefs and to general group outcomes. The former refers to the effects that awareness of sharing beliefs has on these beliefs in the context of the group. The present model proposes that the awareness of sharing beliefs influences the functioning and the status of the beliefs shared. Once the shared beliefs are perceived as validated, they influence group behaviors and are considered relevant to decision making in the group. That is, a group is guided by its shared beliefs because they show the direction of desired action. Thus, leaders of the group take them into consideration and use them to justify their decisions. The latter subcategory of outcomes refers to the effects that awareness of sharing in general has on the group, that is, beyond the effects on the particular shared beliefs. Specifically, the model proposes that awareness of sharing beliefs, through strengthened confidence and sense of similarity, may increase the following factors: identification with the group, cohesiveness, interdependence, mutual liking, perception of homogeneity, differentiation from outgroups, pressure to conform, and sense of power for social influence. Those are powerful consequences that have formative effects on the functioning of the group.

Through awareness of sharing beliefs, society members establish their sense of similarity, which leads to the development of social identity (Bar-Tal, 1990a, 1998a). There is also evidence that a sense of similarity stimulates liking for similar people (Byrne, 1971; Newcomb, 1961), and in turn, liking for group members increases group cohesiveness and interdependence (Cartwright & Zander, 1968; Lott & Lott, 1965). A study by Hogg, Hardie, and Reynolds (1995) demonstrated that when individuals discovered that they shared a belief with group members, it accentuated "liking" them, which was mediated by perceived similarity. In addition, the study showed that liking group members was positively related to identification with the group. The more liking the individuals exhibited on the basis of perceived similarity with other group members, the greater the reported identification with their group. The relationship between perceived similarity and group identification was examined specifically by Roccas (1996), who found, with four different samples of subjects, a high positive correlation between perceived similarity to the ingroup on the basis of shared beliefs, attitudes, and values and identification with that group. In another experimental study, she manipulated the perception of similarity by providing false feedback about the extent to which the subjects (Israeli students) shared the values of their ingroup. After examining the values of the subjects, the feedback was that either their group (other Israelis) shared similar values or their values differed from those of their group. The dependent variable was the extent of identification with the ingroup. The results showed that those subjects who believed that they were similar to ingroup members in terms of sharing similar values expressed more identification with their group than subjects who did not believe that they shared such values with their ingroup. Another line of research indicates that perceived similarity among group members based on shared beliefs increases their perception of group homogeneity and differentiation from outgroups (Turner et al., 1987).

Finally, the awareness of sharing beliefs constitutes by itself a mechanism of social influence. The feeling that beliefs are shared by the majority of group members leads to a sense of rightness and a will to impart them to all the group members. One direction of this influence is reflected in pressure to conform. A consensual group creates pressure on group members to join the consensus (Festinger, 1950). Although group members often willingly adopt the prevailing beliefs of the group by accepting them as valid, this is not always the case. In these cases, group members who are aware of sharing beliefs may exert pressure on deviants. As Turner (1991) noted, on the basis of reviewed studies,

> The more consensual the group and the more isolated the individual (i.e., the less others agree with the deviant), the greater the power of the group to define reality, induce self-doubt in the deviant as to both competence and social position, and threaten her with ridicule and rejection for being different. (pp. 43-44)

Of relevance is a study by Festinger, Gerard, Hymovitch, Kelley, and Raven (1952), which examined the effect of cohesiveness on a series of variables. The cohesiveness of a group was manipulated by notifying participants in the study that they shared beliefs with members of their group. The results showed that sharing beliefs increased liking among group members. But of special importance is the finding that in groups whose members were aware of sharing beliefs, there was higher pressure for uniformity than in groups with no sharing of beliefs. In the former groups, members made special efforts to change the opinions of those who deviated from the group's opinions. Gerard (1954) replicated these results. In addition, by manipulating the awareness of sharing beliefs in one experimental condition, he found that group members in this condition anchored their opinions by relying on their groups. That is, they were affected by what other group members said or did. This anchorage, according to Gerard, "provides the individual with a certain degree of support for his opinion, and hence, a certain degree of attendant subjective validity" (p. 34).

Along the same line, a study by Hall, Varca, and Fisher (1986) showed that when individuals find that they share some beliefs of their group members, they tend to move generally closer to the opinions of their group. Hogg and Turner (1987) reported a series of experiments, using Crutchfield's (1955) paradigm for the study of conformity, which showed the effect of awareness of sharing beliefs with group members on conforming behavior. In these studies, subjects were led to believe that other participants in the experiments were either group members holding similar beliefs or outgroup members with different beliefs. The results showed that categorization as group members and awareness of sharing beliefs increased conformity. Moreover, the studies demonstrated that conformity emerges in the absence of group members and persists in the absence of any direct social influence. Therefore, conformity appears to represent private acceptance of the beliefs prevalent in the group. As the authors observed, the awareness of sharing beliefs, or "the norm" in the

words of the authors, provides consensual validation for perceptions, judgments, beliefs, and so on—"it imbues them with objective correctness, and
leads one to perceive them to be objectively appropriate" (p. 176).

In addition, the awareness of sharing beliefs instigates a general sense of
power among group members on the basis of the aroused sense of similarity,
which indicates unity and solidarity, and on the basis of the confidence in
these beliefs, which arouses a sense of rightness. Group members feel strong
and influential, believing that they are right in their opinions and can influence the decision making of their leaders and the course of group action.

Antecedent Factors

The consequences of sharing beliefs vary as a function of four types of
antecedent factors: factors related to beliefs, factors related to individuals,
factors related to group/society, and factors related to situation/context. The
first relates to both quantity and quality of the shared beliefs. Variables such
as number of shared beliefs, relevance of the shared beliefs to individual and/
or group life, or centrality of the shared beliefs influence the above-described
consequences of having these beliefs in common: They affect the identification of group members, their feeling of similarity, and their sense of the
importance of sharing beliefs. Thus, the more beliefs are shared in a group,
the more relevant and central they are—the more influential are their
consequences.

The second group of factors relates to the personal characteristics of group
members. The consequences of sharing beliefs vary as a function of those personal characteristics that affect, for instance, conformity or sensitivity to information. It can be assumed that individuals who have a tendency to conform
or are sensitive to information about other group members will be especially
affected by the perception that other society members share their beliefs. At
least three characteristics relate to the above-mentioned tendencies: social
desirability, self-monitoring, and self-differentiation. Social desirability refers
to the tendency to rely on others to receive social approval and to avoid negative sanctions (Crowne & Marlowe, 1964; Edwards, 1957). Individuals who
rate high in social desirability are more conforming, more easily persuaded,
more dependent on group norms, and more reliant on group members' opinions than individuals low in social desirability. Self-monitoring refers to the
ways individuals use information in social situations (Snyder, 1979). High
self-monitors are sensitive to social norms, to situations, and to interpersonal
cues regarding how to behave. In contrast, low self-monitors are less tuned to
social information coming from other people and draw on their own internally
generated information. Thus, in comparison to low self-monitors, high self-
monitors make a greater effort to learn about other people and are more likely

to tailor their beliefs, attitudes, and behaviors to fit the demands of the social situation. Self-differentiation refers to the tendency to differentiate oneself from one's group and construct unique self-schema (Brewer, 1991; Jarymowicz, 1991, 1998). Whereas individuals with low self-differentiation define and describe themselves in terms of the group in which they are members, individuals with high self-differentiation view themselves as unique and thus define and describe themselves in differential terms from their group. The former group of individuals is thus more tuned to perceive group characteristics than the latter. This description implies that high social desirability, high self-monitoring, and low self-differentiation intensify and magnify the effects of information about sharing of beliefs with other group members. In addition, the model assumes that the strength of the consequences is also influenced by how important group membership is to the individual. Group members who attribute great importance to being members of the group are especially affected by the awareness that other group members share their beliefs.

The third group of factors relates to the characteristics of the group. Variables such as type of group, level of cohesiveness, or extent of group belief-sharing influence the consequences of sharing beliefs. Cohesiveness, a high extent of sharing beliefs, and an autocratic group increase the pressure of a group on individuals to conform, and therefore, the awareness of sharing beliefs will have increased consequences. Finally, the fourth type of factors is related to the situation or context in which the group members share their beliefs. Different situations, such as external threat, may increase the effects of sharing beliefs. External threat heightens the feeling of solidarity and pressure to conform. Thus, in this situation, the awareness of sharing beliefs has especially increased consequences.

Recently, two studies were performed to test the model directly (Bar-Tal, Raviv, Rosen, & Bruker, 1999). The first study was done among kibbutz members, and the second one was carried out among 12- to 13-year-olds, group members of scout organizations. The results of both studies showed that when respondents become aware that the majority (about 80%) of their group members shared their beliefs, they reported more confidence in the beliefs, more self-satisfaction, more feelings of similarity with group members, more identification with the group, more cohesiveness in the group, and more pride in belonging to the group than when they became aware that the minority (about 20%) of their group members shared these beliefs with them. Also, the first study showed that these effects increased with feelings of solidarity among group members, and the second study showed that these effects increased as the beliefs were more important for group members.

In sum, the presented evidence unequivocally indicates that awareness of sharing beliefs in a group is an important social mechanism. It has crucial social psychological implications, influencing group members as individuals and the group itself: It influences the group members' beliefs and attitudes toward their shared beliefs and toward their group, as well as their behaviors and group functioning. This influence varies as a function of series of variables related to the nature of the shared beliefs, characteristics of the group members sharing the beliefs, characteristics of their group, and the nature of the group's context. These findings point to the power of sharing beliefs in every group, small or large. It thus becomes clear that the study of sharing beliefs should be of great interest for social psychology, as is the study of conformity and minority influence. The relative disregard of the study of sharing beliefs is somewhat surprising in view of the fact that in the early days of social psychology and during the establishment of modern social psychology, this area of study was of interest to social psychologists. The next chapter will review this line of study, including the present growing interest.

2

A History of the Study of Shared Beliefs

Although the study of shared beliefs in a group, or in a society, has never been social psychology's major thrust, it is possible to find through the years various contributions that deal with this social phenomenon. Some of these contributions were explicitly preoccupied with the problem of sharing beliefs by group or society members, whereas others did not focus directly on sharing beliefs, but their findings and theorizing had relevance to the understanding of this phenomenon.

Since the formal establishment of social psychology, it is possible to identify four major attempts to deal with shared beliefs. The first attempt began in the late 19th century and the early 20th century among the first social psychologists, who considered the study of groups in general, and of group mental activities, in particular, an important area of psychology and social psychology. The fathers of modern social psychology Sherif, Lewin, and Asch, who acted in the 1930s, 1940s, and 1950s, led the second attempt to understand sharing of beliefs. However, they were not particularly interested in this phenomenon: Their contribution was especially important for the understanding of group functioning, and the study of shared beliefs was one of its implications. Several decades later, Serge Moscovici, in the European tradition, recovered and reconceptualized the meaning of collective representation proposed at the end of the previous century by Emile Durkheim. Finally, the fourth attempt to study shared beliefs takes place at present. Social psychologists have finally recognized the importance of this phenomenon and are tackling it from different angles. Each of these four attempts will be described in detail.

▨ EARLY STUDIES OF MENTAL SHARING

In the period when psychology began to establish itself as a distinct discipline and social psychology started to emerge, there was a wide interest in people's common worldview (Allport, 1985). Distinguished early psychologists such as Wilhelm Wundt, Gustav LeBon, Sigmund Freud, William James, Carl Jung, and William McDougall were interested in questions of how groups think, how they form common mental products, and what is the nature of the shared thoughts.

I propose to classify the early approaches into two categories. One category consists of conceptions that view the formation and existence of a group's mental products as independent of the individuals who constitute the group (e.g., Freud, 1960; Jung, 1959; LeBon, 1895/1968; Wundt, 1916). The contents of shared beliefs are considered to be predetermined and independent of the wills or desires of group members. The other category encompasses those conceptions that regard group mental products as being formed, shared, and bound to the influence processes within the group (e.g., Durkheim, 1933, 1953; McDougall, 1920, 1939; Tarde, 1969). Belief contents are believed to be affected by the social processes of the individuals who constitute the group. Thus, the differentiating criterion is whether beliefs shared by group members have a superindividual integrity, irrespective of what the specific individuals who compose the group do, or whether the shared beliefs are the products of continuous social influence processes through which the contents of beliefs and the extent of dissemination are determined.

Superindividual View

The conceptions of the first category suggest that beliefs shared (i.e., common views) by group members have a superindividual existence, independent of what specific individuals who make up the group think or do. An illustration of this approach can be found in Wundt's conception of folk soul.

Wundt's folk soul. Wilhelm Wundt, one of the fathers of modern psychology, propagated the superindividual view through the concept *folk soul* (Wundt, 1916). This concept refers to "those mental products that are created by a community of human life and are, therefore, inexplicable in terms merely of individual consciousness, since they presuppose the reciprocal actions of many" (p. 3). Groups, whether a local community, tribe, or nation, develop through reciprocal activity collective mental products (the folk souls), which consist of language, myths, and customs. These elements correspond to the elements of the individual mind (imagination, feeling, and volition). Every group member, as his/her own consciousness develops during childhood, absorbs such folk souls. At the same time and in the same way that individuals synthesize all of their psychic contents, so does the community, or the folk, in a process that takes place beyond the individual psyche. According to Wundt, just as the individual psyche emerges as the result of a progression of superimposed syntheses, the folk soul, too, can be viewed as a synthesis of syntheses. It consists of something creatively new (i.e., collective mind), beyond the sum of its elements, exceeding the sum of the individual mental contents of which the folk is composed. In this meaning, the concept folk soul refers to the superindividual psychic experience, in the same way that the individual soul refers to that of the psychic experience of the individual, as it transcends the scope of individual consciousness. Thus, folk souls are as real as the psychic life of the individuals, and therefore, folk psychology should, according to Wundt, focus on the general characteristics of the folk soul (collective mind), just as individual psychology focuses on the general characteristics of the individual mind.

Group Product

The conceptions included in the second category have the common assumption that shared beliefs are products of continuous social influence processes through which they are both disseminated and adopted by group members. The work of Durkheim on collective representations, which can be considered part of this category, has possibly been the most influential among the early contributions to social psychology.

Durkheim's collective representations. Collective representations are "the totality of beliefs and sentiments common to average members of the same society" (Durkheim, 1933, p. 79). They are socially generated; consist of customs, traditions, values, ideas, and other elements that take shape historically in human culture; and form the milieu in which the individual is socialized and educated. In this respect, they are the images and categories held in a similar form by members of a collective, which allow their common understanding and effective communication. The collective representations are perceptions and ideological interpretations of social and cultural phenomena and serve to explain and justify the society (Durkheim, 1898). Durkheim himself explained the relations between collective and individual representations in the following passage:

> When we said elsewhere that social facts are in a sense independent of individuals and exterior to individual minds, we only affirmed of the social world what we have just established for the psychic world. Society has for its substratum

the mass of associated individuals. The system which they form by uniting together, and which varies according to their geographical disposition and the nature and number of their channels of communication, is the base from which social life is raised. The representations which form the network of social life arise from the relations between the individuals thus combined or the secondary groups that are between the individuals and the total society. If there is nothing extraordinary in the fact that individual representations, produced by the action and reaction between neural elements, are not inherent in these elements, there is nothing surprising in the fact that collective representations, produced by the action and reaction between individual minds that form the society, do not derive directly from the latter and consequently surpass them. The conception of the relationship which unites the social substratum and the social life is at every point analogous to that which undeniably exists between the physiological substratum and psychic life of individuals, if, that is, one is not going to deny the existence of psychology in the proper sense of the word. (pp. 24-25)

Collective representations can be viewed as the emergent products of social life that are shared by participants in a collective. Although they stem from the substratum brain cells of associated individuals, they can neither be reduced to nor wholly explained by the features of these individuals. They have sui generis characteristics. They are independent of any particular mind or set of minds and express different contents from the contents that are purely individual. They are greater than the sum of the individual representations because of their influence and power in the society. In the words of Durkheim (1953),

> Collective representations are exterior to individual minds, it means that they do not derive from them as such but from the association of minds, which is a very different thing. No doubt in the making of the whole each contributes his part, but private sentiments do not become social except by combination under the action of the *sui generis* forces developed in association. In such a combination, with the mutual alteration involved, *they become something else.* . . . The resultant surpasses the individual as the whole the part. It is *in* the whole as it is *by* the whole. In this sense it is exterior to the individuals. No doubt each individual contains a part, but the whole is found in no one. (p. 26)

What make collective representations unique is that they are formed as a result of social action instead of merely through mental process and that they may be both prior and posterior in time to any individual mind. Individuals learn them through the socialization process, as they acquire the cultural products of the collective. Collective representations have qualitative features that distinguish them from individual representations (Durkheim, 1933). They enjoy the moral prestige that is spontaneously associated with all collectively shared beliefs; because these norms are invariably imposed on the individual by public opinion, they engender sentiments that are qualitatively different from those evoked by individual representations. As a result, collective norms have an intensity and compelling force that far exceed those of privately formulated rules. Individuals assume that they derive from and are enforced by some power, real or ideal, that is superior to themselves. This is how collective representations function to legitimize institutional practices and social behavior. At the same time, they also create similarity among collective members and provide communal identity, which, in turn, serves as a basis for solidarity (Durkheim, 1951).

McDougall's group mind. The controversial conception of *group mind* proposed by McDougall (1920, 1939) also falls under the second category. Although in his initial conceptualization (McDougall, 1920), McDougall was not absolutely clear about whether he supports the superindividual view of collective thinking, he later clarified his position, directing it unequivocally toward a second category of conceptions.

The concept of group mind refers to the continuity of shared thoughts, sentiments, and traditions despite the turnover of group members. It holds that highly organized human societies acquire an organized system of mental forces that are largely independent from individual qualities of group members. In other words, groups have collective thoughts, ideas, and memories that exist separately from individuals who compose the group. These mental products are formed in the following process: "When a number of men think and feel and act together, the mental operations and the actions of each member of the group are apt to be very different from those he would achieve if he faced the situation as an isolated individual" (McDougall, 1920, p. 31). But to carry out these high-level mental activities, a group has to have (a) some degree of continuous existence; (b) an idea of the wholeness of the group; (c) intergroup interactions that foster group identity; (d) common knowledge of traditions, customs, and habits; and (e) a system of interdependent roles.

Although McDougall recognized that the group mind does not exist over and above the minds of the group members, but "only exists in the minds of its members" (p. 25), he argued that the group mind goes "over and above any sum of these minds created by mere addition" (p. 26). Moreover, the group mind acquires structures and qualities that are independent of particular group members. It has its own directing and influencing powers, which shape the individual. It perpetuates itself "as a self-identical system," which slowly and gradually changes.

One specific category of contents of the group mind is the group spirit, which serves as a bond to hold the group together. This refers to knowledge about the group and the sentiment of devotion. The first component includes all knowledge that defines the group and differentiates it from other groups. According to McDougall, this knowledge raises the intellectual level of the group because "it leads each member to subordinate his own judgment and opinion to that of the whole" (p. 89). Group members acquire the knowledge about the group, and it guides their behavior.

At a later stage, McDougall (1939) clarified that the concept of group mind does not refer to "some mental entity that exists over and above all individuals comprised in the group and that might continue to exist though all the individual members ceased to be" (p. xii), nor does it exist in its totality in any one individual mind. It expresses the Gestaltist notion that the whole is more than the sum of its parts and that the understanding of the whole requires laws or principles that cannot be arrived at by the study of the parts alone. Accordingly, his conception recognizes

> the organization of the group mind as consisting in the similarities of the structure of the individuals' minds (similarities that render them capable of responding in similar fashion to the common features of the environment, both social and physical) and in those mutual adaptation of individual minds which render them capable of harmonious cooperation and reciprocal supplementation in their efforts toward the realization of a common goal. (pp. xiv-xv)

The whole system is composed of the minds of individuals that reciprocate and complement one another. The collective mental products exert influence on group members. They mold the individual mind, as McDougall said: "Each member of the group so molded bears within him some part of the group mind, some socially molded mental structure that is part of the total structure of the group mind" (p. xvi).

⅏ SHARING BELIEFS IN MODERN SOCIAL PSYCHOLOGY

After the first wave of psychologists who were deeply preoccupied with collective mental products, the interest in this topic faded away. Social psychology, as a distinguished young subdiscipline of psychology, focused mostly on the individual. Floyd Allport (1920), one of the leaders of the individualistic approach, argued that only individuals could be the subject of psychological processes, because only individuals feel, think, perceive, and act. The group is a fictitious entity that exists in individuals' minds and refers to multiplicity of individual processes. Accordingly, an understanding of social phenomena would require the study of individual properties and processes. In Allport's (1920) words, "All theories which partake of the group fallacy have the unfortunate consequence of diverting attention from the true locus of cause and effect, namely, the behavior mechanisms of the individual" (p. 9).

The preoccupation with shared beliefs reappeared in the work of the three founding fathers of modern social psychology: Muzaref Sherif, Kurt Lewin, and Solomon Asch. All three were interested in group behavior and recognized that group membership affects individuals' perceptions of their world. They understood that through social interaction, group members form a common view of the world, which becomes a unique group characteristic. This shared view, which group members make an effort to maintain via processes of social influence, is also a powerful determinant of group behavior.

Sherif's Work on Norms

The study of shared beliefs received a prominent place in the work of Sherif (1936), who was interested in norm formation. He designed a series of experiments to study how individuals in a group form a common norm and how doing so affects their perception and judgment. Specifically, a small group of subjects was exposed to an autokinetic effect; that is, they were shown a single and stable small light that appeared to move in a dark room. The subjects were asked to estimate the distance that the moving light apparently covered. The results showed that when the subjects were exposed together to the situation for the first time, they tended to agree on a distance range of light movement, which Sherif viewed as a norm. In essence, they established a shared belief. This shared belief was established even when the subjects had initially been introduced one by one to the autokinetic effect, giving them the opportunity to form their individual judgment. Subsequent interaction with others showed that subjects tended to converge their previous judgments toward a joint norm (i.e., shared belief). Especially interesting was the finding that when members of the small group were then again asked individually to judge the range of light movement, they perceived it in terms of the previously established group norm. This finding showed that once individuals establish a shared belief in a group situation, it becomes part of their repertoire. Significant variation in the norm established among different groups was observed, suggesting that the shared belief was dependent on the developed consensus, which in fact, arbitrarily established the norm. Sherif (1936) applied this situation to real life experience, suggesting that

> When we are in a situation with other people, our experience and subsequent behavior are modified by the special social conditions around us. The social situation may develop into some form of closed system, with more or less rigid boundaries in which the experience and actions of the individual are regulated by his membership character and his special position in the group. . . . The

slogans and values that develop or become standardized in the group situation become his guides to action. (pp. 84-85)

Of special importance are follow-up studies (Jacobs & Campbell, 1961; Weick & Gilfillan, 1971) demonstrating that the shared norm created by the groups survives across generations of subjects. It means that once a norm (i.e., shared belief) is established, it can be maintained with stability long after the originators of the belief have disappeared. At the conclusion of his experiments, Sherif (1936) said,

The psychological basis of the established social norms, such as stereotypes, fashions, conventions, customs and values, is the formation of common frames of reference as a product of the contact of individuals. Once such frames of reference are established and incorporated in the individual, they enter as important factors to determine or modify his reactions to the situations that he will face later—social, and even nonsocial, at times, especially if the stimulus field is not well structured. (p. 106)

Sherif saw the autokinetic experiment as an important demonstration of how individuals in a collective situation come willingly, and without pressure, to share beliefs. This small-scale study, according to Sherif, can be generalized to real life situations in groups. Individuals, living in groups, adopt common norms (i.e., shared beliefs) that become part of their repertoire. These shared beliefs standardize ways of looking at the world and reactions to the environment. They regulate the lives of group members and guide their behavior. Once the shared beliefs are formed, they tend to persist as a superstructure, independent of particular group members or generations, as long as they are functional in the prevailing societal conditions.

Lewin's Group Life Space

Although Kurt Lewin was not explicitly concerned with shared beliefs, his work about group dynamics has implications for this phenomenon. Lewin (1951) introduced the concept of life space as part of his field theory, and he used it for the analysis of both the individual and the group. In the case of the group, life space refers to the totality of psychological forces that influence the group at any given moment, that is, the group itself and the environment as it exists for the group at that particular point in time. These psychological forces affect the group members in a unitary way—and in response, they form a common view of the environment and the group.

A group has its special meaning in the interdependent relationships among group members. As Lewin (1948) proposed,

The essence of a group is not similarity or dissimilarity of its members, but their interdependence. A group can be characterized as a "dynamical whole"; this means that a change in the state of any subpart changes the state of any other subpart. The degree of interdependence of the subparts of members of the group varies all the way from a "loose" mass to a compact unit. (p. 54)

On the basis of the interdependence group, a high degree of unity was established, although group members fulfill different functions within the whole. The unity is reflected in the formation of common goals, standards, values, and common perceptions, which play an important role for the group. According to Lewin (1947), "It is impossible to predict group behavior without taking into account group goals, group standards, group values, and the way a group 'sees' its own situation and that of other groups" (p. 12).

The above indicates that Lewin recognized the importance of the views that are shared by group members (i.e., shared beliefs); in his conception, such views constitute one of the bases for group formation and subsequently a foundation for the group's continued existence.

Asch's Mutually Shared Field

Another contribution to the study of shared beliefs was made by Solomon Asch. He established several new directions of research in social psychology and, when analyzing group behavior in his comprehensive textbook of social psychology (Asch, 1952), he referred directly to sharing of beliefs. Presenting the opposing views of Floyd Allport, who focused on individuals and disregarded the group entity, and of William McDougall, who formulated the group mind conception, Asch took the middle road. He recognized that psychological processes occur in individuals, but at the same time, he emphasized that each individual is subject to social forces that are at play in groups of which he is part. In his view,

For an adequate formulation of the individual-group relation, we need a way of describing group action that neither reduces the individual to a mere target of group forces of mystical origin, nor obliterates the organized character of group forces in the welter of individual activities. We need a way of understanding group processes that retains the prime reality of individual and group, the two permanent poles of all social processes. We need to see group forces arising out of the actions of individuals and individuals whose actions are a function of the group forces that they themselves (or others) have brought into existence. We must see group phenomena as both the *product and condition* of actions of individuals. (pp. 250-251)

Of special importance for the understanding of group behavior, according to Asch, is the study of psychological interactions in groups and the "mutually shared field" that they produce. The formation of this mutually shared field, which in essence is constituted of shared beliefs, is based on the capacity to perceive ourselves and others as referring to the same situation. Individuals observe and understand the viewpoints of others and form shared actions, feelings, or ideas. These mutual psychological fields enable group actions and in turn, they "bring group facts into existence and produce phenomenal solidity of group processes. These are also the conditions necessary for the idea of a goal that can be achieved jointly" (p. 252). Thus, Asch argues that the formation of shared beliefs among group members is a necessary condition for the interdependent action of group members to achieve group goals. In his view, a *mutually shared field* is the essential feature of groups. While being held in an individual's repertoire, shared beliefs are translated into objective expressions (i.e., group actions), which can be observed. Shared beliefs that have the form of "group consciousness, group purposes, and group goals have an existence in individuals, and in them alone. But they cease to be 'merely' individual facts by virtue of their reference to others" (p. 252). Thus, according to Asch, the shared beliefs of group members are not simply the total sum of individuals' beliefs. These beliefs provide a special characteristic to a group, which implies that a group is more than a mere collection of group members. Sharing beliefs, thus, turns a collective of individuals into a group and enables coordinated joint action.

MOSCOVICI'S SOCIAL REPRESENTATIONS

The work of Moscovici on social representations (1973, 1981, 1982, 1984, 1988, 1993) is the most extensive elaboration of shared beliefs in the modern history of social psychology. On the basis of Durkheim's conception of collective representation, Moscovici presented a theory of social representations that has significantly affected the development of social psychology, especially in Europe and South America. The work of Moscovici has special relevance to the proposed conception of societal beliefs, because it deals directly with shared beliefs in a society. The theory assumes that individuals are part of a group or society and, therefore, that their worldview is determined by representations shared by group or society members.

Moscovici changed the prefix of the concept from *collective* to *social* for the following reasons: He tries to emphasize the plurality and diversity of representations within a group or society, to indicate that they are shaped by an exchange and interaction process, to show that they bridge the individual and the social world, and to reflect the view of changing society. Using the concept of social representations, Moscovici aims more to describe the innovations, dynamics, and changes rather than stable traditions. His conception describes the continuous evolution of concepts and images through communication. This contrasts with Durkheim's focus on relatively static, shared representations in the form of science, religion, or myths embedded in collective memory and inculcated through the educational system. Moscovici's conception pertains to dynamic, commonsense knowledge shared by lay people and constantly produced under the prevailing societal constraints.

In his numerous writings, Moscovici refrains from formally defining the concept of social representations. Much of his effort is directed at describing their contents, discussing their formation, and elaborating their functions. On a general level, social representations constitute "social reality sui generis" (Moscovici, 1984, p. 13), "a system of classification and denotation of allotting categories and names" (p. 30), "a specific way of understanding and communicating what we already know" (p. 17). More specifically, they are "cognitive systems with a logic and language of their own and a pattern of implication, relevant to both values and concept, and with a characteristic kind of discourse," representing " 'theories' or 'branches of knowledge' in their own right, for the discovery and organization of reality" (Moscovici, in his foreword to Herzlich, 1973, p. xiii). Social representations institute a

> set of concepts, statements and explanations originating in daily life in the course of interindividual communications. They are the equivalent in our society of the myths and belief systems in traditional societies; they might even be said [to be] the contemporary version of common sense. (Moscovici, 1981, p. 181)

These definitions imply that social representations are shared ideas constructed in language and imbued with meaning. They are not only held individually by most of the group members but are also reflected in the products of a society, such as books. The scope of contents ranges from science to "everyday thinking and the stock of ideas that give coherence to our religious beliefs, political ideas, and the connections we create as spontaneously as we breathe" (Moscovici, 1988, p. 214). Any contents can become representations when they get "anchored to a context, a network of meanings. To be anchored means that they have a reference and receive a determinative semantic value" (Moscovici, 1993, p. 163).

According to Moscovici, social representations consist of collectively shared concepts and images. Whereas concepts are abstract mental products, images are concrete pictorial mental elements—and together as shared and agreed codes, they refer to people's common knowledge, that is, their commonsense theories about the social world. In other words, these representations constitute the constructed, shared, social reality of group members. They range from generalized hegemonic structures that are shared by society members and entire nations and are reproduced historically, to highly specific knowledge structures that are shared merely by subgroups (Moscovici, 1988). The former are obviously more coercive and prescriptive than the latter.

Insofar as social representations are consensual and informal understandings and images, they stand in contrast to the reified and formal definitions of roles, rules, institutions, and categories, featured, for example, in scientific theorizing and conceptualization. In fact, social representations reflect people's understanding of scientific knowledge and other categories of formal knowledge, by converting this latter type of knowledge into a network of understandable and communicable concepts. Large numbers of individuals in a society share such representations, and they are passed on from one generation to the next. Each new generation acquires them without conscious assent, because social representations are part of the transmitted cultural heritage.

Social representations, as products of social interaction, are formed through interpersonal communication in informal situations, for example, on the street, in offices and hospitals, and through group interactions, for example, in clubs or associations. The novel and unfamiliar are made understandable and familiar through the mediation of the following two interdependent processes: anchoring and objectification. By means of *anchoring,* the novel object or social stimulus is assigned to one of the categories of thought in the stored repertoire of representations. This is done by comparing the new object/stimulus with the existing stock of familiar contents. If, through comparison, the object seems to be similar to the category, then, the unfamiliar acquires the characteristic of the category. In the second process of *objectification,* the novel object or social stimulus, as an unfamiliar and abstract notion or idea, is transformed into concrete and objective commonsense reality. This new version of representation becomes diffused in the course of conversation and communication throughout the social group. Anchoring and objectification are interdependent processes, in the sense that a representation can become securely anchored to the extent that it is also objectified, and vice versa, objectification cannot take place unless a representation has been anchored.

Social representations play a crucial role in the life of any group or society. Without them, a collectivity cannot operate. First of all, they permit an understanding of physical, social, and cultural reality. Social representations turn strange concepts and ideas into meaningful ones, making "something unfamiliar, or unfamiliarity itself, familiar" (Moscovici, 1984, p.24), and they turn "something abstract into something almost concrete" (p. 29). "They make it possible for us to classify persons and objects, to compare and explain behaviors and to objectify them as parts of our social setting" (Moscovici, 1988,

p. 214). As "systems of values, ideas and practices . . . enable individuals to orient themselves in and master their material world" (Moscovici, 1973, p. xiii). In addition, according to Moscovici, social representations guide behavior and enable coordination of group action. Finally, by establishing the awareness of living in a common world, social representations contribute to strengthening of social identity. We can, thus, use social representations as a criterion to differentiate between those who share them and those who do not. The former understand each other and can communicate. Thus, social representations constitute a unifying and homogenizing system that marks group boundaries.

In sum, Moscovici and his collaborators developed what is essentially a theoretical framework that attempts to describe the shared reality of collectives. The conception of social representations, which they formulated taking a constructivist approach, is general and even to some extent amorphous. Rather than defining the concept accurately, Moscovici has extensively described the contents and functions of social representations. Moscovici's major contribution to social psychology is that after seven decades, he returned to focus on the simple but essential observation that individuals as group members share common views. This was a very important reminder in view of the fact that social psychology by this point in time was concentrating mostly on the study of the individual. The introduction of social representations also directed the attention of social psychologists to the study of the contents of beliefs held by groups or societies, such as the study of a group's notions of health and illness (Herzlich, 1973), madness (Jodelet, 1991), or its own identity (Hewstone, Jaspars, & Lalljee, 1982).

These shared social representations form the basis of social life. They allow communication and understanding. But complex societies have additional needs—they need a raison d'être; they need uniting values and goals, the glue that cements their social identity. Societal beliefs, which can be considered a particular category of social representations, fulfill these functions. Whereas social representations are loosely defined and pertain to every component of physical, cultural, and social reality, societal beliefs are well-defined, refer to a limited range of contents, characterize a particular society, and contribute to its identity. The latter play a particularly important role in the life of society members and will be discussed in the next chapter.

SHARED BELIEFS IN CURRENT SOCIAL PSYCHOLOGY

Recently, in addition to the research concerning social representations, which has established itself as a distinguished area of social psychology, a new interest in shared beliefs has emerged from several different directions. This new line of research does not necessarily use the term *shared beliefs* but rather, in the social psychological tradition, the term *shared cognition.*

Several recent publications illustrate this development: the edited volume, *Perspectives on Socially Shared Cognition* (Resnick, Levine, & Teasley, 1991), published by the American Psychological Association on the basis of a conference held in 1989; the recent edited volume, *What's Social About Social Cognition: Research on Socially Shared Cognition in Small Groups* (Nye & Brower, 1996); the review article about "Social Foundations of Cognitions" (Levine, Resnick, & Higgins, 1993), published in the *Annual Review of Psychology*; and the publication of *Group Beliefs* (Bar-Tal, 1990a) and *The Social Psychological Study of Widespread Beliefs* (Fraser & Gaskell, 1990). The latter book, written by a group of European social psychologists, is a good example of current trends in this area. It concerns *widespread beliefs,* a term that is used to describe the general phenomenon when beliefs are shared by many people. In the opinion of the editors, "shared attitudes and beliefs play an important role in defining groups and group behaviors, in the formation and maintenance of social identities, and more broadly in collective realities" (p. 8). The chapters of the book present different types of shared beliefs in different contexts: social representations, ideology, social attitudes, public opinion, collective beliefs, and social beliefs—with economic, political, gender-related, or other contents. Rather than providing any unitary conceptual framework, this book raises the question "to what extent and why do many people share similar views in socially significant domains" (p. 3).

A review of the current preoccupation with the phenomenon of shared beliefs reveals four directions. One direction reframes the study of cognition, which was mostly examined from an individual perspective, as a sociocultural thinking activity or as a social product. Another approach is to explore the consequences of shared beliefs on the individual, whereas the third direction looks at the nature and impact of sharing beliefs by members of groups in general and of small groups in particular. Finally, researchers of stereotypes, one content area of social psychology, recognize that stereotypes have special meaning when they are shared by society members. We shall now consider these different directions of study more closely.

Shared Cognitions

Social interaction has been considered a key process for cognitive development. Years ago, Mead (1934), a leading social psychological theorist, paid special attention to the analysis of interactions in which common symbols are acquired on the basis of language, gestures, emotion, and tone. According to him, acquisition of these symbols is the necessary prerequisite for mutual understanding. Similarly, Vygotsky (1962), the renowned social developmental psychologist, viewed individuals' acquisition of cognitive operations as the result of social transactions. These transactions allow the transmission of common symbolic tools, which are interiorized through the mediation of language and used in joint action. But these lines of thoughts were left relatively ignored, while students of cognition focused on formal and logical operations at the expense of the social basis and factors in cognitive processes. Only recently, the relationship between cognition and social interaction, as well as the functions of shared cognitions, has gained more attention. This approach views cognitive processes as a part of the social processes that constitute social interactions: Other people with their tangible and nontangible products are instrumental in cognitive processes. Insofar as others play significant roles in determining individual cognition, the study of individual cognition is no longer perceived as adequate for explaining even the individual level of thinking.

In this new line of thinking, Cole (1991) suggested that cognition has to be reconceptualized, extending the focus on interpersonal processes to a cultural context. Such a new view of cognition requires reference to transformations, social institutions, and historically accumulated artifacts. According to Cole, the unit of analysis should shift from an individual to a group in a particular cultural setting. Even an interaction between two individuals should be seen as a culture-specific form of cognitive activity in a particular cultural context. Accordingly, cognitive activities in different cultural contexts should be studied, because they may reveal different cognitive processes that lead to particular mental products.

Shared cognitions allow individuals mutual understanding and fruitful communication. It thus becomes clear that part of children's development requires learning of shared cognitions. Without such learning, children have difficulty demonstrating their full cognitive capacity in interactions with adults (Perret-Clermont, Perret, & Bell, 1991; Siegal, 1991). In this vein, of special importance is the work of Gelman and colleagues (Gelman, Massey, & McManus, 1991), who described how children acquire shared cognitions or, in their terms, shared knowledge. Their basic proposition states that children are disposed to attend to certain kinds of information. This suggests that learners determine which information in the environment is relevant for knowledge construction. Children do so on the basis of "skeletal knowledge structures," which lead them to search for particular patterns of information. Skeletal structures of this kind are part of the biological endowment of humans. According to this conception, known as the constructivist theory of supporting environments, shared cognitions arise not just from common exposure to information but also from the fact that humans share common skeletal structures, which are employed in knowledge acquisition. Once the shared cognitions are acquired, they enable a wide range of social cognitive activity, communication, and interdependent action.

A different line of study is taken by Hatano and Inagaki (1991), who investigated the relationship between social interaction and individual comprehension. Examining elementary school classroom interaction in the form of group discussion, they came to a conclusion that "comprehension is essentially a private achievement" (p. 347). But such comprehension is achieved after constructive interactions in which group members express their beliefs, collect information, and receive feedback about their comprehension, which allows them to revise and elaborate their knowledge. Thus, according to Hatano and Inagaki, group interaction facilitates comprehension. Individuals incorporate and assimilate the ideas expressed in the group, but the final outcome is an individual product, because individuals subjectively interpret, select, and organize the provided knowledge.

In reviewing the new approach to cognition, Resnick (1991) suggested that it is based on constructivism, which emphasizes that individuals influence and shape each other's cognitive contents and reasoning processes. In her words, "constructivism forces students of many social phenomena to treat social processes as cognition, leading them to analyze the ways in which people jointly construct knowledge under particular conditions of social purpose and interaction" (p. 2). Shared cognitions, thus, are products of separate and combined processes of reception and joint activity. That is, individuals receive from others knowledge or form it by communicating and acting together.

Shared Beliefs and the Individual

Another direction of studying shared beliefs is well exemplified in the work of Higgins (Hardin & Higgins, 1996; Higgins, 1996) about the functions of shared reality for the individual. This line of research, whose roots can be found in the work of Festinger (1954) on social comparison, is concerned with personal consequences of sharing beliefs. Festinger (1954) posited that people possess a drive to evaluate their opinion and abilities to construct a valid view of reality. A major tenet of the theory is that similar rather than dissimilar others provide the necessary standards for comparison. That is, individuals construct their reality by comparing their beliefs and abilities to group members with whom they share many opinions and attitudes. Such comparison, according to Festinger, validates individuals' view of social and physical reality. But, whereas Festinger focused on the motivational force of social comparison, years later, Hardin and Higgins (1996) concentrated on the meaning and functions of shared reality for the individual. Reviewing a wide scope of psychological literature, they suggested that shared reality is crucial to establish and maintain individual understanding. Thus, once individuals achieve shared reality, they try to protect and maintain it.

According to Hardin and Higgins (1996), shared knowledge is formed both through social communication, when individuals do not have a direct experience with the subject of the knowledge, and through social interaction, in which individuals have joint experiences and, on that basis, form knowledge. Then, "when an experience is recognized and shared with others in the process of social interaction, it achieves reliability, validity, generality, and predictability" (pp. 35-36). The formed shared reality modulates the construction of meaning and regulates social interactions through communication. It plays a prominent role in establishing and maintaining the experience of self in particular situations and over a long period of time in repetitive interactions with significant others.

In another work, Higgins (1996) argued that the development of self-regulation is based on messages received from others, which become shared reality. This is evident from observation of how children achieve self-regulation. When caretakers satisfy children's needs in emphasizing promotion and prevention, their social regulation communicates a particular view of the world. Children adapt this view, which then becomes shared reality, relating not just to the way the world works but also to society's beliefs and values.

Sharing Beliefs in Small Groups

Another direction of investigating shared beliefs emerged in the study of groups, especially small groups, with the assumption that they play a determinative role in group formation and functioning. According to this line of study, one major condition for group formation is the existence of shared beliefs, which underlie social identity of group members. Furthermore, group members can interdependently act only when they form a shared understanding of norms, procedures, and goals. It is, thus, not surprising that groups make an effort to transmit shared beliefs to new members and, at the same time, try to maintain them among veteran members.

Work group culture. John Levine and Richard Moreland have studied small-group processes and especially group socialization for more than a decade in different settings, including workplaces. They proposed the concept, *culture of work groups,* which denotes the shared thoughts and customs of group members (Levine & Moreland, 1991). The culture of work groups guides group members' behavior and allows common interpretations of experiences, which are a necessary part of every group functioning. Shared thoughts consist of (a) knowledge about the group, which includes collective answers to questions such as: What makes our group different? What is our group's past, present, and future? How good is our group? (b) knowledge about group members including answers to questions such as: What kind of person belongs to our group? How do group members differ from one another? or How should group members' behavior be interpreted? (c) knowledge about work, which includes answers to the following questions: Why do we work? What kind of work do we perform? How should we perform our work? Customs are viewed as behavioral expressions of the thoughts shared among group members. They include (a) routines, that is, everyday procedures such as habits and traditions used by group members; (b) accounts, which are verbal descriptions or explanations of matters of interest to group members; (c) jargon, that is, common words, phrases, or gestures; (d) rituals, that is, special ceremonies unique to the group; and (e) symbols, which are material objects that have special shared meaning for group members. New group members have to learn these shared thoughts and customs through the process of group socialization to become full group members (Levine, Bogart, & Zdaniuk, 1996). Learning of group culture facilitates acceptance by old group members and is a condition for gaining influence in the group. But, first of all, group culture has to be shared by all group members to enable common activity. Levine et al. (1996) pointed out that coordinated cognitive activity depends on sharing understanding, which they call *intersubjectivity*. John Levine and Richard Moreland point out that analysis of groups has to pay special attention to shared beliefs, which constitute necessary elements for their functioning.

Group problem solving. Larson and Christensen (1993) come to the study of shared beliefs in small groups from a different perspective than the previously described contribution. They come from the cognitive perspective, trying to bridge between the study of cognition and the study of small groups. In their view, the study of social cognition should not be limited to the analysis of intrapersonal processes of the individual but should address group-level activity. Specifically, it should address those group cognitive activities involved in the acquisition, storage, transmission, manipulation, and use of information for the purpose of creating cognitive products on a group level. In essence, this analysis applies to problem solving by groups and allows a broad understanding of cognitive group processes that were overlooked.

Larson and Christensen (1993) observe that when a group solves problems or makes decisions, it needs to rely on elementary processes of belief sharing that specifically serve group functioning. For example, problem identification on a group level takes place only when members recognize that they all have a common perception of the problem at hand. Sharing the idea that there is a problem is a necessary step for group problem solving activity. Similarly, group members must share conceptualization of the problem, which refers to understanding what kind of information is needed for solving the problem, what kind of manipulations of the information are necessary, and what kind of solutions are acceptable. This type of shared conceptualization of the problem facilitates a selection of adequate problem-solving activities and enables their coordination. Finally, processes of information acquisition, information retrieval, and use of information in groups require the sharing of information in every phase of problem solving. The latter process is the subject of recent review by Hinsz, Tindale, and Vollrath (1997), who presented groups as information processors. Their extensive review of literature suggests that the information processing in groups involves activities among group members including sharing of information, ideas, and cognitive processes. The shared knowledge is essential for group operations.

Group transactive memory. A somewhat different aspect of group mental activity was illuminated by Wegner's (1987) theory of group transactive memory. This theory offers a new perspective on mental interdependence in groups by considering coexistence in a group of individual differences and shared knowledge. The theory suggests that group members possess unique knowledge in their cognitive repertory (i.e., memory), which turns them into experts on particular topics. Group members know about each other's expertise and use it when the need arises. According to Wegner,

> The transactive memory system in a group involves the operation of the memory systems of the individuals and the processes of communication that occur within the group. Transactive memory is therefore not traceable to any of the individuals alone, nor can it be found somewhere "between" individuals. Rather, it is a property of a group. (p. 191)

In describing the organization of knowledge in a group, this theory emphasizes the differences among group members rather than their uniformity. But, the theory points out that for transactive memory to work in a group, group members must hold shared representations of the knowledge held by different members. These shared beliefs must be accurate and validated to ensure the smooth functioning of a group. Recently, Moreland, Argote, and Krishman (1996) reported experiments showing that transactive memory develops especially in situations when group members are trained together. Once it exists, it significantly improves group performance at work.

Consequences of sharing beliefs in small groups. The study of shared beliefs in small groups has become especially relevant for real-life situations in which individuals as group members work together. Researchers of such groups came out with different terms to describe the phenomenon I have called *shared beliefs*: shared mental models, common causal maps, collective mind, shared frames, cognitive consensuality, teamwork schemas, shared meaning, transactional memory, and sociocognition (Klimoski & Mohammed, 1994). Each of these models refers to different units of sharing, including, for instance, categories, frames of reference, values, ideologies, maps, mental models, norms, expectations, or knowledge. Some of the contributions have investigated the consequences of sharing beliefs in small groups. These studies showed that shared beliefs in small groups affect the speed, flexibility, and implementation of a decision (Walsh & Fahey, 1986); facilitate problem definition, generation of alternatives, and evaluation of choices (Walsh, Henderson, & Deighton, 1988); influence the quality of decisions (Innami, 1992); facilitate coordinated action (Smircich, 1983), learning and action (Daft & Weick, 1984), successful performance of a task (Guzzo, Yost, Campbell, & Shea, 1993), and group interaction (Bettenhausen & Murnighan, 1985); enhance the quality of teamwork skills and their effectiveness (Orasanu & Salas, 1993); and improve working relationships (Mitchell, 1986). But, the sharing of beliefs may also have negative effects. Janis (1982) described the phenomenon of "groupthink," which denotes the closure of group members on a particular idea without expression of doubts. Groupthink occurs when there is too much similarity among group members, who seal themselves off from outside influences and refuse to entertain alternative ideas to their consensually validated beliefs.

One conceptualization of the sharing of beliefs in work groups was offered by Klimoski and Mohammed (1994), who introduced the term *team mental model* (TMM). The term suggests that a group is made up of more than just the sum of its individual members' beliefs. The team mental model describes the way group members collectively think or characterize phenomena: It refers to organized knowledge mostly relating to tasks, situations, and working relations. Klimoski and Mohammed suggest that there must be at least a minimal awareness among group members that they share a mental model. Team mental models are especially necessary in the implementation phase of group work, after the decision phase. It is then that groups need shared beliefs so as to coordinate activity, use resources, and perform. Shared beliefs facilitate harmonious interactions, especially in situations of pressure and stress.

Group beliefs. Whereas the contributions previously described focus on the shared beliefs of small groups, and especially in the particular setting of workplace, my own earlier work (Bar-Tal, 1990a) on a particular category of shared beliefs, called *group beliefs,* has general implications beyond the discussion of small groups. It is especially applicable to the analysis of voluntary groups of different types, such as organizations, religious denominations, or political parties.

Group beliefs have been defined "as convictions that group members (a) are aware that they share and (b) consider as defining their groupness" (Bar-Tal, 1990a, p. 36). The special nature of this type of common belief rests in the second part of the definition. These beliefs define the identity of the group and provide the raison d'être for the collective to organize itself. Thus, group beliefs uniquely and formally define group membership, stating the necessary beliefs that a person has to hold to qualify as group member. In other words, they explicitly and specifically express the particular contents that group members have to hold. They define the essence of the group and supply the rationale for the sense of belonging to the group. That is, group beliefs provide the epistemic basis that unites group members into one entity, serve as a foundation for group formation, and form a bond for the group's continuous existence. Examples of group beliefs are, for instance, the Communist Manifesto for communists, the rules of the church (Ordnung) for the Amish society, or the belief in the right to life of the unborn child for the group members associated with the National Right to Life Committee.

My earlier work allowed the analysis of the role of group beliefs in various group processes. First, it suggested that group members have to share a fundamental group belief—"we are a group"—as a necessary condition for group formation. In addition, groups form other group beliefs that define the raison d'être of the group and demarcate its boundaries. They also serve as a cement for the social identity of group members (Bar-Tal, 1998a).

The developed conceptual framework suggests that group beliefs function as a prism through which it is possible to analyze various types of group dynamics: how groups merge, form subgroups, split, and disintegrate. Groups can merge only when their group beliefs are similar. Subgroups are formed when group members partly hold the same group beliefs but are divided with regard to issues on which they form subgroups. Groups split when group members strongly disagree about their group beliefs, and groups disintegrate when group members lose interest in group beliefs.

Stereotypes as Shared Beliefs

The study of stereotypes is a particular area of social psychology that has recognized the importance of shared beliefs. There is clearly a major difference between the case when beliefs about the contents of the stereotype are held by one person and the case when these beliefs are shared by group or society members. Ashmore and Del Boca (1981) differentiated between stereotype and cultural stereotype. According to their view, " 'stereotype' should be reserved for the set of beliefs held by an individual regarding a social group and the term 'cultural stereotype' should be used to describe shared or community-wide patterns of beliefs" (p. 19). The cultural stereotype widely shared by members of a group should receive the special attention of social psychologists, because it plays a powerful role in intergroup relations.

Tajfel (1981) also pointed out the importance of social context of stereotypes. Social context, according to Tajfel,

> refers to the fact that stereotypes held in common by large numbers of people are derived from and structured by the relations between large-scale social groups or entities. The functioning and use of stereotypes result from an intimate interaction between this contextual structuring and their role in the adaptation of individuals to their social environment. (p. 148)

However, social psychologists have only recently begun to elaborate on the consensual nature of stereotypes (i.e., Gardner, 1993; Haslam, 1996; Stangor & Schaller, 1996).

Stangor and Schaller (1996) differentiated between individual and collective approaches to the study of stereotypes. The collective approach refers to stereotypes as one category of the collective knowledge that a society holds: "It is part of the social fabric of a society, shared by the people within that culture" (p. 4). Stereotypes as collective belief systems have special importance because they guide group collective behavior: "Once group stereotypes exist in a culture, expected patterns of behavior for those group members follow, and these expectations determine both responses to group members and the behavior of the group members themselves" p. 13). Collective stereotypes, thus, can be considered as cultural norms that "are represented and perpetuated across individuals, across generations, and across time" (p. 13).

According to Stangor and Schaller (1996), stereotypes are maintained as norms; language and media are responsible for their transmission. Language transcends the individual and allows storage of the stereotypes on a collective level. It enables communication, through which the stereotypes are disseminated. Media as the major agent of dissemination teach and reinforce the uses of stereotypes.

Recently, Schaller and Conway (in press) proposed a social evolutionary framework to explain the evolution of shared stereotypes. According to this framework, stereotypes, like other socially shared cognitions, emerge and change as a result of processes similar to those that govern the evolution of biological structures. For sharing stereotypes, communication is the basic process that determines its selection. The more a particular stereotype is communicated to individuals, the more likely it is to become shared across a population of people. The likelihood of communicating a stereotype is an interactive function of its features as a belief, the characteristics of the group members, and the properties of the group's cultural norms and expectations.

Haslam (1996) claimed that the sharing of stereotypes does not derive from exposure to the same information but rather from group membership; underlying this are processes of social influence to seek agreement with other group members about the contents of stereotypes. Specifically, Haslam elaborated that stereotyping derives from the fact that the self is necessarily defined in terms of a social identity, which means that it is shared with other group members. Individuals who perceive themselves as group members agree and expect to agree with others who categorize themselves as members of the same group. In fact, individuals as group members actively seek to validate their own beliefs by social reality testing, that is, by comparing their own beliefs with beliefs of other group members, because those who share social identity are also identified as sources that can consensually validate subjective beliefs. As a result, group members tend to adopt the beliefs shared by other group members and to form a shared reality. They may attribute disagreement to perceived relevant differences in the stimulus situation, or they may recategorize those with whom they disagree as outgroup members. Haslam described an informational process through which stereotypes, as an example of beliefs, become shared. In a series of studies, he demonstrated that stereotypes become shared through perceptions of shared identity rather than by exposure to information per se. Group members endorse shared stereotypes through mutual influence, because they reflect shared ingroup norms (see review by Haslam et al., 1998).

The analysis of Gardner (1993) about stereotypes as consensual beliefs has implications for understanding shared beliefs. First, he points out that viewing stereotypes as consensual beliefs implies two units of analysis: the group and the individual. The first unit allows discussion about the shared content and the extent of sharing, whereas the second unit focuses on whether the particular individual shares the belief, how his/her attitudes or perceptions reflect sharing a belief, or does he/she evoke stereotype automatically. The analyses indicate that stereotypes as consensual beliefs have social relevance to the individual by influencing aspects of social behavior. Gardner proposed that consensually defined stereotypes, being based on social support and relying on common sources of information, have special characteristics. First of all, they are viewed as facts interpreting social reality. Second, they are based on cognitive factors rather than motivational or attitudinal ones. Third, they are often activated automatically and processed efficiently. Fourth, they are typically stable and do not change easily. Fifth, they are easily communicated.

These characteristics of consensual stereotypes can be generalized to shared beliefs in a group or society. The previous analysis was not done because of the particular content of stereotypes but because of their consensual nature. That is, this analysis suggests that consensual beliefs in a group, including stereotypes, have special characteristics as a consequence of being shared by group members.

The present book concerns a particular category of shared beliefs, namely societal beliefs, which are shared by society members. The next chapter will present this category of shared beliefs.

3

The Nature of
Societal Beliefs

THE CONCEPTION OF SOCIETAL BELIEFS

Societal beliefs, which are the focus of this book, are defined as enduring beliefs shared by society members, with contents that are perceived by society members as characterizing their society. The focal part of the definition points to the fact that societal beliefs characterize a society. Society members perceive this characterization and recognize that societal beliefs influence societal functioning. In this vein, it should be noted that not necessarily all societal beliefs contribute to the sense of social identity. Such a contribution is surely made by those dominant societal beliefs that constitute the ethos of the society. Societal beliefs then constitute societal knowledge accumulated by society members, that is, knowledge about their society. Society members share societal beliefs, which also appear in various cultural products, public debates, leaders' speeches, media information, and educational material. These beliefs endure for a long time and are part of the individual and public repertoire.

The endurance of societal beliefs is an important characteristic. Some societal beliefs may persist and survive over centuries, others over decades, whereas others are held only for a number of years before they vanish. Temporariness and transience are, however, not part of their nature.

An important reason for the durability of societal beliefs is that although societal beliefs are stored in individual minds, they exist nevertheless independent of the specific individuals who hold them. They are maintained by various societal institutions and transmitted by various societal channels of communication, which perpetuate them. A belief becomes a societal belief when it is spread among society members who consider it as such. This happens through a long process of social influence and dissemination, and once this status is achieved, it does not disappear overnight. Society members change their societal beliefs neither frequently nor suddenly. Revolutions, which when they occur, change existing systems and structures, are rare and, contrary to what their name suggests, happen as the result of a long run-up of change in societal beliefs. In most societies, most of the time, there is continuity of societal system, structure, and characterization. Societal beliefs, as beliefs that characterize a society, are pillars of a society and allow its continuation. But their durability does not imply that societal beliefs are unchangeable. They may change as part of a continuous social-historical process. This change depends on changes in reality as perceived by society members. As long as society members consider societal beliefs to be meaningful, relevant, and identity-serving, the beliefs continue to function and exist. But, societal beliefs cease to fulfill their functions when they become irrelevant to the new reality; then, they lose their status and may fall into oblivion. In other cases, the contents of societal beliefs may be modified and adapted to a new perceived reality. These processes will be further elaborated in the next chapters.

According to the preceding definition, what differentiates societal beliefs from other types of beliefs is their scope of contents, specific features, and functions. Group beliefs define, formally and uniquely, the "groupness" of any given group, exclusively characterize it, and are especially applicable to analyses of voluntary organizations and groups (Bar-Tal, 1990a). In contrast, the contents of societal beliefs are of wide scope and inclusive. Many beliefs characterize a society, and societies may hold similar societal beliefs. For example, more than one society may hold a societal belief that states "We are democratic" or "A number one problem of our society is drug addiction" or "We are engaged in violent conflict." But each particular society may view these beliefs as its characteristics. Moreover, the concept societal belief is used to analyze large social systems, where often there are no formal beliefs to define boundaries of the groupness. Societies, as social systems with structures, institutions, defined procedures, and sometimes even specific territories, do not always have beliefs that are necessary and sufficient to qualify people for membership. As an example, it is not clear what kind of beliefs a person living in Italy has to hold to be a member of Italian society. But all societies have characterizing beliefs, societal beliefs. Thus, the concept societal beliefs is especially applicable to characterize societies, which may not have clearly defined beliefs that are required for membership.

Societal beliefs provide a basis for the development of awareness of similarity, social identity, communication, interdependence, and coordination of societal activities—all of which are necessary conditions for the functioning of social systems. It is, thus, important that society members adopt these beliefs. Indeed, societies exert special effort to impart and maintain societal beliefs among their members. Society members, on their part, internalize these beliefs, which are viewed as part and parcel of that society (Turner, 1982). Being a member of a society indicates, in most cases, an acceptance of certain beliefs shared by members of this society (Bar-Tal, 1998a; Turner, 1991). Societies differ with regard to the number of societal beliefs shared by their members and the extent of sharing beliefs. In orthodox and totalitarian societies such as the Amish society or Nazi Germany, members share many societal beliefs, and, in fact, sharing societal beliefs is an essential requirement of these types of societies, which leads to great uniformity. In contrast, in democratic or open societies, sharing societal beliefs is not enforced, and therefore, fewer beliefs may be shared by society members. Nevertheless, even in some of the latter societies, members hold societal beliefs and, on the basis of the extent of their internalization, it is possible to distinguish between new society members (e.g., new immigrants) and rooted society members. It should be noted that in one state, a number of societies can be found; in some cases, these societies may be separated as, for example, the Palestinian and Jewish societies in the State of Israel, which has its own system of societal beliefs; in some cases, societies may have a common basis of shared societal beliefs, being part of a national society, and at the same time a separate system of societal beliefs as, for example, ethnic societies have in Canada. Many states are multisocietal, as they include different societies that flourish on the basis of such foundations as ideology, convictions, ethnicity, religion, national affiliation, race, or regional residence. The boundaries of the societies are determined by the self-identity of their members. What is focal for the present framework is the fact that each society develops its own system of societal beliefs. They are the fabric that gives essence to the society and provides the basis for societal action. They are one of the fundamental elements that turn an aggregate of individuals into a functioning society.

Societal beliefs are not exclusively connected with individuals' cognitive repertoire, because they can also be found in various cultural products of the society. On the individual level, societal beliefs illustrate Abelson's (1986, 1988) observation that "beliefs are like possessions." They tend to relate also to topics that are not directly experienced and not sensibly verifiable as, for example, are our beliefs about democracy or conflict. "They serve a social reality function—they are tools that enable us to act competently in the world around us" (Abelson, 1986, p. 229). What is most important is that they are held or experienced in the same way possessions are: They are owned, they are part of the cognitive repertoire, and they are seen as characterizing the person, also as a society member. According to Abelson (1986), one source of a belief's value is indeed its "sharedness." Societal beliefs are of high value for society members, because they "bring people closer and provide a basis for collective action" (Abelson, 1986, p. 237).

Societal beliefs, however, are not merely individual manifestations; they are also considered a societal characteristic. This perspective has been relatively neglected in social psychology but is widely addressed by sociologists, political scientists, and anthropologists. The view that societies, through a complex interaction between human experience and thinking, form characterizing belief systems shared by the society's members has been expressed by many social thinkers, including Karl Marx, Emile Durkheim, Karl Mannheim, Talcot Parsons, and Robert Merton, to name just a few of the most prominent social scientists. This position is well expressed in the sociology of knowledge perspective, which proposes that social knowledge is developed, transmitted, and maintained in social situations and that as such, it shapes the reality of society members. In the view of Mannheim (1952), "the analysis derived from the content of individual thought can never achieve this basic reconstruction of the whole outlook of a social group" (p. 59). Such reconstruction can be done with knowledge of a society that is grounded in its particular features. In turn, Parsons (1951) argued that "the sharing of a common beliefs system is a condition of the full integration of a system of social interactions" (p. 352). The stability of a social system depends on the degree to which society members internalize the shared beliefs and produce an integrative collective belief system.

Anthropologists through the years have been preoccupied too with the shared knowledge of a society. They realized that such shared knowledge is an important part of a culture (e.g., D'Andrade, 1984; Dougherty, 1985). Roberts (1964) pointed out,

> It is possible to regard all culture as information and to view any single culture as an "information economy" in which information is received or created, stored, retrieved, transmitted, utilized, and even lost. . . . In any culture information is stored in the minds of its members and, to a greater or lesser extent, in artifacts. (pp. 438-439)

And D'Andrade (1981) similarly suggested,

> It is not just physical objects which are products of culture. . . . Behavior environments, consisting of complex messages and signals, rights and duties, and rules and institutions, are a culturally constituted reality which is a product of our socially transmitted information pool. (p. 180)

Quantitative models have recently been developed to assess the extent to which cultural knowledge uniquely characterizes a particular society. One such model is Weller's (1987) common elements model of shared knowledge, which examines the extent to which society members share a particular body of knowledge that they consider cultural knowledge.

The present conception analyzes societal beliefs from a social psychological perspective to provide a unique contribution, complementing the work of other social sciences that have studied belief systems in a society. Social psychology has devoted considerable effort to examining the nature and structure of beliefs and how they are acquired and changed, but mainly on the individual level. It is important to apply this knowledge to the analysis of beliefs shared by a group or by society members. That is, research done in social psychology concerning the beliefs and attitudes formed by individuals in a group framework can shed special light on societal systems of beliefs.

The following analysis of societal beliefs will consist of a description of their contents, characteristics, and functions.

⁂ THE CONTENTS OF SOCIETAL BELIEFS

Any analysis of societal beliefs must refer to their contents. Society members perceive the contents of societal beliefs as characterizing them. These contents can touch on various issues, experiences, memories, expectations, justifications, or concerns. They may include such products as myths, collective memories, symbols, ideologies, self-images, images of other societies, goals, values, or societal aspirations. They can be drawn from the remote past to provide a common foundation and history of the society. They can also derive from the present and relate to current characteristics and concerns of the society, and they may also consist of future goals and visions. Societal beliefs constitute the fundamental conceptual knowledge of the society. These beliefs must be relevant to the present conditions and state of the society. That is, they must afford an understanding of where the society comes from and what its present concerns and future aspirations are. Societal beliefs, thus, shed light on the past, give meaning to the present, and offer society members a sense of the predictability of the future.

Societal beliefs can be either descriptive or prescriptive in nature. Descriptive societal beliefs touch on past experiences and events and on present concerns and issues, whereas prescriptive beliefs refer to values, norms, or future goals. These prescriptive beliefs, defining the desired condition of the society to itself, are based on descriptive beliefs: The desired goal, values, or aspirations are derived from past and present conditions or experiences.

The contents of societal beliefs are organized around different themes, which in many cases are related to each other. For example, a theme of societal beliefs can pertain to security concerns of society members in view of threats coming from another group. Such a theme may be related to a theme of poverty, that characterizes a society, because limited resources can be directed either to increase security or to fight poverty. In principle, themes constitute the organizational framework for societal beliefs.

Societal beliefs, as well as the themes in which they are organized, are not of equal importance. Particular societal beliefs and their themes may play a more central role in societal life than others. The most central themes and the relevant societal belief(s) are the dominant characteristic of a given society. They reflect the ethos of a society. Societal beliefs related to such themes have special effects on societal life. An example of such central themes can be found in societies engaged in violent and protracted conflict. In these societies, societal beliefs about the conflict are of special importance, and therefore, the ethos of these societies can be characterized as an ethos of conflict. This specific case will be discussed in Chapter 8.

Several themes of societal beliefs will be described and illustrated extensively in separate chapters, but for now, a few examples of contents will be presented. These examples are based on the writings of social scientists who refer to shared beliefs characterizing particular societies. Some of the examples are based on empirical findings and others on conceptual analyses. The examples are taken from different societies and, in a few cases, even from past periods.

Jessop (1974), in his analysis of the British political culture, pointed out several beliefs widely prevalent in British society, which can be considered societal beliefs because they are widely shared and characterize the British society. On the basis of survey data of the 1950s, 1960s, and early 1970s, he showed, for example, that the majority of British people believed that Britain needs the royal family and that the royal family plays an important role in British life, symbolizing the British people. Also, he observed a widespread belief in the necessity of symbolic religious institutions. Most Britons believed in the need for religious education in schools, prayers in the House of Commons, chaplains, and state religion status for the Anglican church. They also believed that their society is stratified into classes.

In another study done in the United States, Coleman (1941) provided a list of beliefs that are shared by American society members and that characterize this society. Among these beliefs, he noticed a belief urging "freedom from entangling alliances," a belief in equal opportunity, distrust of strong government, importance of associations in societal life, and beliefs stressing local responsibility and initiatives. This list was repeated years later by Williams (1970), who pointed out that Americans shared a number of beliefs that prescribe their desired goals and behaviors (i.e., values). American society can be characterized by values of occupational achievement, emphasis on work, moral orientation, efficiency, progress, material comfort, equality, freedom, patriotism, and democracy.

Examples of societal beliefs in the former Soviet Union can be inferred from the large-scale study done by Inkeles and Bauer (1959), who administered questionnaires and interviewed many hundreds of Soviet refugees at the end of World War II to tap the beliefs of the Soviet people in general. Their data suggest that the great majority of Soviet citizens believed in the importance of state planning, public ownership, and state control over most areas of economic life. Additional widespread societal beliefs in the Soviet Union were that it is the role of the government, and society at large, to provide welfare benefits, medical care, education, and job security. These beliefs, typifying a communal, socialist welfare type of society, were clearly perceived as characterizing Soviet society (White, 1974) by the Soviet citizens and by the world outside what was then the Union of Soviet Socialist Republics. In addition, it was noted that one of the basic Russian societal beliefs pertains to the importance of strong central authority to govern Russia (Flenley, 1996). The central authority was called "the Palladium of Russia," and historical events were interpreted to support belief in its necessity, stating that periods of weakened central authority inevitably ended in successful foreign invasions. Thus, disunity among the Kiev princes facilitated the Mongol conquest; disintegration of the central power brought occupation by Swedes and Poles. On the other hand, strong central rulers brought stability, prosperity, and strength.

A study of Japanese society reveals a number of examples of societal beliefs. Benedict (1967) suggested that any attempt to understand Japanese society after World War II must begin with the recognition of its beliefs (i.e., societal beliefs) about societal order and hierarchy. In her own words,

> Japan's confidence in hierarchy is basic in her whole notion of man's relation to his fellow man and of man's relation to the state and it is only by describing some of their national institutions like the family, the state, religious and economic life that it is possible for us to understand their view of life. (p. 43)

An additional example of a societal belief in the present Japanese society is provided by R. J. Smith (1983). In his eloquent analysis of the Japanese society, he proposed that one of its distinguishing societal beliefs concerns striving for perfection for the benefit of the society. In his opinion, this belief derives from premises rooted in Japanese myths and based on Confucian teaching and Buddhism.

Another example of societal beliefs may be taken from the Protestant and Catholic societies in North Ireland. Whereas the Protestants' leading societal belief refers to their desire to remain part of Britain (Morrow, 1995), the Catholics' leading societal belief refers to their aspiration to be part of the Irish Republic (O'Malley, 1990). An analysis of Burmese society by Pye (1962) illustrates societal beliefs anchored in religion. He observed that belief in Buddhism "seems to be at the very basis of the Burman's sense of identity both as an individual and as a member of a community" (p. 189). The belief in being Buddhist is the most profound basis of the society, which affects almost all domains of societal life including many of its secular aspects. It also provides foundations for most Burmese social and political structures.

The above examples of contents indicate that societal beliefs serve as an organizing framework of knowledge about the main features of the society for society members. In other words, they provide the epistemic basis by which society members know their society. They present a picture of the society from the society's point of view. It is a society-centered image, but it plays an essential role in societal behavior, and as such, the study of the contents of societal beliefs is an important prerequisite for understanding any given society. These contents are identifiable and can serve as well-defined units of analysis, which can be studied in different ways, by means of different research methods, mainly through questionnaires and through content analyses of the tangible products of the society.

In the first method, societal beliefs, or ethos, are elucidated directly from society members by questioning them with either open-ended questions or closed questions, for example, presenting items (i.e., beliefs) to which society members express their agreement. Using questionnaires, different sample groups of society members can be asked about societal beliefs. Polls can also be used to inquire about the prevalence of societal beliefs. For example, Bar-Tal and Zafran (2000) developed a scale to assess the prevalence of societal beliefs that are part of the conflictual ethos, described in Chapter 9. The same chapter describes an analysis of societal beliefs of the American ethos, done by McClosky and Zaller (1984), who used surveys in their investigation.

A second method for study of societal beliefs or ethos pertains to use of content analysis. It is possible to content-analyze the appearance of societal beliefs in various cultural, political, and educational products such as leaders' speeches, school textbooks, literary texts, newspaper articles, films, and so on. These products are used to transmit societal beliefs, and this method does not require the cooperation of society members but only the availability of such materials. An example of the use of content analysis is a study that investigated the prevalence of societal beliefs of intractable conflict ethos in school textbooks used by Israeli schools (Bar-Tal, 1998b).

▨ THE FUNCTIONS OF SOCIETAL BELIEFS

The observation that beliefs or attitudes fulfill functions for both individuals and societies is not a new one. As early as the 1950s, two main theories were put forth which came to describe the functional basis of attitudes and beliefs (Katz, 1960; Smith, Bruner, & White, 1956). These theories imply that the repertory of beliefs and attitudes that a person has is not accidental and that individuals select and hold those beliefs and attitudes that satisfy their needs. Another assumption is that individuals differ with regard to the functions their attitudes or beliefs actually serve. In the words of Katz (1960), "By concerning ourselves with the different functions attitudes can perform, we can avoid the great error of oversimplification—the error of attributing a single cause to given types of attitudes" (p. 168). Moreover, any given belief or attitude held by any given individual may serve one or more functions, whereas the same belief or attitude may serve different functions for different individuals.

In the last decade, the subject of the functionality of attitudes and beliefs appeared again, having disappeared for a few decades, and began to interest social psychologists (see Eagly & Chaiken, 1993; Herek, 1986; Pratkanis, Breckler, & Greenwald, 1989). Of particular interest to the present conception is the work of Tetlock (1989) about the function of political beliefs, which can also be applied to societal beliefs. Tetlock pointed out that political beliefs are shaped by the "fundamental values they are trying to advance in particular policy domains, by the degree of conflict or tension among those values, and by the role and accountability relationships within which they must work" (p. 130). He also acknowledged that beliefs may be grounded in various motives, such as concern for cognitive mastery or protection of self-image. Lane (1973), a political scientist, noted,

> For organizations and societies, the internal functions served by belief systems are those of integration, coordination, morale building, leadership legitimization, defining equity and justice within the system, and providing formulas for conflict resolution. (p. 94)

The present conception pays special attention to the functions that societal beliefs fulfill, an approach implying that the contents of societal beliefs are not accidental, as society maintains those societal beliefs whose contents satisfy its needs. Because a society has many different needs, the various functions that come to address them will now be elaborated on. As a general proposition, it should be stated that societal beliefs play an important role in the life of a society. They fulfill functions for the society as a whole and for society members as individuals. Societal beliefs provide one of the bases that makes a society, and they constitute an important mechanism that maintains the society. Society members need societal beliefs to live together as a collective. Specifically, they create uniformity and provide rationale for being a society. As indicated, societal beliefs allow society members to maintain their social structure, to carry their unique culture, and to develop their own social system by enabling awareness of similarity, communication, development of common worldview, common identity, interdependence, and coordination of activity. Therefore, societal beliefs are an inherent part of the societal system, and society cannot exist without societal beliefs.

The present conception assumes that societies tend to form and maintain those societal beliefs that are functional for coping with reality as perceived by society members. This assumption indicates that societal beliefs help society members to adapt to the perceived reality. This is done through several specific functions fulfilled by societal beliefs. Society members as individuals and as members of a collective have different needs, which arise as a result of the interaction between their own dispositions and between the particular situations in which they find themselves. Satisfaction of these needs is crucial for every society, because it allows society members to live under particular conditions. Thus, for example, a society that lives under conditions of intractable conflict, which will be analyzed in Chapter 9, maintains societal beliefs that facilitate coping with these determinative conditions. Different conditions require different sets of societal beliefs, and therefore, societies that live under different conditions have different societal beliefs.

The present conception focuses on four major functions that societal beliefs fulfill: epistemic, social identity, the preservation, and action guidance. Those are four general functions that beliefs in any society can be observed to fulfill. Each society has to satisfy these four functions to exist. They are basic functions that enable society members to relate to their society and function as its members. It should be remembered, however, that these are not the only functions that societal beliefs fulfill. Societies have additional functions that arise as a result of their particular history, conditions, structure, or goals. At present, the four basic functions will be presented, and later, when specific societal beliefs will be described, their additional specific function will be outlined.

The Epistemic Function

On the most basic level, societal beliefs fulfill the elementary epistemic function of providing knowledge about the society. Their contents and themes enlighten society members about fundamental questions such as, How was the society formed? What were its major formative experiences? What is its uniting basis? What is the rationale for its structure and functioning? What are its major concerns? What are its goals? In essence, through societal beliefs, society members learn about themselves.

The epistemic function is of crucial importance in satisfying the basic human need to comprehend the world in which we live. This need seems to be fulfilled by the knowledge function of attitudes, proposed by Katz (1960). In his conception, an attitude functions to make sense of the world and enables people to make sense out of their experience.

> Individuals . . . seek knowledge to give meaning to what would otherwise be an unorganized chaotic universe. People need standards or frames of reference for understanding their world, and attitudes help to supply such standards. . . . People are not avid seekers after knowledge as judged by what the educator or social reformer would desire. But they do want to understand the events which impinge directly on their own life. (pp. 175-176)

Individuals strive to perceive their world in a meaningful way in which events, people, things, or symbols, beyond being isolated stimuli, come to be apprehended in an organized way that provides meaning to the perceived information (Reykowski, 1982). Individuals try to reduce uncertainty and ambiguities to live in an environment that is comprehensible (Berkowitz, 1968). They try to find order in the social and physical world they live in (e.g., Berger, 1969; Geertz, 1973).

The sense of understanding is a precondition for a feeling that the world is organized, predictable, and controllable. As Fiske and Taylor (1991) pointed out, "General knowledge about ourselves and others provides us with the expectations that enable us to function in the world" (p. 15). Knowledge allows a sense of understanding and thus a sense of control (Heider, 1958; Kelly, 1955; White, 1959). Individuals who have knowledge feel that they can predict what may happen in the future and thus control their fate (Forsyth, 1980).

Societal beliefs fulfill the important function of providing a meaningful and comprehensible picture of the societal world for society members. Insofar as they are shared beliefs by society members and characteristic of the society, they are accepted as truthful and valid. They are viewed with trust because they are shared by members of the same social category, who establish and maintain them as part of the social agreement that underlies any society or group (Hogg & Abrams, 1993; Turner, 1991).

In terms of contents, societal beliefs provide unique knowledge about the society on a wide range of themes. This knowledge sheds light on an array of experiences, concerns, issues, or images that characterize the society. Societal beliefs fulfill the epistemic function by providing meaningful, coherent, and

organized knowledge about the society. They provide explanations, justifications, information, interpretations, evaluations, reasonings, rationales, and
expectations about themes that are relevant to societal life. They construct
"a rational reality" that allows individuals to understand the society of which
they are members. Especially important is their role as the prism for understanding current issues, such as conflict, unemployment, or crime, which preoccupy society members. Current issues involve temporary problems and also
long-standing concerns faced by the society. Societal beliefs illuminate and
bestow meanings on these. Thus, societal beliefs enable society members to
feel that they comprehend the society's issues.

In sum, it can be said that by fulfilling the epistemic function, societal
beliefs crucially affect society members' understanding of their world. They
influence what kind of information gets attention, how new information is
interpreted, and how inferences are made when information is missing. Societal beliefs, thus, provide coherence and organize many society members'
experiences.

The Social Identity Function

As already noted, some societal beliefs fulfill the unique function of contributing to the formation, maintenance, and strengthening of social identity, a
crucial requirement in the formation of any society or group. Individuals have
to identify themselves as group members for the group to exist. This condition
is widely accepted by social scientists. For example, Deutsch (1968) proposed
that "a psychological group exists (has unity) to the extent that the individuals
composing it perceive themselves as pursuing promotively interdependent
goals" (p. 468). Similarly, Merton (1957) suggested that a second criterion for
a group "is that the interacting persons define themselves as 'members' "
(p. 286). It is, thus, not surprising that the study of social identity has become
one of the central areas of interest in social psychology. The previously men-
tioned work by Tajfel and his collaborators (Tajfel, 1978, 1981, 1982; Tajfel &
Turner, 1986) initiated this line of interest, which was followed by Turner and
his collaborators (Turner, 1991, 1999; Turner et al., 1987). According to them,
self-concept consists of a collection of self-images that includes both individ-
uating characteristics and social categorical characteristics. The former represent personal identity, whereas the latter express social identity. Social identity
combines identifications—of varying degrees of importance—with different
groups. The formation of social identity is based on a self-categorization
process in which individuals group themselves cognitively as the same, in
contrast to some other class of collectives. On this basis, the uniformity and
coordination of group behavior emerge.

Clearly, self-categorization is fundamental for self-definition as a society member, but it is only an initial phase; it must be followed by acceptance of additional beliefs that provide meaning to social identity (Bar-Tal, 1998a; Turner, 1991, 1999). Society members, as thinking creatures, cannot be satisfied with mere self-categorization for forming society membership. They need an elaborated system of beliefs that justifies and explains their belonging, describes their characteristics and concerns as society members, and explains the meaning of their social identity.

Abelson and Prentice (1989) recognized, in their analysis of beliefs, that beliefs may fulfill social identification functions. In their opinion, beliefs that serve this function are central, stable, and highly characteristic of a group. These beliefs are shared, and group members care whether other members hold them. In this vein, Aberle, Cohen, Davis, Levy, and Sutton (1950) included in their definition of a society two provisions that refer to what we have called here societal beliefs: "The members must share a body of cognitive orientations and they must share certain goals that have common modes of feeling and willing" (p. 101).

Some societal beliefs provide the knowledge that is required constructing social identity. The most salient example appears in the ethos of a society. These core beliefs not only define the raison d'être for society formation, as groups beliefs do (see Bar-Tal, 1990a), but also extend the epistemic basis for the formation of social identity by adding shared beliefs that go beyond the mere definition of the society's "we-ness." They describe the particularity of the society, frame its experience, focus on its concerns, and outline its aspirations.

The contribution of societal beliefs to the formation and maintenance of social identity is achieved not only through the contents of the beliefs that characterize the society but also through the awareness that they are shared. Society members experience a sense of commonality when they are aware that other society members share the same beliefs. In this way, societal beliefs contribute to the sense of unity and solidarity of society members. Sharing the same beliefs shapes society members' identity, giving them a sense of belonging and cohesiveness. When combined into an ethos, these beliefs also are factors that allow differentiation among societies. In addition to such determinants as territory, language, customs, or physical features, ethos characterizes a particular collective and helps to demarcate its societal boundaries.

The Preservation Function

Societal beliefs are an important mechanism for the preservation of the existing societal system and structure. They provide the knowledge that gives meaning to the existing societal order. This function of societal beliefs has been widely discussed by social scientists: From Marx and Weber to Parsons and Habermas, it has been agreed that beliefs play a crucial role in maintaining the societal system. In most cases, it is not usually in the nature of societal beliefs to instigate dramatic social change or spark revolutions, but rather to maintain and strengthen societal institutions, symbols, or values. In this vein, Levinson (1964), a psychologist, observed that every society needs shared beliefs or, as he labeled them, ideology. He suggested that "societal stability requires that the most common (model) ideologies held by its individual members shall be congruent with, and thus serve to maintain the norms of the existing social structure" (p. 307). Societal beliefs support the visions and goals that the society aims to achieve in the future, and they glorify the past. They justify and explain societal acts, and in essence, they provide the rationale for societal structure and functioning.

The mere fact that societal beliefs are shared provides the basis for society's stability and continuation. Society members, by adopting societal beliefs, are persuaded and even committed to continue the societal order. There is, indeed, social psychological evidence indicating that individuals who achieve a shared reality act in ways that protect and maintain it (Hardin & Higgins, 1996).

Thus, it is not surprising that those sectors, groups, and individuals in the society who have a vested interest in the maintenance of the system and structure make a special effort to disseminate and propagate societal beliefs among society members. They actively take responsibility for spreading societal beliefs through societal communication channels, among them educational institutions.

But, this should not be understood to mean that societal beliefs advocate complete stagnation. They may express society members' dissatisfaction with various domains of societal life and reflect desires for change. Thus, for example, American society, being characterized by societal beliefs pertaining to the problem of violence and crime, does not accept this state of matters. The prevalence of these societal beliefs is an energizing force to improve a troubling situation without changing the societal system and structure.

The Action Guidance Function

Another important function of societal beliefs is to motivate and guide societal action. Smelser (1962) recognized that "in all collective behavior there is some kind of belief that prepares the participants for action" (p. 79), and beliefs "create the common culture within which leadership, mobilization and concerted action can take place" (p. 82). Similarly Cancian (1975), who discussed shared beliefs, proposed that they "affect behavior by specifying what action will cause others to validate a particular identity. Therefore beliefs that are perceived to be shared by groups will be related to action, while personal beliefs of an individual may not be" (p. 135). Societal beliefs supply many of the reasons for societal behavior. These reasons rationalize, justify, and instruct the direction and type of action that the society takes. A clear instance of the use of societal beliefs for justifying, explaining, and motivating actions can be found in the rhetoric used by leaders. Society members need a rationale for their coordinated behaviors, because it is a basic human need to perceive oneself as acting on a rational basis and thus having reasons for one's behavior. Leaders are often the ones who provide these reasons, and they often base them on societal beliefs.

Societal beliefs not only lead forward to action but also may come to justify or explain past action. American social scientists suggested early on that human action was the basis for social knowledge (e.g., Mead, 1934; Thomas & Znaniecki, 1918): From their behavior, individuals learn about themselves and the environment. From another perspective, Bem (1967, 1972) also suggested that individuals, as observers of their own behavior, form beliefs to explain it. Thus, we may conclude that society members also form societal beliefs after a behavior has taken place because they want to make sense out of action already performed. Societal beliefs that have emerged in this way serve to give meaning to the experiences of society members. As such, they fulfill the role of knowledge, as was elaborated earlier, in the discussion of the epistemic function of societal belief.

4

Formation, Dissemination, Maintenance, and Change of Societal Beliefs

The formation, dissemination, maintenance, and change of societal beliefs are key processes in every society. They constitute an important part of societal functioning, and the present chapter will discuss each of them.

FORMATION OF SOCIETAL BELIEFS

A societal belief passes through a long process from the moment it originates as a belief held by an individual society member, or shared by several of them, until it is shared by the society as a whole and perceived as characteristic of the society. What is of importance for the present discussion is the instigating basis for societal belief formation: I would like to propose that the content of the potential societal belief is based on distinctively society-related experiences of the society members. That is, the collective experiences of society members, which have relevance to the whole society, are the basis for forming knowledge that can shed light on the society.

55

Experiential Basis of Societal Beliefs

The specified proposition states that the contents of societal beliefs are based on collective experiences of society members, whether real or imagined and/or on implications that are drawn from these experiences. A wide range of collective experiences can serve to instigate the formation of the belief; these experiences may involve various types of events or gradual processes, conditions, practices, or ways of life; they may relate to societal structures and institutions, social phenomena, and so on; and they can be derived from different domains of life, such as politics, economics, religion, culture, or others. In principle, any collective experience that is meaningful in the eyes of society members can serve as a basis for the formation of beliefs, which eventually may become societal beliefs. Common collective experiences that play this role are wars, conflict, political alliances, disasters, injustices, rebellions, famine, persecutions, hunger, a particular regime, exploitation, victories, economic successes, a particular economic or political system, inequalities, and so on. Societal beliefs can refer directly to these collective experiences and describe them, and they also can consist of implications drawn from the collective experiences. Often, both the collective experience and its implications serve as a basis for the formation of a societal belief. Usually, there is no single societal belief formed on the basis of a collective experience, but rather a number of beliefs organized around a particular theme.

A societal belief based on direct experience is, for instance, associated with British society: Britain has a royal family that serves as a key symbol (Jessop, 1974). In this case, the societal belief describes the experience of living in a society that has a royal family. Also, Israeli society distinguishes itself by a societal belief about the existence of conflict between its secular and religious society members, a belief resulting from directly experiencing such conflict (Levy, Levinsohn, & Katz, 1993). A final example is the societal belief prevalent in Mexican society that it is characterized by inequality; this is based on the perceived experience of a majority of its members (Mesa-Lago, 1976).

Besides being based on direct collective experience, societal beliefs can, as noted before, be formed using the implications drawn from such collective experience: these implications may refer to evaluations, prescriptive values, desirable goals, learned lessons, and so on, all based on the collective experience. The following example will illustrate how societal beliefs originate this way. The tragic experiences of Jews during the Holocaust not only led to the formation of societal beliefs based directly on the collective experience itself but also served as the basis for drawing the conclusion that Jews cannot trust anyone but themselves; this became a societal belief in Israeli society (see Chapter 8 for elaboration of this example). Another example is that of some societies, which as a result of the collective experience of living under a totalitarian regime, have formed the societal belief of aspiration for democracy. Thus, Spanish society formed such a belief, as an aspiration, during the dictatorial rule of Franco (Perez-Diaz, 1993). Indeed, Iniguez, Valencia, and Vazquez (1997) suggested that the collective experience of the Spanish Civil War, in which nearly 1 million people were killed, caused the Spanish people to realize the importance of "democratic order as the context that reduces the conflict, the fight, that the war represents" (p. 250).

The collective experiences that serve as a basis for the formation of societal beliefs are usually real and consist of either past or current collective experiences. But a society might also generate societal beliefs from imagined experiences. In most cases, these experiences have supposedly occurred in the distant past. An example is the myth about the legendary Swiss patriot, Wilhelm Tell, who supposedly secured the independence of Switzerland in the 14th century. This myth originated in the 15th century but spread only toward the end of the 18th century and subsequently became a societal belief transmitting patriotic devotion and the value of national liberty (Kohn, 1956). Of a similarly mythical provenance is the Jewish societal belief that Jews were slaves in Egypt more than 3,000 years ago: The majority of Jews today still consider this belief as central to their cultural religious heritage (Eban, 1984). In any event, what is important is not necessarily the belief's basis in reality, but the meaning attributed to it by society members and the function it fulfills for the society. Societal beliefs based on imagined experiences may at times feature more centrally in the societal repertoire than societal beliefs that are based on real experience. This is especially so because imagined experiences are likely to fulfill the function of providing social identity by referring to contents that describe the more or less remote origins of the society.

Real collective experiences that serve as the basis for the formation of societal beliefs have to involve at least some members of the society, and often, they involve many. In any case, these experiences have to have relevance for the whole society. Even though terrorist attacks that have taken place in Israel throughout the last decades have directly involved relatively few members of Israeli society, they have nevertheless served as a basis for the formation of societal beliefs about Israel being a state affected by terrorism and about the insecurity of the country (Arian, 1995). On the other hand, many Israeli Jews of the older generation have either directly or indirectly experienced the Holocaust, and this too has formed the basis for various societal beliefs (Liebman & Don-Yehiya, 1983). Another example of societal beliefs based on direct collective experiences of many society members is discussed by Lira (1997), who described the preoccupation of the Chilean society with human rights issues following the Chilean dictatorship that ruled the country for 17 years (1973-1990). During these years, out of a population of 10 million, 1.6 million people were forced into exile, 50,000 people were detained, and about 3,000 were murdered. As Lira analyzes this experience, the Chileans' collective memory in the 1990s regarding the regime's abuses served as a basis for evolving societal beliefs regarding the importance of guarding human rights. Recently, Schwartz (1991) proposed that the American people's direct experience of the extraordinary funeral rites for President Abraham Lincoln, following his assassination, were responsible for transforming Lincoln into a sacred symbol of American society, expressed in various societal beliefs.

Collective experiences from the ancient past can also be recovered to serve as a basis for the formation of societal beliefs. Thus, for example, contemporary Israeli society has formed societal beliefs on the basis of the Jewish defense of Mount Masada during the rebellion against the Romans in 73 C.E., which ended with the collective suicide of the defenders; and on Bar Kochba's rebellion against the Romans, which took place from 132 to 135 C.E. (Liebman & Don-Yehiya, 1983; Zerubavel, 1995). The formation of a societal belief based on the former event was documented and described by Ben-Yehuda (1995), who investigated how a narrative recorded by Flavius Josephus and neglected for nearly 1,800 years was turned into a central myth of Israeli society. This myth (i.e., societal belief), shared by the Israelis, has become a primary symbol of heroism, patriotism, self-determination, and lonely struggle in a hostile world.

Flavius Josephus describes about 960 Jewish rebels against the Roman occupation who left Jerusalem for the desert fortress of Masada, where they fought Roman legions under siege. Seeing that Masada's fall was inevitable, its defenders committed collective suicide rather than surrender. This is the only remaining account of events that were forgotten for many centuries. Only in 1923 was the story translated into modern Hebrew. In 1933, an Israeli educator, Shmaria Guttman, visited the mountain and realized that the impressive landscape together with the powerful story could successfully help constitute a major myth for the reviving nation. This was done consciously and intentionally, as the political leadership realized the need for this type of myth in a society engaged in violent struggle to achieve independence. After Israel was founded, the Masada narrative remained a central one, which fulfilled and still continues to fulfill important symbolic functions for the society. The Masada story has had wide cultural currency in Israel. It has been disseminated by all societal institutions and channels of communications, such as the youth movements, mass media, school textbooks, art products, tourist industry, political leaders, and the Israeli army—all of them acting to turn it into a functional major societal belief that is transmitted to every Israeli up to the present day. The example of the Masada myth shows how a society reconstructs collective memory to fulfill its needs. It adopts the images of old events and experience to contemporary functions.

The proposition that a society's past is usually reconstructed and re-appropriated to serve current attitudes and needs, especially when it defines the social identity of society, is well supported by historians and sociologists (Halbwachs, 1992; Kammen, 1991). Moreover, as indicated, some prevailing societal beliefs, which are part of a society's collective memory, can be shown to have been "invented" to serve various current societal functions, especially the formation of identity (see Anderson, 1991; Kammen, 1991). In general, collective memories whether invented or not provide a stable image on which new societal beliefs are formed. Connerton (1989) pointed out that "our experience of the present very largely depends upon our knowledge of the past. We experience our present world in the context which is causally connected with the past events and objects" (p. 2). Beliefs about the past help to make sense and to legitimize the present social order.

Collective experiences that serve as a basis for the formation of societal beliefs can be either one-time events or continuous states of a society. In the former category are events that last a relatively very short time, such as fateful battles, for example, the Catholics' defeat by the Protestants at Derry, Aughnim, and Boyne in the 17th century, which nourished societal beliefs among both Catholics and Protestants in Northern Ireland (Cecil, 1993), or the Serbian defeat at Kosovo by the Ottoman Turks in 1389 for Serb society (Volkan, 1996), or the signing of the U.S. Constitution in 1787 for American society (Martindale, 1960). A one-time event can also be of a prolonged nature, such as the French Revolution of 1789, which was crucial for French society and has been the basis for many of its societal beliefs (e.g., Hunt, 1984). Another example is the major impact of Nazi rule in Germany between 1933 and 1945 for German society; this experience formed many different societal beliefs (e.g., Aycoberry, 1981). Some of these events—for example, revolutions, determinative battles, genocides, or wars—have such strong impact on societies that societal beliefs emerge as a reaction to them soon after the collective experiences. An example of such a collective experience is the fall of the Berlin wall separating East and West Germany and the reunification of the two countries. This experience had an important impact on German society, and new societal beliefs were formed on its basis and quickly institutionalized (LeGloanes, 1994). Another dramatic collective experience in recent history was the U.S. dropping of atom bombs on Hiroshima and Nagasaki in Japan in the summer of 1945. This tragedy was followed immediately by the formation of new Japanese societal beliefs about pacifism and nonviolence, opposition to the use of nuclear power, antipollution, and disarmament (Ishida, 1989). Such quickly formed societal beliefs not only keep events alive in the collective memory, but also give meaning to collective experiences. Other events do not have such an immediate impact but, over time, acquire importance for a society, for example, the immigration of the Turkish guest workers to Germany during the 1960s and 1970s. This immigration changed the nature of German society, which became multicultural, and, as a result, societal beliefs about German multiculturalism were formed (Brubaker, 1992; Waever, Buzan, Kelstrup, & Lemaitre, 1993).

Societal beliefs are also formed on the basis of continuous conditions in a society. In this vein, Marxist social thinkers proposed that societies form shared belief systems on the basis of prevalent social conditions and economic modes of production. Other continuous collective experiences that can serve as a basis for societal belief formation are experiences of individualism, threat, democracy, or religious domination. Thus, America's self-sufficient and self-reliant way of life has served as a basis for evolving a societal belief about American society's individualism (Williams, 1970). Similarly, the continuous influence of Catholicism in Italy has generated many societal beliefs (Kogan, 1983).

A society undergoes many different collective experiences, and society members form many different beliefs on their basis, which may then become characteristic of the society as a whole. Only very few such beliefs are disseminated among a majority of society members, become shared, and are considered societal beliefs: that is, beliefs a significant part of society members regard as characteristic of their society. Two questions that arise in this context are (a) what kind of processes turn beliefs into societal beliefs and (b) what are the features of these beliefs that facilitate these processes. The next section of this chapter tries to answer these questions.

DISSEMINATION OF SOCIETAL BELIEFS

The formation of societal beliefs, as described above, is only the first phase in the process of their acquisition by society members. After their formation, beliefs have to be disseminated if they are to be acquired and considered by society members as societal beliefs. The process of dissemination is two-fold: Beliefs are both transmitted and negotiated. Transmission describes the spreading of the beliefs among society members, whereas negotiation refers to their adaptation through social influence. Each will now be elaborated.

Transmission

A belief has to be transmitted to society members to be acquired by them. The transmission takes place through various channels of communication available in the society. These range from the informal and personal, such as interpersonal interactions in small groups, to institutionalized formal channels of information, including cultural, political, and societal sources. Of special importance are the mass media, which distribute information to large numbers of society members. Transmission takes various forms: Often, societal beliefs are expressed orally, for example, in leaders' speeches, or they appear in printed form, for example, in books, journals, or newspapers. Painting, sculpture, and even dance communicate societal beliefs, even though often in a less obvious way.

Medin's (1990) book provides an enlightening example, describing how the Cuban leadership transmitted Marxist-Leninist beliefs together with Cuban nationalism and shaped them into societal beliefs of the Cuban ethos. This was a challenging task for the revolutionary Cuban leaders, because the overwhelming majority of the Cuban people were far removed from the conceptual world of Marxism-Leninism at the time Castro took power in Cuba. Almost from the beginning, the leaders used all possible channels, institutions, and mechanisms to impart what the authors call "the revolutionary social consciousness." Education played an important role in the transmission efforts. First, through a literacy campaign, the illiterate population was systematically exposed to socialist ideology. Then, the school system, through school textbooks, curricula, and teachers' training, was mobilized to transmit the beliefs of the new ethos. In this attempt, the Cuban leadership also used the Revolutionary Armed Forces (FAR). As one of the commanders said, "Among its many duties, the party's principal task in the FAR is the Marxist-Leninist education of the soldiers and noncommissioned and commissioned officers" (Medin, 1990, p. 147)

In addition, the leaders made a special effort to found mass organizations among different sectors of Cuban society to transmit the new societal beliefs. These efforts were complemented by monopolizing the cultural channels, which were reorganized and given the task of indoctrinating the masses: The cinema, literature, theater, and popular music were all used to transmit the new societal beliefs composing its ethos. Medin (1990) points out that during the 30 years of Cuban Revolution, the leadership succeeded in shaping a new ethos: Marxism-Leninism plays "a prominent part, not only in projecting political messages, but also in conveying cultural, artistic, social, and other messages" (p. 1). These messages penetrated deeply into Cuban society, and many of its members hold them as truthful, characterizing beliefs.

Societies differ with regard to the number and variety of channels that transmit beliefs. This is a matter not only of the availability of certain modes of communication in certain societies but also of their local popularity and acceptability. For example, in some African countries, radio and television play an important role in spreading knowledge, whereas in European societies, information is more readily accepted when it is printed (Edelstein, 1982).

The more available channels transmit the belief, the wider its dissemination and the more likely it will be acquired by society members.

In the process of transmission, society members have the opportunity to be exposed to the contents of the belief, which is the first necessary condition for its acquisition but not a sufficient one. Whether a belief will be acquired in the transmission process and become a societal belief depends on a number of conditions. First, to be acquired by society members, the belief has to be comprehended by them (see Sniderman, 1975). Comprehension, which means that society members can relate beliefs to their stored knowledge (Winograd, 1972), facilitates acquisition and storage in the repertoire (Bransford, 1979).

Second, the contents of beliefs have to be perceived as valid to become societal beliefs. Society members have to attribute to them high confidence, perceiving them as verities. This is a necessary condition because societal beliefs define the reality of society members, and this reality has to be firm and certain. Society members rely on societal beliefs in their judgments and decisions, and thus, reduced confidence in societal beliefs may shatter their sense of reality.

A third feature that is necessary for turning a belief into a societal belief is its perceived relevance to the society by society members (Sperber, 1996). By relevance, we mean that the contents of beliefs must be perceived as having implications for societal life (Bar-Tal & Saxe, 1990). Society members have to be able to take an interest in them and feel that these beliefs concern them as part of the society. Relevance has special consequences in this vein. Research in social psychology showed that individuals pay special attention to relevant beliefs and acquire them and store them more easily than irrelevant ones (Wyer & Srull, 1980, 1986).

In addition to comprehension, validity, and relevance, a belief has to fulfill certain needs of society members to be acquired and considered a societal belief (see Chapter 3). This feature of functionality was underlined in the previous chapter. It can be said that individuals are more likely to acquire beliefs that satisfy their needs (see Pratkanis et al., 1989; Sperber, 1996). As Smith (1968) suggested, "a person acquires and maintains attitudes and other learned psychological structures to the extent that they are useful to him in his inner economy of adjustment and outer economy of adaptation" (p. 86). As specific societal beliefs are presented at length in the next chapters, their different functions will be described as well.

Social scientists have proposed several models to describe additional conditions that influence the process of social knowledge transmission. For example, Boster (1991) developed an Information Economy Model (IEM) to describe and explain the factors that influence the degree and patterns how beliefs are shared in a group; we could say that this is another way of describing the transmission process. He suggests that the degree of sharing depends on the quantity and quality of information and distribution of the opportunities to learn the content of beliefs. Learning shared beliefs is easier when the information provided by societal sources is of good quality, consistent, coherent, and redundant. Learning is also easier when the beliefs are equally and readily available in the society. Moreover, individual variables influence how shared beliefs are learned. Personal characteristics such as individual ability, motivation, and opportunity to learn shared beliefs, as well as ways of learning the beliefs, determine individual differences in acquisition of shared beliefs. Finally, Boster suggests that different themes are learned differently, because themes vary in the extent to which learning them is based on direct observation or is acquired through the mediation of external experts. He found that beliefs based on a person's own observation are better learned than beliefs provided by external sources.

The work of the anthropologist Sperber (1985, 1996) on the epidemiology of beliefs is of relevance to our present discussion about the transmission of beliefs. Sperber (1985) borrows the medical concept of epidemiology, which refers to the spread of diseases, and applies it to the dissemination of cultural representations. According to his analysis, only a very small fraction of all mental representations become shared cultural representations. Shared cultural representations circulate within a human society and are continuously retransmitted through various communication channels. However, unlike viruses or bacteria, these representations are altered and integrated with various personal ideas. In his later work, Sperber (1996) differentiates between intuitive beliefs, which are the output of perception and unconscious inference, either on one's own or through communication with others, and reflective beliefs, which are interpretations of these intuitive beliefs. In his opinion, intuitive beliefs owe their distribution to common perceptual experiences and to communication, whereas widespread reflective beliefs owe their distribution almost exclusively to communication. Of special interest to us is the transmission of those reflective beliefs that are deliberately spread via social processes. Their successful transmission depends on how the new beliefs are communicated and how they are cognized. Sperber claimed that beliefs are socially distributed on condition, first, that they are easily comprehended and are perceived as accurate; and second, that there is an incentive to recall and tell them to other society members. To turn into socially accepted beliefs, they have to be transmitted by societal sources that are respected and trusted.

Sniderman (1975), a political scientist, proposed three phases to the process of acquiring political beliefs. The first is the phase of exposure, in which society members are exposed to beliefs. Exposure depends on the location of the communication channels, interpersonal and societal, and the attentiveness and receptiveness of society members. Once society members absorb the belief, they have to comprehend it to store it in their memory. Finally, to adopt it as their belief, society members have to perceive a reward value in its acceptance. According to Sniderman, the process depends on the personality characteristics of society members, and he particularly focused on the trait of self-esteem: low self-esteem, he showed, tends to inhibit the acquisition of political beliefs by impeding exposure and comprehension.

Once the belief is transmitted and acquired by society members, the process of negotiation begins, which determines its particular meaning and its status as a societal belief. Although beliefs are rarely announced as societal beliefs by leaders of the society, their status as societal beliefs is negotiated among society members.

Negotiation

Negotiation is the process of social influence through which society members interpret beliefs, attribute to them societal meaning, and eventually come to regard them as societal beliefs. Through negotiation, contents of societal beliefs may be modified according to the interpretation of society members and adapted to their needs (see Lincoln, 1989). Individuals are active interpreters of the absorbed information: They ascribe meaning on the basis of their own personal repertoire, the content of the message, medium of communication, and source of information (Gamson, 1988; Neuman, Just, & Crigler, 1992).

Wilson and Canter (1993) formulated a model that describes the formation of shared beliefs in small groups through the process of negotiation. According to their analysis, each group member brings to the group his or her own set of beliefs. Through negotiation, that is, by considering other members' beliefs, it is determined how shared beliefs may be formed and used in joint decisions. The process of negotiation is more complex in large social systems with many members and various channels of communication, where members differ in the power they have to determine the contents of societal beliefs.

Walsh and Fahey (1986) tried to account for such differences in power by introducing the concept of *negotiated belief structure,* which proposes that the formation of shared beliefs is based on the interplay between beliefs and the internal politics of the group or society. Whereas in some societies, a limited number of powerful society members negotiate the meaning of societal beliefs and other society members passively acquire them, in other societies (egalitarian societies), the negotiation is widely carried out, and many society members participate in the negotiation. However, even in the latter type of society, there are still society members who passively and obediently acquire them. Much of the negotiation is done by the elite of the society. They have the power, resources, access, and means to participate in the negotiation.

Of special importance in the dissemination process are a society's epistemic authorities. They have an important role in transmitting beliefs to society members, and often, they also form them.

Role of Epistemic Authorities

Epistemic authorities are sources of information that exert determinative influence on the formation of individuals' knowledge (Bar-Tal, Raviv, Raviv, & Brosh, 1991; Kruglanski, 1989; Raviv, Bar-Tal, Raviv, & Abin, 1993). Individuals have high confidence in the validity of information provided by epistemic authorities. They accept this information as true and factual, assimilate it into their own repertoire, and rely on it. A source can become an epistemic authority to the extent that individuals believe that it/he/she possesses characteristics that produce such an authority. Authority can derive generally from the fact that the bearer has a certain social role (e.g., professor, prime minister) or that the information appears in print or in media news, and so on; authority can also be specific, by referring to particular individuals (e.g., news commentator, a leader) (Bar-Tal, Raviv, & Raviv, 1991). In principle, any characteristic may turn a source into an epistemic authority, and any source can, potentially, serve this function: The perception that an information source is an epistemic source is in the eye of the beholder.

Each society has its epistemic authorities. Nevertheless, in most contemporary societies, there are well accepted and even institutionalized epistemic authorities that have the power to impart beliefs to society members. For many society members, newspapers provide valid information and so do radio and television. Certain newscasters and commentators are perceived as especially reliable sources of information. Some people also perceive as valid any information coming from formal sources, such as governmental institutions. Leaders in official positions, such as presidents, prime ministers, ministers, or supreme court judges, are also frequently perceived as epistemic authorities by the mere fact of fulfilling leadership roles. Also, in modern societies, experts, and especially academic specialists, are viewed as epistemic authorities in their area of specialization. With regard to the dissemination of those beliefs that become societal beliefs, a special role is played by intellectuals, who have special weight and influence on other society members. However, every society has additional epistemic authorities who influence the knowledge of society members. Such a list must not omit religious leaders, who have much influential power in almost every society, at least on some society members.

Epistemic authorities not only transmit beliefs that are perceived as valid, but they also may take an active role in the formation of beliefs on the basis of a society's experiences. They may draw implications and indicate the relevance to society. To generate beliefs is one of the important roles of some sources perceived as epistemic authorities. Political and religious leaders, for example, are expected not only to make decisions but also to construct a meaningful reality for their followers. They provide knowledge that may become societal beliefs.

MAINTENANCE OF SOCIETAL BELIEFS

Once society members acquire societal beliefs through the processes of transmission and negotiation, they maintain them through processes of conservation, socialization, and acculturation. The process of conservation maintains society's unique culture, including societal values, attitudes, beliefs, and patterns of behavior, among veteran society members, that is, those who have already been socialized into society. The process of socialization refers to the inculcation of the societal culture in a new generation of society members, and the process of acculturation refers to imparting the societal culture to new society members (see Berry, 1997). All three processes are necessary for keeping societal beliefs accessible in the societal repertoire, and they are not completely separate. They overlap to some extent, because they rely on communications through the same societal channels. Nevertheless, each should be defined and described in its own right.

Conservation of Societal Beliefs

The conservation of societal beliefs is probably the most basic societal process, because it involves the continuous and consistent communication of societal beliefs by societal channels of communication. This process of communicating the societal beliefs that characterize the society is responsible for making the society unique and differentiated from other societies. Through the process of conservation, societal beliefs appear in the public debate: Some refer to issues that concern the society, some serve to explain current problems, and some provide justifications for actions. Societal beliefs appear frequently in mass media, leaders express them in their speeches, and intellectuals debate them. Also, as indicated, societal beliefs are often enshrined in various cultural products, such as literature or films, which keep them available in the society's repertoire. Some of the beliefs, especially those directly related to a society's identity, are expressed through particular mechanisms whose role is to conserve societal beliefs. A society's holidays, memorial days, ceremonies, rituals, customs, and symbols all serve to maintain its societal beliefs related to social identity (Swidler & Arditi, 1994). These mechanisms express societal beliefs, reminding society members of their existence and importance. In one specific analysis, Connerton (1989) discussed the role of commemorative ceremonies in maintaining societal identity. He proposed not only that these ceremonies transmit the beliefs through speeches but also that their typically habitual performance also facilitates the maintenance of societal beliefs.

Socialization of Societal Beliefs

Because one of the key components of a society is its societal beliefs, and because sharing them is an important condition for being considered a society member, the society actively and intentionally strives to pass societal beliefs to the new generation. This process, part of socialization, is essential if the society desires to continue to exist as a unique entity. Socialization begins with the birth of the new society members and continues throughout their lives. The literature about political socialization is relevant to the analysis of the transmission of societal beliefs, especially in view of the fact that many societal beliefs have political contents. It is beyond the scope of the present book to review the vast amount of accumulated knowledge that deals with the acquisition of political beliefs by children and adolescents; such reviews were done elsewhere (e.g., Dawson & Prewitt, 1969; Greenstein, 1965; Hess & Torney, 1967; Ichilov, 1990; Jennings & Niemi, 1974; Renshon, 1977). But still a few general remarks are in order. Informal but crucial socialization agents are family members, mass media, or peers who communicate or even inculcate societal beliefs. But the formal institution par excellence through which society transmits its societal beliefs to new generations is the educational system.

Children and adolescents acquire societal beliefs in the educational system through formal instruction and through informal interactions with teachers and peers. School textbooks have an important mediating role. As major mechanisms for mass learning, they construct the social reality of the students, providing knowledge regarding various societal themes such as collective memory, values, goals, self-image, and so on (Bourdieu & Paseron, 1990; Luke, 1988). Societal beliefs are part of the knowledge transmitted by school textbooks. They appear prominently in the history, geography, social science, or language textbooks, which represent and analyze the concerns of the society or its particular identity as expressed in history, culture, and language. The school textbook carries the knowledge that leaders of the society think should be possessed by society members:

> Textbooks are a sign that some larger community exists. The community exists insofar as it shares collective knowledge. The textbook is therefore a carrier of

the publicness of the public school. It suggests the possibility, indeed the certainty, of shared collective identity (Gitlin, 1995, p. 23).

The Acculturation Process of Societal Beliefs

Acculturation takes place in societies that absorb new society members and assimilate them. These new members can be immigrants, refugees, or even national minorities. They do not always desire to assimilate culturally into the new society, and the society does not always agree to assimilate them. But, when such desire exists, part of the process of becoming new society members is the acquisition of societal beliefs. When the society strives to assimilate the new society members, it exerts effort to impart its cultural heritage to them. This includes imparting values, patterns of behavior, attitudes, and beliefs, including societal beliefs (Berry, 1997). Different mechanisms can be employed to achieve assimilation, sometimes even coercive ones. The new members are often directed to acquire the language of the society, to learn its history and culture. An example of such acculturation attempts can be found in Israeli Jewish society, for example, which actively tries to acculturate new Jewish immigrants who have come from many different countries in the world. Among other things, societal beliefs are imparted to them through various channels and institutions such as the mass media, schools, or special classes for immigrants (Eisenstadt, 1954; Gitelman, 1982).

Although most work in the social psychology of groups concerns small-group processes, the work of John Levine and Richard Moreland (1991, 1994) about small-group socialization has relevance for the analysis of the acculturation process in societies. They claimed that new members joining any group are required to acquire its culture, which involves beliefs shared by members, customs, and the behavioral expressions of these beliefs. The shared beliefs pertain to knowledge about the group as a whole, knowledge about group members, and knowledge about the group's tasks. In a later contribution, Levine et al. (1996) elaborated two factors that influence acquisition of group culture: the motivation and ability of the new member and the motivation and ability of the group members. The first set of factors explains individual differences. Among these factors, Levine et al. (1993) noted the level of knowledge of the new member, contacts with other group members, assessment of the probable rewards of membership, the member's own social skills, and access to information about the group. The other set of factors refers to structural features of the group and the strength of the group culture. Group members have the responsibility to transmit group culture to new members: Their way of transmission, as well as their own degree of internalization of group culture, influences the success of new members' acculturation.

░ CHANGE OF SOCIETAL BELIEFS

Societal beliefs are durable, but not stable, as they may change with time. Their content may be modified, and some societal beliefs may even disappear. Societal beliefs remain in the societal repertoire as long as they at least fulfill their epistemic and identity functions for society members. That is, as long as society members believe that the societal beliefs illuminate the society in a valid way and characterize that society, the beliefs maintain their status, especially if they also satisfy other needs of society members. But when societal beliefs cease to fulfill these epistemic needs, society members stop considering them valid and eventually change them.

Societal beliefs do not change overnight but through a prolonged, sometimes years-long process. This change is a natural universal process that takes place in every society, as a result of the changes it goes through. Technological development, economic change, development of new ideas, or political change are only some examples of the changes that may occur in a society. New collective experiences require the formation of new societal beliefs to shed light on them. In this vein, the prominent anthropologist Murdock (1960) noted that cultural change, including a change of collective ideas, takes place when the situation changes. According to him,

> Among the classes of events that are known to be especially influential in producing cultural change are increases or decreases in population, changes in the geographical environment, migration into new environments, contact with peoples of differing culture, natural and social catastrophes, wars, economic depression or death or rise to power of a strong leader. (p. 249)

Thus, not only gradual societal changes bring change of societal beliefs but also major short- and long-term events that have a profound effect on societal life and were described in the beginning of the chapter as formative collective experiences.

Inglehart (1990), who defined culture as these attitudes, along with values and knowledge that are widely shared within a society, provided an extensive analysis of cultural change due to economic, technological, and political change. Because societal beliefs are part of cultural knowledge, his analysis is of interest to our discussion. Inglehart proposed that social change is always circular in nature: Economic, technological, and sociopolitical changes influence the culture, and these changes in culture affect, in return, the economics, society, and politics in advanced industrial societies. Among current economic, technological, and political factors of change, he noted the evolution of the high-tech industry, the limitation of welfare services, a shift toward individual autonomy, greater interest and participation in political processes, major waves of immigration from Third World countries, and growth of economic prosperity. On the cultural level, Inglehart noted emphasis on quality of life, individual permissiveness, emphasis on self-realization, and increase in democratic attitudes.

On the basis of data collected from two dozen societies around the world about cultural change, Inglehart (1990) found that societies differ in beliefs, values, attitudes, and behaviors, even when their conditions are similar. This means, according to Inglehart, that societies attribute different meanings to similar situations because of different historical experiences. Studying data collected over a period of 15 years (1973-1988) and then tracing the data back into the 1950s, Inglehart found durability in societal beliefs. Most of the beliefs did not change overnight. But he noticed gradual change over the years: "Change in a central component of people's worldview seems to take place, in large part, as one generation replaces another" (p. 423). The young generation adopts more and more postmaterialistic values, which include a broader orientation toward such issues as the environment and nuclear power, toward roles of women, homosexuality or divorce, political outlook, or motivation to work. Economic, political, and technological changes have created different experiences for the young generation. These experiences affect the belief system of society members.

Two specific examples of a societal change that has led to change in societal beliefs are the unification of Germany and the disintegration of the Soviet Union. In both cases, powerful collective experiences within the two societies involved changed their realities and caused the evolution of new societal beliefs. In the case of Germany, the new societal beliefs pertain to such themes as a new identity, the nature of the welfare state, the relationship between state and religion, Germany's role in Europe, and the nature of capitalism (see Grosser, 1992). In the case of Russia, the change was even greater, and the new societal beliefs refer to such themes as new political and national identity, democracy, capitalism, and the nature of social institutions (White, Gill, & Slider, 1993).

Another example of changes in the society that lead to changes in societal belief is the emerging demand in British society for abolition of the monarchy, which has served as the symbol of British society for many centuries; on its basis, societal beliefs were formulated. With changes in the cultural and political context and in the popular perception of the royal family's behavior in recent decades, old societal beliefs about the royal family no longer fulfill the needs of the society, and therefore, new symbols are sought. Another instance of change of societal beliefs has been taking place in European societies, such as France or Germany, which are rapidly becoming multicultural societies. The change of experience leads to a change of societal beliefs about the nature of society. These societies search for a new identity that can incorporate the new societal demography (see Brubaker, 1992; Fulbrook, 1994). Also, U.S. society has gone through major changes of societal beliefs regarding the integration of blacks, as reported by Carmines and Merriman (1993):

> The percentage of White Americans who think Whites and Blacks should go to the same school increased from 30 percent in 1942 to 90 percent in 1984. . . . Whites' support for fair employment practices increased from 42 percent in 1944 to 96 percent in 1972 . . . the percentage of Whites who agreed that Blacks have a right to live wherever they can afford increased from 65 percent in 1964 to 88 percent in 1976. (p. 237)

Societal beliefs change through the process of negotiation, in which leaders, the intellectual elite, media sources, economic decision makers, and other groups take part. The negotiation, which takes the form of public debate, may go on for years, until a new societal belief evolves. For example, Israeli society is now negotiating the contents of societal beliefs pertaining to the meaning of Zionism. The collection of opinions compiled by Ginossar and Bareli (1996) exemplifies the act of negotiation pertaining to the relationship between Zionism and the Jewish religion; between Zionism and the idea of the "whole Israel," the so-called "land of Israel," including the West Bank; the relationship between Israel and the Jewish Diaspora; and the relationship between Zionism and civic society and democracy.

The change of societal beliefs depends on various internal societal factors— among them, the availability of free information, the extent and type of pressure to conform, and the availability of communication channels among society members. A free flow of information in the society, low pressure to conform, and availability of various communication channels in society facilitates change of societal beliefs. In any event, the process in which societal beliefs are changed is not always a peaceful one. Frequently, the change of societal beliefs is accompanied by vivid public debate, disagreement, and sometimes even by conflict. This is the case with the above-mentioned change of societal beliefs concerning Zionism in Israeli society.

In the case of conflict, various groups in a society may struggle over acceptance of certain societal beliefs, and the outcome of this conflict may well have serious implications for the society. The conflict can be over societal beliefs pertaining to goals, ideology, values, or structure. Chapter 6 discusses a conflict in Israeli society between "doves" and "hawks" over societal beliefs about security. The two groups disagree about what conditions can guarantee national and personal security. Whereas doves believe that the only peaceful resolution of Israel's conflict with the Arab states and the Palestinians requires withdrawal from territories occupied in the 1967 war, and that only this can strengthen the security of Israel, hawks believe that security must be maintained first of all by holding on to these territories, so as to control hostile forces and to allow enough warning time in case of sudden war.

Such conflicts can lead to violence, because opposing groups in a society may come to consider their societal beliefs as essential and view the societal beliefs of the other group as threatening their basic values or denying their existential needs. Perceiving the situation as a zero-sum conflict, the opposing groups may resort to violence to impose their own societal beliefs on the whole of society. An example of such conflict was the civil war in Spain between 1936 amd 1939, in which two parts of the society fought over a societal belief regarding socialism, agrarian reforms, church-state relations, and other matters that determined the nature of the society (Preston, 1978). At present, a violent conflict over societal beliefs is taking place in Algerian society between fundamentalistic and secular forces—each has a different outlook as to what should be the dominant societal beliefs of the society.

However, each society also holds some central and fundamental societal beliefs that constitute a societal ethos. These beliefs play a key role in defining the society's identity and therefore rarely change. They are usually considered fundamental societal beliefs that determine the "we-ness" of the society and provide its raison d'être. Their change would indicate a radical change in the very essence of the society. An example of such a fundamental belief is a societal belief held by the Jewish Israeli society pertaining to its ties with the Land of Israel. This is a fundamental belief, underlying the Jewish claim leading to its return to Israel after 2,000 years of exile (Schweid, 1985; Shimoni, 1995). The societal belief that claims that "American society is democratic," or the societal belief to the effect that "The French Revolution bestowed its values on modern France" are other examples of fundamental societal beliefs that do not change easily. These types of beliefs may change, however, during revolutions, as happened following the Bolshevik Revolution in Russia or following the nonviolent Islamic revolution in Iran.

All the described cases suggest that societal beliefs are dynamic, shared representations that reflect the political, economic, and cultural conditions in a society. As the conditions change, so do the societal beliefs. But, at the same time, it should be remembered that societal beliefs, in turn, are responsible to some extent for the prevailing political, economic, and cultural conditions in the society. Society members who hold particular societal beliefs view their world in a particular way and act to maintain the conditions that can preserve their worldview. Thus, societal beliefs and societal conditions are interlocked. A change in societal conditions leads to change in societal beliefs, and a change in societal belief leads to change in societal conditions.

5

Societal Beliefs About Patriotism

One theme of the most universal of societal beliefs, found in nearly every society's ethos, refers to patriotism. These beliefs are so wide-spread because patriotism is a sine qua non in the life of a society (especially in the framework of a nation-state), providing the basic sense of belonging, love, care, and devotion of members toward their society. Naturally, therefore, societies make serious efforts to impart societal beliefs about patriotism—with their affective and behavioral implications—to their members through the available cultural, social, and political mechanisms.

From an early age, even before people are aware that they live in a society or understand what this means, they develop a sense of belonging, accompanied by positive attitudes toward various characteristics of their own society. They develop a sense of connection, not only with other people who share their life space—the people who raised them, who are their friends, or with whom they interact in the course of everyday life—but also with the larger community of their society, the great majority of whom they have never met. This experience of connection, which reflects a kind of membership in their extended group, is the basis of patriotism. Frequently, in the modern world, this extended group is the nation, and the present chapter will often refer to this collective as a societal unit.

AUTHOR'S NOTE: This chapter, although extensively rewritten, is based on a previously published article: Bar-Tal, D. (1993). Patriotism as fundamental beliefs of group members. *Politics and the Individual, 3,* 45-62. It is used here with permission of that journal.

▥ THE CONTENTS OF PATRIOTIC BELIEFS

I propose that in its fundamental and general form, patriotism reflects the attachment of society members toward their nation and the country in which they reside. Attachment, in this definition, implies a binding affection between people and their society and the land. Patriotism, thus, is especially found in any ethnic group or society that has an attachment to a certain geographical place. This attachment, which reflects basic human motives and is associated with positive evaluation and emotions, is expressed in many societies by societal beliefs connoting contents of belonging, love, care, and loyalty. These societal beliefs are the most salient expressions of patriotism, and they are communicated in many societies, although this is done in different ways in different societies. Societal beliefs are learned, and on their basis, motivational-emotional reactions are formed. That is, society members who form beliefs of the type "I love my country and my people," "I am loyal to my country," "I am proud of my people," also develop the evaluational and emotional feeling of attachment. In line with this view, patriotism should be seen not as motivational-emotional expressions only, but holistically, together with the accompanying beliefs on which the attachment is based. These beliefs, on the one hand, serve as antecedents of the motivation and emotion and, on the other hand, function subsequently as their expression, explanation, and justification.

Patriotism hinges on people's desire to belong to a society that society members positively evaluate. That is, patriots want to be part of their society, define themselves as members of it, and feel some kind of "we-ness." Even when, as a result of special circumstances, patriots leave their country, they always wish to return. This profound sense of belonging to the society is deeply rooted, because individuals are born into a society, perceive themselves to be its members, and are perceived as such in the environment where they live. However, people may not, throughout the entire course of their life, wish to remain part of the society. Individuals may move to new places and develop new patriotic feelings (i.e., attachment to a new society and country). But, without developing a sense of belonging, individuals cannot experience patriotism. Only on the basis of this, additional beliefs and emotions associated with attachment can be developed. An emotion that expresses patriotism most directly is love of the society and the country. This statement may be considered a necessary but not a sufficient condition for patriotism; tourists, for instance, may fall in love with a country or a nation, too, but this would hardly make them patriots. What distinguishes the former from the latter is the sense of belonging. The objects of love are usually the people, the culture, the landscape, the flora and fauna of the country, and so on. Patriotism also reflects concern about the society; that is, patriots have an interest in what happens to their people and country. This cognitive component comes as an addition to belonging and love and implies the requirement of caring about the well-being of the society and the country. And finally, patriotism refers to devotion and loyalty, which imply possible action for the sake of the society and country.

Indeed, it should be noted that for many people, patriotic beliefs have behavioral implications motivating voluntary action for the benefit of the society and country. In extreme cases, patriots may be willing to sacrifice their lives. This component allows us to differentiate between passive and active patriotism. Passive patriotism is related only to the cognitive-affective aspects of attachment and consists of the beliefs and emotions that people have toward their society and country. Active patriotism involves behaviors that are carried out as a result of patriotic beliefs. The range of patriotic behaviors varies and depends on societal requirements, as well as on personal tendencies. In any event, patriotic behavior almost always involves some kind of personal sacrifice.

Moving to empirical data, it was found that patriotic societal beliefs about love for one's country, loyalty, and commitment are widespread among society members. Rose (1985) reported a broad survey that compared patriotism in 15 countries by studying nationwide samples. He concluded his study as follows: "Patriotism is the norm in every country surveyed: the differences in national pride are a matter of degree, not of kind" (p. 86). According to Rose's survey, in the United States, 96% have a sense of pride in the country, in Ireland 91%, in Iceland 89%, in Mexico 88%, in the United Kingdom 86%, and in Spain 83%. Even in the Federal Republic of Germany, where national pride was found to be lowest, 59% reported pride in the country, and only 29% were not proud (12% could not decide). Rose suggested that several factors may influence this sense of pride: Thus, for instance, a struggle for independence at any point in the last two centuries increases the level of patriotism, whereas major defeat in an unjust war and/or occupation by a foreign power may decrease it.

In a more recent study, Blank (1997) assessed German patriotism. Studying a national sample of Germans in the former West Germany and East Germany, he found that about 60% of the Germans in West Germany expressed at least some love of their mother country. In East Germany, the percentage was higher—about 70%. In addition, the survey showed that about 62% of the Germans in West Germany reported an inner obligation to Germany, whereas about 64% of Germans in East Germany felt this obligation. Also, about 58% of the West Germans and about 63% of the East Germans felt proud to be German.

Hirshberg (1993), who discussed U.S. citizens' patriotic self-image, reported from national samples taken in the 1980s that 95% to 99% were proud to be American. In his view, American patriotism is based on the belief that the United States is the best country in the world, because it has the best sociopolitical system of liberal democratic capitalism, expressed in the commitment to freedom, a cherished value for Americans. According to Hirshberg, these beliefs bolster positive feelings about the United States.

Similar strong feelings of patriotism have also been observed among Russians (Gozman, 1997). Smith (1976) noted that "Russians are perhaps the world's most passionate patriots. Without question, a deep and tenacious love of country is the most powerful unifying force in the Soviet Union, the most vital element in the amalgam of loyalties that cements Soviet society" (p. 303). This patriotism originates in the far past and was strengthened each time Russians had to defend their country against foreign invaders. The czars as well as Communist leaders used this emotion to mobilize the Russian people for various national projects and to lead them to great sacrifices. Thus, for example, the heroic defense of the Soviet Union during World War II, which has been called the Great Patriotic War, led to enormous Russian sacrifice to save the homeland, Mother Russia.

Any discussion of patriotism should clarify the status of—and possible interrelations between—the objects of the attachment: the society (or frequently in our times, the nation) and the country. These two are both necessary components of the definition. On the one hand, a person cannot feel patriotically toward a nation without reference to the geographical place to which the nation is attached. On the other hand, a person cannot have patriotic feelings toward a specific geographical place without relating it to a nation that resides there. The objects of the attachment are, therefore, both nation and country, and these two elements are interwoven. The nation and country constitute one unit for a patriot. This relationship is reflected everywhere in the nation's (or group's) history and culture. Empirical support for this is presented in a study by Doob (1964), who mapped the scope of patriotic beliefs by German-speaking inhabitants of South Tyrol (in Italy) and North Tyrol (in Austria). His mapping indicates that these beliefs refer to the land (e.g., "Our landscape is beautiful," "Our churches and castles are artistic"), history (e.g., "Our country has an old history," "We have been able to produce famous people in most spheres of culture"), people (e.g., "We are unified people"), and culture (e.g., "Our festivals are particularly beautiful," "We must cultivate our culture").

Two points should be noted with regard to the relationship between nation and country: (a) Patriots do not always agree about the boundaries of the country toward which they feel patriotically and (b) patriots do not always agree about the groups that constitute the nation. In the former case, the disagreement may concern a region or regions; that is, patriots feel patriotically about at least certain parts of the country, but not necessarily about all of them.

This is so because from prehistorical times, groups have wandered across continents in search of a place to settle. They conquered lands and took up residence in them. But wars and conquests have continued until the present day, and therefore, the world's boundaries have changed many times. Comparison of the maps of Europe in 1812, 1815, 1848, 1919, 1945, and 1997 vividly illustrates such change. In cases where boundaries changed and regions passed from hand to hand, some members of a nation may not form patriotic sentiments toward a certain part of the country that other members of the nation do feel patriotic about. Thus, for example, not all Germans today consider Sudetenland and Pomerania to be part of Germany; not all Frenchmen in the 1950s considered Algeria to be part of France; and not all Israelis have patriotic feelings toward the West Bank and the Gaza Strip. Moreover, people may change their patriotic feelings and redirect them, for instance, toward their new countries and nations. For example, American patriots of today are descendants of Englishmen, Scots, Poles, Irishmen, Italians, Mexicans, or Japanese who arrived in that country relatively recently. Or again, Bedouins who came to Jordan from the Arabian peninsula about 80 years ago are now patriotic Jordanians, and many current Israeli patriots were assimilated Jews in other countries until fairly recently.

In the case of patriotism toward the nation, the disagreement may concern the composition of the nation. A group of patriots may, for example, hold that certain ethnic, racial, or religious groups do not constitute part of the nation. Disagreement of this type arises in nations or groups that are heterogeneous in their composition. Thus, for example, there have always been Americans who do not view Blacks as part of their nation; many Germans in the 1930s and 1940s excluded Jews from the German nation, although the Jews considered themselves German patriots of the Jewish religion.

Within the framework of the discussion about societal beliefs that reflect patriotism, it is important to note the study by Sullivan, Fried, and Dietz (1992). This study provides a unique opportunity to demonstrate that society members who hold societal beliefs of patriotism attach to them different meanings and implications. Using a methodology that allows an identification of different understandings of patriotism, the researchers found five alternative perspectives about the meaning of patriotism that have an effect on political attitudes and behaviors: (a) iconoclastic patriotism, which rejects the appeal of political symbols and patriotic images and focuses instead on critical political activity; (b) symbolic patriotism, which focuses on traditional symbols, rituals, and slogans that express emotional attachment; (c) instinctive environmental patriotism, which focuses on the commitment to the land and its preservation; (d) capitalistic patriotism, which combines love of the country with economic growth and development of natural resources; and

(e) nationalistic symbolic patriotism, which focuses on the best of the country and its particular superior standing in the world. Moreover, the observed five perspectives were found to be related to patterns of political participation, behavioral expressions of patriotism, and voting behavior. These obtained findings support the assumption presented in Chapter 4, which suggests that society members interpret societal beliefs and attribute subjective meaning to them.

The subjective understanding of patriotic beliefs is obviously beyond political control, but of special interest for the present discussion about the contents of patriotic societal beliefs is the observation that societies formally add specific beliefs pertaining to patriotism to beliefs about belonging, love, care, loyalty, or sacrifice (e.g., Page, 1915; Snyder, 1976). They may add, for example, societal beliefs requiring support of a particular ideology or specific government policy, devotion to a particular leader, or rejection of another society. I have called this phenomenon *monopolization of patriotism* (Bar-Tal, 1997b).

The monopolization of patriotism is especially salient under totalitarian regimes, because they set the boundaries of patriotism, harnessing it for the total support of the dominant ideology, government policies, and ruling leadership (Curtis, 1979). Indeed, patriotism serves as one of the major legiti-mizing mechanisms of totalitarian regimes. This type of coupled patriotism will always portray the dominant ideology, policies, and leaders as good for the nation and as reflections of true patriotism. Instances of the monopoliza-tion of patriotism can be found in Nazi Germany, Fascist Italy, and the Communist Soviet Union.

Nazism subsumed patriotism as part of its ideology and saw the National Socialist party as embodying the German nation. The Nazi version of patrio-tism required acceptance of Nazi ideology and support of the Nazi regime (see Bullock, 1962; Frei, 1993; Hildebrand, 1991). In Hitler's own words, "The fate of the community of the German people is bound with the existence of this Movement, and the fate of the German Reich is dependent on the strengthening of the community of the German people" (Baynes, 1969, pp. 231-232).

A similar monopolization of patriotism can be observed during the fascist regime of Mussolini in Italy during the period 1922 to 1943, when the regime identified patriotism with support for fascist ideas and the regime (Gregor, 1979; Halperin, 1964; Tannenbaum, 1972). The monopolization of patriotism that took place in the Soviet Union (Brzezinski, 1957) is best summed up in the following quotation: "Boundless love of the Soviet people for the Socialist motherland, the unity of all the fraternal people around the Party of Lenin, and Stalin and the Soviet Government" (Barghoorn, 1956, p 9).

⁊ THE ESSENTIALITY OF PATRIOTISM

Patriotism probably first appeared when human beings, living in groups, stopped wandering and settled in particular places. It is likely that they began to develop an attachment to a place from this point onward. And although the organization of groups and societies has seen changes through the ages, patriotism has persisted as a human phenomenon. Through the ages, the attachment could be to village, city, region, and/or country, depending on the political-societal systems of the group or society. Today, tribes, ethnic groups, and nations still strongly appeal to patriotic sentiments and make all possible efforts to feed and maintain them. The following section will describe the development of this phenomenon. To do this, it is necessary to first focus on the process of society formation. Patriotic beliefs appear in the process of society formation and the emergence of society members' social identity. They are part of the set of basic beliefs that serve as a foundation for societal existence.

The crucial phase in the process of society formation is the emergence of beliefs concerning societal existence (i.e., "We are a society"). Individuals have to believe that they constitute a society and that they have something in common uniting them. These beliefs fill the purpose of self-categorization and become part of the reality of the individuals who constitute the society (Bar-Tal, 1990a; Turner et al., 1987). That is, once individuals categorize themselves as society members, awareness of their membership becomes part of their self-concept, forming their social identity. Tajfel (1978, 1981, 1982), in a seminal analysis of the development of social identity, defines it as "that part of an individual's self-concept which derives from his knowledge of his membership of a social group (or groups) together with the value and emotional significance attached to that membership" (Tajfel, 1978, p. 63). This perspective assumes that individuals' self-concept also derives from their membership in certain societies or groups. The self-perception as a society member, together with one's evaluation of the society, determines one's own social identity.

On the assumption that people have a basic need to evaluate themselves positively, social identity theory posits, as already indicated, that people who define themselves in terms of societal membership are likely to evaluate their society positively (Tajfel, 1978, 1981, 1982). That is, they seek to establish a positive social identity.

It can be assumed that an individual will tend to remain a member of a group and seek membership of a new group if these groups have some contribution to

make to the positive aspects of his social identity, i.e., to those aspects of it from
which he derives some satisfaction. (Tajfel, 1981, p. 256)

This pursuit is not surprising in view of the fact that society membership
also comes to fulfill individuals' emotional needs. People usually take pride
in the accomplishments of their group, which thus enhance their self-esteem.
We can, then, say that society membership not only defines one's identity but
also serves as a basis for one's own self-evaluation. Indeed, when social identity in terms of a particular group membership is unsatisfactory because individuals cannot achieve satisfactory positive evaluation of the society, one way
of coping with this situation is to leave this group and join a more positively
evaluated society (Tajfel, 1978, 1981).

I would like to suggest, for societies that settle in one place, that together
with the development of self-categorization and the emergence of social identity, patriotic beliefs and emotions appear. Patriotism adds an important element to society membership. It provides the binding glue among individual,
society, and place in which the society resides. The appearance of the sense of
belonging and feelings of love, concern, loyalty, devotion, and pride toward
the society is an integral part of society formation.

Individuals construct the meaning they attribute to a society not only
through self-social categorization but also via shared attachment to the society. Patriotism is an important addition to social identity, and both constitute a
crucial cognitive-motivational basis for a society's existence. With very few
exceptions (for example, Jews or Gypsies, dispersed in the past in various
countries), patriotism and social identity are the part of individuals' repertoire
that makes them society members. Awareness of being a society member and
the attachment to the society and the country provide the sense of "we-ness."
Both elements are essential for the construction of the society members'
shared social reality. These cognitive-motivational social aspects of patriotism
make an individual in reality a society member. Moreover, because society
members are aware of sharing these patriotic sentiments, they constitute the
uniting bond. It is thus not surprising that the ethos of each society contains
societal beliefs of patriotism.

As a particular example, Curt (1946) described the birth of American patriotism during the first half of the 18th century. Due to the unique experiences
of the colonial Americans and their special demographic makeup, new ideas
began to form among the people. White settlers began to be attached to America and to express patriotic beliefs; they no longer saw themselves as foremost
a part of the British empire. This provided the basis for the emergence of a
new identity. With the crystallization of the new identity, patriotic beliefs took
a firm hold just before the Declaration of Independence in 1776, by which
time founding fathers of the United States spoke about "our country," "one

people," "flag of the United States," "loyalty," "dedication," and "love of the country." These patriotic beliefs served as a basis for the establishment of the new American society and its separation from the British kingdom.

The present conception of patriotism also extends our understanding of societal disintegration. In analyzing this process, I argued elsewhere (Bar-Tal, 1990a) that it takes place when society members lose their confidence in those beliefs that define their distinctive social identity or when these beliefs become peripheral in the society members' repertoire. Now, I should like to add that societies whose members do not develop patriotism may dissipate and eventually disappear. A society with members who do not desire to belong, do not love the society, do not feel loyalty toward it, are not concerned with the society's well-being, and are not willing to act on its behalf have difficulty surviving. With few exceptions, most societies cannot exist for any considerable length of time without the patriotism of their members. Only few societies, under unusual circumstances, such as Jewish societies in exile during the past centuries, succeeded in constructing societal mechanisms other than patriotism for survival. McDougall (1920) expressed this idea:

> The group spirit, involving knowledge of the group as such, some idea of the group, and some sentiment of devotion or attachment to the group, is then the essential condition of all collective life and of all effective collective action. (p. 66)

A sociobiological theory proposed by Johnson (1989, 1997) strengthens the point about the necessity of patriotism for a society's survival. As part of an evolutionary approach, he suggests that patriotism is the product of an interaction between genetically based predispositions and socialization processes that cultivate and redirect these predispositions. It is an important mechanism that provides the bond holding large-scale societies together. Patriotism allows integration, serves as a basis for solidarity and, most important, leads to self-sacrifice for the benefit of society, which is a necessary requirement for society's survival. Johnson's theory, which is based on kin selection, a concept explaining genetic altruism with reference to kinship, extends the scope of self-sacrificial behavior to the non-kin.

In his view, patriotism is based on evolutionary forces of nepotism and reciprocity. Nepotism refers to kin selection, which leads to kin-based cooperation and altruism. Kin is distinguished from non-kin by means of the three following mechanisms: (a) association between familiarity and kinship through which human beings learn and identify all the cues that indicate membership in the society, (b) matching between genotype and phenotype by learning cues that allow recognition of a stranger as society member, and (c) connection between kinship and territory allowing recognition of a society member by location. Reciprocity, another evolutionary force, explains how individuals who are nonrelatives engage in altruistic exchanges. It suggests that society members who are not directly related are ready to repay the benefits that they enjoyed receiving as being part of the society. This repayment is reflected in their readiness to perform altruistic sacrifices on behalf of the society.

Besides this evolutionary aspect of the development of patriotism, Johnson also acknowledges the role of socialization. Societies exert special efforts to develop patriotism through national language, common history, compulsory common education, common social values, monuments, ceremonies, litera-ture, and other societal, cultural, political, or educational mechanisms (see Ben-Amos, 1997; Kashti, 1997; Reykowski, 1997, for further discussion of these socialization mechanisms).

Books by Samuel (1989) and Hayes (1974) are examples of the analysis of societal socialization of patriotic beliefs. A collection of articles in the book, *Patriotism: The Making and Unmaking of British National Identity* (Samuel, 1989), describes how cultural products that transmit beliefs contribute to the formation and maintenance of British patriotism. One of these is constituted by national figures who function as objects of identification and/or patriotic exemplars. Some of these figures are real people who acted for the benefit of the nation or otherwise possess desired patriotic qualities, for example, Lord Nelson or the Duke of Wellington, and some are fictional characters who are imaginary symbols of the nation, for example, Britannia, John Bull, Robin Hood, or St. George. However, both categories serve as patriotic myths. The beliefs about them are imparted to society members and provide concrete patriotic figures for identification. Another element in the makeup of patrio-tism is the image of soldiers, which especially reflects loyalty and discipline. Soldiers are presented as the ones who make extraordinary contributions for the country, because they are prepared to sacrifice their lives in national wars. Also, in the case of Britain, the monarchy plays a special role in maintaining patriotism. The royal family serves as a symbol with which society members identify and toward which they develop attachment. Samuel also stresses that attachment to the country's landscape is an important component of patrio-tism. All the above ingredients contribute to the formation of patriotism by being transmitted through music, paintings, literature, theater plays, and films. British writers (e.g., J. B. Priestley, Joseph Conrad, Robertson Scott, Richard Jeffries, George Orwell), poets (e.g., Robert Bridges, Philip Larkin, Christopher Hussey, Edmund Spenser), painters (e.g., David Wilkie, Hubert van Herkomer, Thomas Faed, James Thornhill), playwrights (e.g., William Shakespeare, John Walker), and composers (e.g., Cecil Sharp, Ralph Vaughan Williams, Ivor Gurney) played important roles in the formation of British patriotism. They planted various patriotic beliefs in their creative works, which as cultural products have been consumed by society members, who absorb these beliefs and internalize them. In this way, patriotic societal beliefs have been disseminated, becoming possessions of the masses.

Hayes (1974) analyzed the patriotism of the French. He argued,

> All Frenchmen are supremely loyal to France. And the explanation of this fact is attributed only in part to achievements of French intellectuals in discovering common denominators of various French philosophies and patriotisms. It is attributable even more to the invention and skilled use of new engines of education and propaganda. (p. 13)

Hayes's focus was on the cultural construction of (French) patriotism. He provided detailed descriptions of how the political system, education, the military forces, the churches, the press, radio and cinema, national associations, and national symbols and ceremonies were used for this purpose. Similar analyses have also been done with regard to the development and maintenance of American patriotism (e.g., Kammen, 1991; Zelinsky, 1988). Clearly, what we learn from these studies is that patriotic societal beliefs and feelings are acquired, and the societies exert considerable effort to impart patriotism to new generations of society members and to maintain these beliefs and feelings throughout their lives. Societies consider them essential for their functioning and survival.

THE FUNCTIONALITY OF PATRIOTISM

Patriotic beliefs have always played an important role in the life of society members, serving both narrower personal and broader communal needs.

Of special importance among the personal needs that patriotic beliefs fulfill is that of belonging and identification. In his theory of human motivation, Maslow (1970) suggested that "belongingness" is a basic human need. Because the society has a determinative role in personal survival, individuals strive for a place not only in their family but also in their society. They want to be affiliated, be part of a social entity, and have meaningful relations with it. Patriotic beliefs help to satisfy this need. They indicate that a person is a member of a society, that together with other individuals, he or she constitutes a social entity, that the society is attached to a land, and that other society members share the same beliefs. The sense of shared attachment is related to a strong feeling of belonging.

Patriotic beliefs not only strengthen the sense of belonging, but also support the definition of an individual's social identity. In fact, the sense of belonging and social identity are profoundly related. Social identity can be formed on the basis of a sense of belonging. As Hogg and Abrams (1988) pointed out,

> Identity, specifically social identity, and group belongingness are inextricably linked in the sense that one's conception or definition of who one is (one's identity) is largely composed of self-descriptions in forms of the defining characteristics of social groups to which one belongs. This belongingness is psychological, it is not merely knowledge of a group's attributes. Identification with a social group is a psychological state very different from merely being designed as falling into one social category or another. It is phenomenologically real and has important self-evaluative consequence. (p. 7)

Patriotic beliefs and emotions of love, care, or devotion toward the society strongly express social identity. Society members with high confidence in patriotic beliefs, which are central in their cognitive repertoire, have especially strong identification with the society.

With regard to group functions, among the important societal needs that patriotic beliefs serve are unity, cohesiveness, and readiness to act for the society's welfare. First, a minimal degree of unity is a necessary condition for a society's existence. Society members ought to believe that they are united through some kind of commonality, and unity indicates that they belong to the same social entity. Patriotic beliefs reinforce this sense of unity, irrespective of possible differences among society members, for example, in attitudes, goals, values, or ideology. Patriotism implies a common interest and a common fate. In this respect, patriotism enhances integration and feelings of solidarity and minimizes ingroup differences by focusing on a commonality and allegiance.

Patriotic beliefs draw the line between one's own society and other outgroups. In other words, they unite society members by emphasizing their similarity in contrast to the different outgroups and provide one of the criteria for differentiation between one's society and outgroups. In this respect, the point made by Sherif (1951) can be understood. He suggested that "the most important consequence of group structuring is the delineation of *ingroup* from *outgroup*. The development of ingroup and 'we experience' is accompanied by the demarcation and setting of boundaries from outgroups" (p. 395).

The personal willingness of people to be society members has been identified as an important condition for group existence. Social scientists have defined this willingness as group cohesiveness, "the resultant of all the forces acting on members to remain in the group" (Festinger, 1950, p. 274). This concept expresses attraction of society members to their society and the willingness to belong, which in reality provide the basis for the formation of the society. Patriotism can be viewed as one of the forces acting on members to remain in the society. The attachment expressed by love, care, or loyalty serves as a crucial bond. Patriotic beliefs not only increase cohesiveness but also, conversely, can be regarded as an indicator of a society's strength. It can be assumed that the stronger the prevailing patriotic beliefs, the more cohesive the society.

The relationship between patriotism and cohesiveness is further clarified by Turner et al.'s (1987) view of cohesiveness. He suggested "that group cohesion or mutual attraction between ingroup members is a function of mutually perceived similarity (identity) between self and others in terms of the defining characteristics of the ingroup self-category" (p. 59). In the same vein, Hogg and Abrams (1988) pointed out that similarities shared with large numbers of other people increase the social attraction of the group. That is, the development of social identity, which produces psychological belongingness, leads individuals to perceive intragroup similarities, which in turn enhance intragroup attraction. Individuals tend to like people who are members of the same group.

In the case of patriotism, society members are aware of their shared attachment to the society and the country. This common experience serves as a basis for feelings of similarity. Patriotic feelings both increase the sense of similarity among society members and at the same time reflect the level of their attraction to the society. In this way, patriotic beliefs can be seen as enhancing cohesiveness, thus serving as the psychological cement that keeps people in a society. It is hard to imagine a member of a society who would not harbor at least a minimum of fundamental patriotic beliefs. A person who does not have this confidence signals that he or she does not want to be a society member and that the society does not serve for him or her as a positive reference. The more society members feel this way, the less cohesive is the group.

Finally, patriotic beliefs mobilize society members to act on behalf of the society (see Stern, 1995). They play an important role as motivators that raise people's concern about society, to act for its welfare and even sometimes to sacrifice their own lives. Without such a readiness, the society cannot exist. Patriotism, thus, is a mobilizing, cognitive-affective force that not only binds individuals together but also provides the necessary ideology, explanation, and justification for action on its behalf.

Beliefs concerning patriotism cause people to give up personal comfort and to contribute their efforts, time, or money for the benefit of their society. The goals for which patriots are mobilized differ from society to society and may change over time. Also, there are individual differences with regard to patriots' level of willingness to commit themselves, as well as with regard to the goals they consider important. Although the leadership may set goals and mobilize patriots to achieve them, the latter may not consider them important and set their own goals. But the common motive in different acts of patriotism is the willingness to do something for the benefit of the society and country, even when this may involve personal cost.

6

Societal Beliefs
About Security

THE NATURE OF SECURITY BELIEFS

Every society is preoccupied with its security, but for some societies, this is a focal concern: Beliefs about security not only become societal beliefs but also occupy a central place in their ethos. Such a preoccupation develops when the society is concerned with a situation of insecurity, characterized by serious and prolonged threats to various aspects of societal life, the state, and/or the well-being of society members (Klare & Thomas, 1991; Pick & Critchley, 1974; Smoke, 1975). Such situations appear especially during intergroup conflict. In this case, collective experiences of insecurity, which lead to formation of beliefs about security, are dependent on the level of perceived threat and also on the perceived ability to cope with this threat (Bar-Tal & Jacobson, 1998). The greater the perceived threat and the more difficult people think it will be to cope with it, the more insecurity the society experiences and the more prominent become societal beliefs about security. Examples of societies greatly preoccupied with security are the Protestant and Catholic societies in Northern Ireland, the Kurdish society in Turkey, Algerian society, or Tutsi society in Rwanda. In all of them, society beliefs about security play a central role.

The present approach places security (or insecurity) in a sociopsychological conceptual framework, viewing security as a set of beliefs and feelings

AUTHOR'S NOTE: Although it is extensively rewritten, this chapter is based on a previously published article: Bar-Tal, D. (1991). Contents and origins of the Israelis' beliefs about security. *International Journal of Group Tensions, 21,*237-261. It is used here with permission of that journal and its publisher, Plenum Publishing Corp.

that are part of human repertoire. People as individuals and/or as society members experience security or insecurity with regard to their own personal life and/or with regard to their society. This approach stands against the prevalent perspective in political sciences, which views security as an objective and well-defined phenomenon that can be maintained and strengthened with tactics and strategies (e.g., Nye & Lynn-Jones, 1988; Pick & Critchley, 1974; Smoke, 1975). As a result, the political perspective focuses on such problems as military capability, deterrence, alliances, and so on. In contrast, the social psychological approach views security as necessarily related to human needs and based on cognitive processes through which society members evaluate their situation. Security or insecurity is thus viewed in terms of beliefs and feelings and, as a result, it is marked by individual and societal differences.

The Contents of Security Beliefs

Societal beliefs about security frequently pertain to at least four categories of contents. The first category of contents expresses the extent of insecurity or security feelings. Society members form beliefs about the level of insecurity on the basis of their perception of threats and their perceived ability to cope with them. They may share these beliefs, agreeing, for example, that their society is under a serious threat with which it cannot easily cope. In such a case, the beliefs express a high level of insecurity.

The second category of contents of security beliefs refers to the type of threat that society members collectively experience. Threats can be of different types, and different societies may well perceive different threats as relevant to them. A partial list of threats may include existential threats such as annihilation or genocide; threats to independence, self-determination, autonomy, or freedom; threats to territory; threats to superiority; threats to social economy; threats to social values or ideology; or threats to the well-being of society members. The threats can originate either from other societies or from internal forces within the society. Thus, for example, an external threat can be another society's or nation's expressed goal to conquer part of the society's territory, and an internal threat can derive from the extremely high rate of crime within the society.

The third category of beliefs about security consists of contents providing support for the coping of the society with the threat(s). These contents feature security as an important goal and value and glorify the means that are instrumental in achieving security. Thus, such beliefs ascribe status and prestige to the personnel whose role it is to maintain security, as, for example, in the case of intergroup conflict, to soldiers or other security forces. Other contents include slogans, myths, symbols, or models that raise the awareness of secu-

rity needs and motivate society members to engage in activities that are functional for security maintenance. In general, this category of beliefs plays an
important role in setting the sociopsychological conditions that enable the
society to cope with threats.

The fourth category of societal beliefs refers to the conditions that are
believed to be necessary for the achievement of security. The conditions can
be territorial, military, political, economical, and so on. They specify what
society has to do to cope with the threat and to be able to maintain security.
Thus, for example, in the case of territorial conflict, the conditions may refer
to military strength necessary for deterrence, development of military industries, and/or large reserves of military forces. Conditions depend on various
factors such as the nature of the threat, the perceived capability of society to
cope with the particular threat, and the context of the threat.

The Functions of Security Beliefs

The most important function of societal beliefs about security is to satisfy
the need of maintaining safety, which involves the basic human needs for a
sense of protection, surety, and survival (Maslow, 1970). These are basic
human needs that characterize every person. Their fulfillment is a prerequisite
for normal personal and societal life. Individuals strive to satisfy these needs
by "recruiting all the capacities of the organism in their service, and we may
then fairly describe the whole organism as a safety-seeking mechanism"
(Maslow, 1970, p. 39). Societal beliefs about security fulfill their function by
supplying information indicating that society is very concerned with the needs
of its members, that achievement of security is society's superior objective.
These beliefs also specify the conditions that are necessary for the achievement of security. In addition, security beliefs play an important role in the
mobilization of society members for coping with perceived threat. They call
for joint efforts of all society members to cope with the threat, for
volunteerism, for action that can improve security, and especially for taking
roles that have the responsibility to maintain security. In addition, these
beliefs call for sacrifices by society members to achieve security, even the
willingness to die to establish the society's security. Finally, beliefs about
security raise confidence in society's ability to cope with the threat and provide hope for a better future, because society members have to believe that
they can successfully withstand the threats and dangers.

Beliefs about security are essential for coping with threat: Without them,
a society may have great difficulty in overcoming the various dangers to
which it is exposed. Therefore, a society makes every effort to impart these
beliefs to its members. In times of threat, it uses all societal channels to

transmit these beliefs and employs control mechanisms so that society members absorb them, maintain them, and act according to them.

Societal beliefs about security are often imparted by external sources, because usually the great majority of society members are not directly involved in situations of relevance to security and do not have direct access to information about it. Society members, then, receive the information from leaders or the mass media and through various cultural products. These intermediaries define to society members the level and nature of the threat and specify the measures needed to strengthen security. Society members receive this information, and when this information is persistent, related to societal life, and of central importance, it may become the basis of societal beliefs.

THE ROOTS OF SECURITY BELIEFS

Societal beliefs about security are formed on the basis of perceived military, political, economic, and cultural conditions and collective experiences. Declarations of hostility, claims to territory, terrorist attacks, ideological competition, economic depression, or famine are all examples of situations that signal threats with which the society has to cope. Whether the situation is actually perceived as threatening—that is, by identifying the threatening situation, evaluating it, and making inferences—depends on previously stored knowledge (Fiske & Taylor, 1991; Kruglanski, 1989; Markus & Zajonc, 1985). The influence of existing knowledge is especially pronounced in situations that provide ambiguous information about threats and/or ways to contain them. In reality, this is the case for the majority of threat situations, because only rarely is information about threats unequivocal. Such situations may be a declaration of war, direct attack, continuous terrorist attacks, explicit verbal threats, or deep economic depression. However, many situations are not as clear, and therefore, cognitive factors play a role in their identification and evaluation. Two types of knowledge especially affect the formation of societal beliefs about security: (a) collective memories and (b) ideology and political attitudes. Both often serve as a prism through which new information is perceived and understood.

Collective memory may tune the society to attend to particular information and to interpret it in a particular way, while disregarding other relevant information. For example, collective memories of past traumas involving war, genocide, or occupation may sensitize society members to look for information that indicates possible threat and danger. This is how Volkan (1996) analyzed Serbian behavior in the Bosnian crisis. He suggested that Serbian behavior was greatly influenced by the society's traumatizing loss to Muslim

Turks in the 14th century. Centuries after the loss, Bosnian Muslims were perceived by the Serbs as extension of the Ottomans, and Serbs often referred to them as Turks who constitute a threat.

A society's political ideology may influence the formation of beliefs about security in a similar way. When political beliefs are central to the repertoire of society members—especially when these attitudes constitute a coherent system, that is, an ideology—they exert a special effect on the way society members view their world. The beliefs affect what information will receive attention and how it will be encoded and organized. Thus, political beliefs function as an interpretive framework and thereby influence evaluations, judgments, predictions, and inferences (Fiske & Taylor, 1991; Markus & Zajonc, 1985; Vertzberger, 1991). Beliefs about security may well be part of such an ideology or set of political beliefs. Because in any particular society, groups of society members differ in their political beliefs, this difference may be one factor that causes differences in beliefs about security. These differences may regard, for instance, evaluation of the potential threat and the way to cope with it.

The present chapter analyzes two cases of societal beliefs about security: American society and Israeli society.

▓ SOCIETAL BELIEFS ABOUT SECURITY IN THE UNITED STATES

One of the salient examples of societal beliefs about security can be found during the Cold War in the United States. Following World War II, the Soviet Union and the United States engaged in serious competition and conflict, which even involved a real threat of nuclear war. Most Americans believed that the communist Soviet system and the capitalistic American system could not coexist, because the Soviet system was perceived as inherently expansionist, seeking dominance, threatening U.S. religious and moral values, and opposing U.S. socioeconomic order. The Soviet communist ideology seemed in total opposition to the American ethos (e.g., Bialer, 1985; Free & Cantril, 1967; Frei, 1986). Historically, with the exception of World War II, the Soviet Union had long been perceived as a great threat to the United States. Soviet activities in Poland, Finland, the Baltic States, Iran, Greece, Berlin, East Germany, Hungary, Cuba, Czechoslovakia, Angola, Nicaragua, and Afghanistan, as well as the oppression and purges of the Soviet citizens, provided unequivocal evidence of the threat that the Soviet Union posed to the United States. In addition, the Soviets themselves continuously and constantly communicated that the United States and the Soviet Union were indeed locked in an ideological, political, economic, scientific, and cultural conflict, which they often even presented as being of a zero-sum nature.

All of this contributed to the evolution of societal beliefs about security in contemporary American society. How great Americans' sense of insecurity was in view of the Soviet threat is illustrated by Jules Henry (1963), who argued that "the most important single fact in American history since the Revolution and the Civil War is the pathogenic fear of the Soviet Union" (p. 100). In 1947, the term *national security* came into general use, as the U.S. government accepted a new doctrine for "containing" Soviet power. It was during this period that societal beliefs about security evolved, concerning the Soviet danger and ways to cope with it (Smoke, 1984).

Through decades, these beliefs about security remained dominant in American society (see Almond, 1960; Schneider, 1984). T. W. Smith (1983) provided the results of surveys done in the 1950s, 1960s, and 1970s, mapping attitudes toward the Soviet Union and communism. This work indicates that although Americans did change their attitudes as a function of changes in the relations between the United States and the Soviet Union, they felt consistently threatened by the Soviet Union and communism. For example, in the 1950s, over 80% of Americans viewed the Soviet Union unfavorably. The results of Gallup polls reveal the contents and prevalence of security beliefs during the Cold War. Thus, for example, in May 1949, 66% of the Americans believed that Russia "is trying to build herself up to be the ruling power of the world." This percentage rose to 81% in November 1950, and a large majority of Americans continued to hold this belief through the years (see Gallup, 1972, 1978). In May 1949, 60% of Americans believed that the Soviet Union did not want peace. In July 1950, 68% believed that "Russian expansion in Asia and Europe should be stopped." In November 1952, 57% believed that the United States should continue to give money and send troops to help Europe build up a defense against Russia. Between 1972 and 1976, about 80% constantly expressed some degree of feeling threatened by communism, and 85% expressed some concern about the Soviet Union. Even in the 1980s, 70% of Americans believed that war with Russia was unavoidable, and 56% believed that the "Soviet Union is like Hitler's Germany—an evil empire trying to rule the world" (Yankelovich & Smoke, 1988).

These beliefs held by the American public about the Soviet Union generally followed the lead of various important opinion sources (e.g., Erikson, Luttberg, & Tedin, 1980; Schneider, 1984). Therefore, of special importance for understanding the scope of conflict attitudes are the studies that examined the beliefs of American elites.

In two extensive surveys reported by Holsti and Rosenau (1984), data about beliefs of over 2,200 American leaders were collected in 1976 and 1980. The respondents represented every sector of American public leadership, including business executives, labor officials, educators, clergy, and so on. The analysis of their responses indicated that the great majority of

American leaders believed that "the Soviet Union is generally expansionist rather than defensive in its foreign policy goals" (84% in 1976 and 85% in 1980). Moreover, although the elites differed with regard to their conception of the conflict, its scope, and so on, they basically agreed that it existed (Holsti & Rosenau, 1986).

Also, Herrmann (1985) pointed out that although the American elites may disagree with regard to perceptions about the nature of the conflict, they agreed that the "USSR is interested in power and seeks to improve its influence vis-à-vis the United States" (p. 377). Similarly, in his analysis of American national leaders' commitment to containment, he found that the overwhelming majority of the American elite samples of 1979 and 1982 perceived the Soviet Union as a threat, although opinions differed about the level of the threat and the intensity of commitment to containment (Herrmann, 1986).

🏛 SOCIETAL BELIEFS ABOUT SECURITY IN ISRAEL

Another example of societal beliefs about security can be found in Israeli society. Because these beliefs play a very central role in the ethos of Israeli society, the discussion about them will be more extended. Security has been one of the most central problems to Israeli Jews since the beginning of the Yishuv (pre-state Jewish settlement) through the foundation of Israel and up to today. This concern is not surprising in view of the country's protracted and violent conflict with Arab states, and especially with the Palestinian people. From the Israeli perspective, the conflict directly concerns the existence of Israel and the well-being of the Jews who live there. That is, Israeli Jews believe that there is a real threat to the security of Israel as a state and to its Jewish citizens (see Arian, 1995; Stone, 1982). Almost half a century after the establishment of the State of Israel, the goal of achieving security still tops the public agenda. This goal plays a decisive role in setting the conditions for a peace agreement with Arab neighbors and therefore has a determining function in Israeli politics. Any territorial compromises, according to Israel's position, must be conditional on reliable assurances concerning the security of the country and its citizens. It is, thus, not surprising that lay people express deep concerns about security problems, that people who are involved with maintaining security are highly valued, that leaders compete on how they contribute to the security of the State, and that political parties use *security* as their passwords. In addition, the media almost daily evaluate the state of security, suggest solutions, and make comparisons with the past (see, e.g., Bar-Tal, Jacobson, & Klieman, 1998; Horowitz, 1984).

Through the years, security has frequently been used to justify government decisions, even those that do not directly concern security; security has been the rationale not only for military initiatives and responses but also for activities in the political, societal, and even educational and cultural domains. Security has also been used as the most important objective in negotiations with Arabs, because this is the only legitimate consideration accepted by the international community and by the great majority of the Israeli Jews. Such central and intensive preoccupation with security turned the beliefs involved into central societal beliefs.

The Contents of Societal Beliefs About Security in Israel

It is possible to identify at least four themes in societal beliefs about security in Israeli society.

Beliefs about insecurity. Societal beliefs about insecurity are dominant in the Israeli ethos: Israeli Jews believe that Israel lacks security. This is so because, from the beginning of the Zionist venture in Palestine at the end of the 19th century, Jews have continuously been subject to, and coping with, various types of threat. The unwelcoming and often hostile attitudes of Turkish authorities in the Ottoman empire, the Arab population, the British mandate, and Arab states—all of these contributed to Jewish beliefs about insecurity.

Surveys reported in Stone (1982) refer directly to Israeli Jews' worries about the security situation. The surveys, conducted between 1970 and 1979, indicated that, with the exception of a brief period before the 1973 Yom Kippur War when a significant drop in security worries was noticed, a high percentage of Israeli Jews continuously expressed worries regarding security. From 1970 to 1971, about 70% of Israeli Jews expressed this attitude; in 1972, about 60%. In 1973, there was a drop to 30% expressing worries and then, following the war, a very high percentage of Israeli Jews voiced this concern (70% to 90%). From 1976 to 1978, this percentage dropped slightly to 60%, and as a result of the Camp David agreement, it even briefly reached the level of 50%. In the 1980s, concerns about security increased again, especially with the onset of the Palestinian uprising, the Intifada. The 1993 Oslo agreement with the Palestinians first increased the sense of security, but it dropped sharply with the wave of terror in 1994 and 1995, and again, the sense of insecurity became prevalent. In a national survey by Yaar, Hermann, and Nadler in March 1995, 64.4% of Israelis said they felt that their personal security had decreased since the peace process began, and 58.8% claimed that the security of Israel was in worse condition than before. In September 1997, the national survey performed by Gallup (Shalev, 1997) showed that only 33% of Jews in Israel evaluated their personal security as satisfactory (either *very good* or *good*).

Type and extent of threat. The second theme commonly found in security beliefs bears on the type and extent of perceived threat. Threat ranges from the annihilation of Israel, war, terrorist attacks, and loss of a Jewish majority in Israel to personal injury. Data collected among Jewish inhabitants of Israel's four largest urban areas suggested that Israelis are pessimistic about the possibility of war involving their country (Stone, 1982). Between 1973 and 1977, at least 70% and often more than 90% of respondents thought there would be another war with the Arab countries in the coming years. In 1988, 70% of respondents still expressed this belief (Levy, 1988). In his surveys, Arian (1995) reported that after the Gulf War in 1991, 54% of Israelis thought that war with Arab countries was either probable or very probable. By 1994, this percentage had dropped to 43%, with the beginning of the peace process.

Also, between 1973 and 1979, at least 60% and sometimes more than 80% of Israeli Jews agreed that "the Arabs' aim is not the return of occupied territories but the destruction of Israel." Arian's 1986 surveys showed a stable perception of existential threat among the Jewish population of Israel. In 1986, about 5% of the population thought that the ultimate goal of the Arabs was to recapture some of the territories lost in the 1967 war. About 20% reported that they thought the Arabs' goal was to get all the territories lost in this war. About 35% thought that the Arabs really wanted to conquer the whole of Israel, and the same percentage believed that the ultimate goal of the Arabs was to conquer the State of Israel *and* destroy the Jews living there. This distribution hardly fluctuated in surveys done in 1987, 1988, 1990, 1991, 1992, 1993, and 1994 (Arian, 1995).

Specific assessment of security worries indicates that although, unsurprisingly, many Israeli Jews expressed a high level of worry about terrorism (between 1968 and 1979, almost continuously at least 70%), they did trust the fighting ability of the Israeli Defense Forces (between 1968 and 1977 no more than 40% of Israeli Jews expressed a worry about this issue). In the 1990s, worries about personal safety because of terrorism climbed. In 1993, 84% of Israelis were either very worried or worried that they or members of their family would be injured in a terrorist action; the percentage in 1994 was 76%, and in 1995, 85% (Arian, 1995). Also, in the course of the late 1980s and early 1990s, more Israelis believed that the Israeli Defense Forces had become weaker. But with a view to the future in 1994 and 1995, more Israelis believed that the Israeli army would strengthen itself again than that it would be weakened.

Valuing security. The third theme of societal beliefs about security makes security the central value and cultural master symbol of Israeli society. First, the word itself has become a key concept in Israeli society: A large majority shares the societal belief that security considerations come before anything else. Security, as we said, has been the supreme reason and justification for various types of decisions, policies, and actions: in the distribution of national resources, manpower, planning, individual development, censorship, and legal matters, as well as in relation to the Arab minority, the definition of gender roles, and so on (e.g., Bar-Tal et al., 1998; Kimmerling, 1993; Yaniv, 1993).

In evolving its beliefs about security, the society used myths and symbols that stress heroism, courage, determination, and the continuing struggle for national survival (Ben-Yehuda, 1995; Liebman & Don-Yehiya, 1983; Zerubavel, 1995). A master image of Israeli society, thus, draws on the duel between the brave young David, who stands for the new Israeli society, and the gigantic Goliath, who symbolizes the enemies of Israel (Gertz, 1984). Another founding narrative is that of the historical Maccabee family, who led a successful struggle for independence against the Greeks from 147 to 166 C.E. Among other episodes from ancient Jewish history, the defense of Masada and Bar Kochba's rebellion receive prominent focus. After a long Roman siege, the defenders of Masada decided to commit mass suicide rather than fall into the hands of the enemy; Bar Kochba led a brave but unsuccessful rebellion against the Roman occupation.

From contemporary history, Jewish resistance during the Holocaust, especially the uprising in the Warsaw ghetto, and Jewish partisans receive a special place in the Israeli collective memory and have been turned into models of heroic struggle. Moreover, Israeli society glorifies those involved in maintaining security, as well as the institutions and organizations whose function it is to secure national survival and personal safety. Societal beliefs glorify underground military organizations in the prestate period, the Israeli army, army units, and individual soldiers who fought bravely, and special security operations and missions. Commemoration of those fallen in various associated actions occupies a prominent place on the national calendar.

All of the society's political, educational, and cultural institutions participate in the formation, transmission, dissemination, and maintenance of these beliefs, and this is done formally and informally, directly and indirectly, by means of various channels and mechanisms such as rituals, ceremonies, school curricula, books, films, army training, leaders' speeches, the media, and so on (see Ashkenazy, 1994; Bar-Tal, 1998b, 1998c; Gertz, 1998; Popper, 1998).

Conditions to guarantee security. The last theme of societal beliefs about security concerns the conditions deemed necessary to establish security.

These beliefs are at the roots of Israeli society's profound polarization. Until the historical visit to Jerusalem of Egyptian President Anwar Sadat in November 1977, societal beliefs regarding the conditions for security were nearly uniform. In view of the refusal of Arab states to recognize the State of Israel, and as a result of the repeated violent attempts to resolve the conflict, Israelis believed that only military strength together with continued occupation of the territories gained in the 1967 war could prevent future wars. But the successful negotiations with Egypt, which ended with a peace treaty in 1979, indicated that the Israeli-Arab conflict could be resolved peacefully. From this turning point, Israeli society became divided in its beliefs concerning the conditions that would guarantee the security of the State and its citizens. Although some (i.e., doves) believe that a prerequisite for security is peace, to be achieved through partial or full withdrawal from the territories occupied in the 1967 war, others believe that only by holding on to most of the territories can security be guaranteed (Arian, 1995; Inbar & Goldberg, 1990; Stone, 1982). The achievement of security has been and continues to be the supreme objective of all society members, and the majority consider this national objective the only legitimate reason for occupying the territories. The disagreement within Israeli society concerns the question of whether or not the occupied territories are crucial for maintaining national security. Thus, peace and security have been tied to different visions, depending on the ideology and political beliefs of the group. This polarization is a vivid example of how societal beliefs can change because of a new experience and how society can become divided as a result of such changes.

A review of the polls reflecting such changes shows that between 1971 and 1979, the majority of Israelis either were not willing to return any territories in exchange for peace or were willing to return only a small part of them (Arian, 1995; Stone, 1982). This majority ranged, with some periodic exceptions, between 50% and 75%. Very few Israelis were willing during this period to return most of the territories (12% to 21%). In effect, these polls showed a consensus, because a great majority of Jewish society members up to 1979 did not agree to any significant withdrawals from the occupied territories in exchange for peace. In the 1980s, opinions changed: Although about 50% were not willing to return any territories in exchange for peace, or were willing to return a small portion only, about 50% were willing to return a large part of the territories, most, or all of them. The latter group slowly increased during the 1990s (Arian, 1995; Shamir & Shamir, 1993).

In 1995, after the Oslo and Cairo agreements with the Palestine Liberation Organization, which constituted a first phase in efforts for a peaceful resolution of the Israeli-Palestinian conflict, the survey of Arian (1995) showed the following distribution regarding preferred solutions for the territories: 15% of Israelis preferred annexation of the occupied territories and transfer of the

Palestinians; 15% favored annexation without transfer (but without rights for Arabs); 7% preferred annexation with full rights for Arabs; 25% favored Palestinian autonomy; 8% preferred return of most of the territories to Jordan, 18% favored Jordanian-Palestinian federation, and 13% preferred a Palestinian State. This survey also shows that the question of giving up territories in exchange for peace is the most divisive issue. Arian found, referring to specific areas, that 80% were ready to relinquish the Gaza Strip; 46%, Arab urban areas in the West Bank; 30%, western Samaria; 19%, the Jordan Valley; 18%, Gush Etzion; and 9%, East Jerusalem. With regard to a peaceful conflict resolution with Syria, the Israeli public is also divided. According to Yaar et al.'s (1995) survey, only 12.8% of Israelis support a full withdrawal from the Golan Heights in return for peace with Syria and realization of major conditions; 37.9% support partial withdrawal, and 46.3% object to any kind of withdrawal.

The Origins of Israel's Societal Beliefs About Security

Israel's societal beliefs about security are most immediately based in the intractable conflict with the Palestinians and the Arab states (Ben-Dor, 1998; see Chapter 9, this volume). The history of Jewish-Arab relations is marked by continuous conflict that has involved verbal threats, economic boycott, territorial claims, violent engagements, terrorism, and war. These experiences played a crucial role in the formation of societal beliefs about security. But, in addition, two factors have influenced the perception, interpretation, and evaluation of the information coming from the experiences of the Israeli-Arab conflict: namely, Jewish collective memory and political ideology.

The continuous threat to Jewish existence is probably one of the most important themes in Jewish collective memory (see Chapter 7). Spending 2,000 years in exile, where the concern for security was a central preoccupation because of constant persecution, expulsion, discrimination, and pogroms, left its mark on the Jewish ethos. In addition, the Holocaust, that is, the German Nazis' attempt to systematically wipe out the Jewish population of Europe, has become the focal experience in Jewish history, leaving its marks on all considerations of security.

Many Israeli Jews perceive threats made by the Arabs as a continuation of anti-Semitism. They view the current conflict through the perspective of the past, and this enhances their feelings of insecurity. Only very recently, Israel's President, Ezer Weizmann, said, "It is characteristic of Jews to be insecure. This trait has been imprinted on us" (*Ha'aretz*, October 15, 1997).

Against this background, it is not surprising that Arian (1995), in two national samples (done in 1987 and 1994), found that the more Israeli Jews express fears based on past experiences, the more they tend to feel threatened by the present situation and the less they hold conciliatory beliefs about the future of the occupied territories. Similarly, Bar-Tal and Antebi (1992) found that hawkish Israeli attitudes toward resolution of the Israeli Arab conflict are best predicted by fears originating in the past.

Political ideology and beliefs also have had an effect on societal beliefs about security. Thus, Israelis who subscribe to the concept of the "Land of Greater Israel"—according to which the Jewish people have a natural and historical right to Judea and Samaria (i.e., the West Bank)—have a different conception of security and solutions for safeguarding it than other Israelis, who believe that Israel should be democratic and Jewish, or that Israel is the homeland of two nations, the Jews and the Palestinians.

Arian (1989) investigated the relationship between ideology and security beliefs, finding that political identification is strongly associated with security beliefs. Those who support hawkish parties are likely to believe that war is more likely than peace ($r = .34$) and are less conciliatory with regard to solutions about the territories ($r = .45$) than those who support dovish parties.

An illustration of the relationship between political attitudes and beliefs about security was provided in the analysis of political platforms of parties contending for Israel's 1988 elections. The analysis showed that the security conception of the hawkish Likud party was embedded in its ideology regarding the exclusive Jewish right to the "whole land of Israel." The Likud platform states that

> The right of the Jewish people to the Land of Israel is an eternal right which cannot be undermined and is part of the country's right for security and peace. Zionism is the liberation movement of the Jewish people. The State of Israel has the right to sovereignty in Judea, Samaria, and the Gaza Strip. (Likud platform, 1988, p. 1)

It is not surprising, then, that the Likud party stated that sovereignty over all of the so-called "Land of Israel" is a necessary condition for warranting security.

> Withdrawal from Judea, Samaria, and Gaza means narrow borders and a lack of strategic depth, necessary for sufficient warning in case of war and sufficient time for military preparation. (undated Likud flier)

> The autonomy settlement which was agreed in Camp David guarantees that in Western Eretz Israel there will be no territorial division, no Palestinian state, foreign sovereignty, or foreign self-determination. (Likud platform, 1988, p. 1)

The security beliefs of the Labor party were dictated by two convictions: (a) the will to preserve "the Jewish national nature" of the State of Israel, which "is based on a large and stable Jewish majority"; and (b) the desire "to consolidate the state as a democratic enlightened society with equal rights to its citizens" (Labor party's platform, 1988, p. 7). In line with these two objectives, the Labor party's conception of security consisted of three elements:

> Peace, withdrawal from territories which are not densely populated, and demilitarization of the rest of the territories. The Labor's platform stated that the military strength of Israel is a condition for advancing peace. Peace is an important component of security . . . withdrawal from territories densely populated by Palestinians in a peace settlement is a significant contribution to the security of the State of Israel. . . . The permanent borders must be defensible, which will decrease the risk of acts of aggression and enable Israel to defend itself efficiently with its own forces. Israel will retreat to pre-1967 eastern borders and will keep territories, which are not densely populated by Arabs, necessary for its security. Demilitarization and security arrangements, which will be included in the peace agreements, will be carried out additionally to the establishment of permanent borders and not in place thereof. (Labor party platform, 1988, p. 7)

I have analyzed the scope and roots of beliefs about security held commonly by Israeli society. These beliefs, as will be shown in Chapter 9, are part of the Israeli ethos, which is characterized as an ethos of conflict. They play a central role in the ethos, because the threats deriving from the conflict are determinative experiences of the Israeli society.

7

Societal Beliefs About Siege

THE NATURE AND BASIS OF SIEGE BELIEFS

Another theme of societal beliefs that can be observed in different societies pertains to the experience of being under siege, that is, perceiving that the rest of the world has highly negative intentions toward one's society. That is, society members who hold this societal belief believe that their society is surrounded by a hostile world. The focus of the core societal belief is on *negative intentions* and *the rest of the world*. Negative intentions refer to the desire and motivation of the world to inflict harm or to hurt the society, implying a threat to the society's well-being. The crucial part of the belief relates this threat to the rest of the world. This element is unique to siege beliefs; many societies probably believe that at least one other society has negative intentions toward them. But in the siege case, the situation is far more extreme and serious. Not only do members of the society believe that their society is in conflict with another group, or surrounded by hostile neighbors, but they believe that the rest of the world, as a whole, is hostile toward them. *This creates the tragic perception that the society is alone in a hostile world.* In actual fact, the concept *world* does not necessarily include all the societies or nations in the world. For hostility to be experienced in this generalized sense, it is enough if the belief refers to those nations that are relevant to the belief holders, that is, those nations in the world that function as reference groups—either

AUTHOR'S NOTE: This chapter, although extensively rewritten, is based on a previously published article: Bar-Tal, D., & Antebi, D. (1992). Siege mentality in Israel. *International Journal of Intercultural Relations, 16*, 251-275. It is used here with permission of that journal and its publisher, Elsevier Science Ltd.

because there is a desire to have positive relations with them or because they affect the welfare of the society. Clearly, these reference nations may change with time depending on political, social, and economic conditions. But what is of importance in this situation is the sense of loneliness the society experiences in the midst of a hostile international community.

Usually, the described core societal belief occurs with additional societal beliefs that may reflect such contents as feelings of loneliness, threat to societal existence, lack of trust in other nations, expectations that no nation will extend help in time of need, or the need to secure the existence of the society without resorting to external help. Whenever the siege theme is central in the society's repertoire of beliefs, we can say that society members possess a siege mentality. In this case, siege beliefs not only feature prominently in the cognitive repertoire of society members, but also come with important affective and behavioral implications that have a major effect on the life of society members and on the decisions of their leaders.

The recent past and the present offer a number of examples of societies characterized by societal beliefs about siege: the Soviet society immediately following the Bolshevik Revolution; the Japanese society in the early 1930s; the Jewish society in Israel; the Albanian society in the 1960s, 1970s, and 1980s, the South African White society prior to the elimination of apartheid; and North Korean, Iraqi, and Iranian societies today. The roots of the siege experience in these societies are not, of course, necessarily identical. It is possible to differentiate at least three causes for the evolution of siege beliefs. The siege experience can be evoked by the society's leaders, who decide to isolate the society from a hostile world for various internal causes. Alternatively, it may stem from perceived maltreatment of the society by the world. Finally, the siege beliefs may be maintained because of the imprint left by past collective experiences, something that greatly affects the present perception of the world. It should be noted, however, that these bases are not mutually exclusive and may be found in one society. But usually, one basis is more dominant than others. Therefore, each category of cases will now be elaborated, and specific examples will be provided.

Self-Isolation

A society may isolate itself from a world it perceives as hostile and harboring negative intentions toward it. In this case, it is society's decision, usually that of its leaders, to live in isolation, without any clearly observable maltreatment from the "rest of the world." It is hard to decide whether this isolation is based on the perception of a hostile world or on internal needs. The perception is subjective and real for the perceivers. But in some cases, self-imposed isolation serves various internal needs that underlie the perception of world threat. In this vein, Simmel (1955) observed,

> Within certain groups, it may even be a piece of political wisdom to see to it that there be some enemies in order for the unity of the members to remain effective and for the group to remain conscious of this unity as its vital interest. (p. 98)

Obviously, there is a major difference between purposely inventing an enemy or enemies and subjectively perceiving all the nations of the world as enemies. The former is an extreme case of the above-described observations, but in principle, it serves the same needs as the latter case: Self-imposed isolation based on siege beliefs allows preservation of the society's political and/or cultural system without external influence; it enhances cohesiveness, solidarity, and unity; it enables control of the society, as well as development of self-reliance and autonomy; and it results in the permanent mobilization of society members.

One example of a self-perpetuated siege mentality is that of Albania during more than three decades, from the 1960s until 1995, when the communist regime collapsed. The process of partial isolation began after War World II when Albania became part of the so-called Eastern Bloc with the Soviet Union and China as its major patrons and had no relations with the West. But following a change in Soviet leader Khrushchev's policy toward Yugoslavia, relations between the European Eastern Bloc and Albania started to deteriorate, until in October 1961, ties were broken completely. Then, in 1978, Albania also detached itself from China, embarking on a self-imposed isolationist policy (Biberaj, 1990; Costa, 1995; Prifti, 1978). During the rule of Enver Hoxha, and even in the years after his death in 1985, Albanian leaders constructed a national atmosphere that most resembled that of a besieged fortress. They persistently propagated beliefs about the negative intentions of "the world," constantly feeding the public information about alleged "imperialist-revisionist conspiracies" against "socialist" Albania. The external threat was supposed to come from the West as well as from the East, that is, from the entire rest of the world.

Another example of self-initiated siege mentality is the present case of North Korea, which, following the changes that took place in Eastern Europe, isolated itself from the rest of the world, attributing especially negative intentions to capitalist countries. The present leader, Kim Jong-il, the son of Kim I-sung, has explained that

> To prevent imperialist ideology and culture from infiltrating into our country remains the key to protecting our socialism and guaranteeing the development

of socialist culture. The imperialists are attempting to infiltrate bourgeois culture into the socialist world, thus to paralyze the revolutionary spirit of the people here. (Lee, Park, & Rhee, 1993, p. 29)

In line with this thesis, North Korea views other countries with extreme suspicion, minimizing relations with them (except with China) by maintaining a "closed door" policy (Savada, 1994; Yang, 1994).

Maltreatment

The second category of causes leading to the formation of siege beliefs is based on observable, clear-cut behavior. We can identify different types of collective experiences that have led societies to the perception that they are being maltreated by the rest of the world. It is possible to assume that in the past, persecuted societies such as Jews; exploited societies such as the Indians in South America or Blacks in North America; or societies that suffered extermination and genocide such as the Armenian society in Turkey, Jews and Gypsies in Nazi Germany, or the Indian tribes in North America; experienced isolation and maltreatment by other groups and thus formed societal beliefs about siege (the particular case of Jews will be elaborated later). In different parts of the world, particular social groups are still suffering maltreatment. Thus, it is very likely that the Tutsi tribe in Rwanda, the Muslims in Bosnia, or the Kurds in Turkey have formed societal beliefs about siege.

It also happens that the international community decides to cut relations with a particular society, and usually such a decision is accompanied by punitive actions such as embargoes, boycotts, sanctions, or even violent hostile activities. It is not surprising when the isolated society then perceives itself as being besieged by the rest of the world. The international community may have different reasons to oust a nation; most often, it is the threat that the given society constitutes to the international community. The threat can originate for various reasons. One such reason can be the establishment of a regime based on an ideology that threatens other political systems, for example, in the Soviet Union in 1918. Following the Bolshevik Revolution, the communist regime threatened the basic principles, norms, and values of other societies. As a result, isolation was imposed on the Soviet society, and some countries (the Russians claimed there were 14) intervened in the Civil War between 1918 and 1920 by sending military units to fight the new communist regime and by imposing economic sanctions (see Fisher, 1951; Kennan, 1960). In this period, societal beliefs about siege appeared among the Bolsheviks. They perceived the actions of the intervening countries as a capitalist conspiracy to crush the emerging state (e.g., Ponomaryov, Gromyko, & Uhvostov, 1969).

Lenin and other Soviet leaders expressed this belief frequently on different occasions. On November 7, 1918, Lenin (1965) said,

> The capitalists of the whole world in terror and hatred hurried to rally together for the revolution's suppression. And the Socialist Soviet Republic of Russia is a particular thorn in their side. The combined imperialists of the world are prepared to attack us, to involve us in more battles, and to impose more sacrifice on us. (p. 167)

Another example is Japan in the 1930s, when there was a widespread conviction about the world's negative intentions toward it. The immediate event that increased the availability and centrality of this belief was the vote of the League of Nations in 1933, approving almost unanimously an anti-Japanese resolution following Japan's military action in Manchuria. As a result, Japan withdrew from the League of Nations. The Japanese leadership felt that the world was hostile toward their country (see Barnhart, 1987; Morley, 1974). Hashimoto Kingoro, a prominent army leader, expressed this belief in the following way: "At the time of the Manchurian incident, the entire world joined in criticism of Japan. They said that Japan was an untrustworthy nation" (Tsunoda, de Bary, & Kenne, 1958, p. 797).

In present times, the isolation of another society by the international community may take place when a given society performs acts that violate the internationally accepted code of behaviors, for example, in the case of Iran, which supports terrorism, or Iraq, which attacked another state, Kuwait. What counts in these cases is probably not just the violation of the above-mentioned code—this is something that many societies do—but the extent of the threat that such violating actions seem to pose to the well-being of other countries. Thus, for example, Iran's support of terrorism in different countries destabilizes other societies, disturbs their life, and brings violence and stress to civilian populations. Iraq's occupation of Kuwait threatened the supply of oil, the major source of energy in many countries.

In the case of Iran, the United States, as the one remaining superpower, presses other countries to limit their contacts and trade with Iran. In the case of Iraq, the U.N. Security Council passed a resolution on August 6, 1990, imposing an economic and trade embargo on Iraq, following the Iraqi occupation of Kuwait. Later, following the Gulf War, the U.N. Security Council imposed a wider range of sanctions on Iraq to force its leaders to eliminate all their weapons of mass destruction and the means to produce them (Cordesman & Hashim, 1997). These steps led to the strengthening and formation of siege beliefs, as expressed by an Iraqi official in an interview with a Western journalist: "Is there another country in the world whose government is opposed by every one of its neighbors, and by the only superpower which also funds the main opposition group, and by the world media" (Cordesman & Hashim, 1997, p. 155).

It is rare for the international community to isolate another society for violating moral law in its internal practices. But this is what happened with South Africa. The South African government, representing the country's white minority, institutionalized discrimination against the non-white part of the society. Almost all the countries of the world united against South Africa's apartheid system, which was seen as a morally repugnant practice of racial discrimination. In 1960, the Commonwealth of Nations expelled South Africa from its organization. In 1963, the Organization of African Unity called for a total boycott of South Africa, and various U.N. agencies and other international organizations excluded South Africa from their activities. In 1973, the U.N. General Assembly declared apartheid a crime against humanity; the most serious sanctions taken against South Africa were economic, with countries around the world limiting their trade with and investments in South Africa to differing extents (Grundy, 1991; van der Stoel, 1988).

The South African government viewed the global effort to end apartheid as "total onslaught" (Grundy, 1991). The government's White Paper on Defense and Armaments in 1982 blamed the imposed isolation especially on the Soviet Union. It stated,

> The ultimate aim of the Soviet Union and its allies is to overthrow the present body politic in the RSA (Republic of South Africa) and to replace it with a Marxist-oriented form of government to further the objectives of the USSR, therefore all possible methods and means are used to attain this objective . . . this onslaught is supported by a worldwide propaganda campaign and the involvement of various front organizations and leaders. (Grundy, 1991, pp. 101-102)

In view of the sanctions imposed by the international community, and especially following the expulsion of South Africa from the British Commonwealth, white South Africans began to perceive themselves as a nation pushed with its back to the wall by a hostile world (see, e.g., Brown, 1966). Legum and Legum (1964) have cited numerous expressions of South African political leadership that demonstrate the above-mentioned perception: "The world is against us. But we have stood before—belied, slandered, and spied upon" (Dr. Hertzog, Minister of Post and Telegraphs, *The Star,* December 16, 1960).

Imprinting Past Experiences

Finally, societal beliefs about siege may characterize a society with long-remembered experiences involving the negative intentions of the world at large. If such experiences lasted through a long period of time, or if they were particularly intense, a society may go on having societal siege beliefs even when the situation has changed and the conditions that justified the beliefs have disappeared. The siege beliefs, then, are based on a trauma that leaves its marks on generations through decades and even centuries (Krystal, 1968). Under the new circumstances, society members will search for evidence to validate their societal beliefs about siege and continue to maintain these beliefs through educational, cultural, and political mechanisms and institutions. An example of this case is the Israeli Jewish society, which maintains societal beliefs about siege mainly on the basis of 2,000 years of Jewish history. We shall have a closer look at this particular case as an example of a society with siege beliefs.

𝍫 ISRAELI BELIEFS ABOUT SIEGE

Jewish history shows that from the destruction of the Second Temple and the beginning of the forced exile in the Roman era and continuing through the Middle Ages, the Reformation, and the Industrial Revolution until the present time, Jews have consistently and continuously been subjects, in almost every place they lived, of what we would call today massive anti-Semitism. Throughout this long history, they experienced persecution, libel, social taxation, restriction, forced conversion, expulsion, and pogroms (e.g., Grosser & Halperin, 1979; Poliakov, 1974). As a result, as Liebman (1978) rightly pointed out, "Jewish tradition finds anti-Semitism to be the norm, the natural response of the non-Jew. . . . The term 'Esau hates Jacob' symbolizes the world which Jews experience. It is deeply embedded in the Jewish folk tradition" (p. 45).

But the climax of these experiences took place in the 20th century with "the final solution to the Jewish problem," the systematic genocide that we now call the Holocaust (see Dawidowicz, 1975). The fact that 6 million Jews perished while "the world" remained indifferent (e.g., Morse, 1968) served crucially to strengthen the siege mentality of the remaining Jews and left its marks on future generations and their experience (Bar-Tal, 1990b). In the Jewish point of view, the Holocaust does not stand alone as one grim event but is a metaphor for Jewish history itself (Stein, 1978). This is of critical importance for understanding the Israeli siege mentality, as it is expressed, for instance, in the following insightful observation:

> The Holocaust remains a basic trauma of Israeli society. It is impossible to exaggerate its effect on the process of nation-building. . . . There is a latent hysteria in Israeli life that stems directly from this source. . . . The trauma of the

Holocaust leaves an indelible mark on the national psychology, the tenor and content of public life, the conduct of foreign affairs, on politics, education, literature, and the arts. (Elon, 1971, pp. 198-199)

In addition, the Israeli-Arab conflict, although very different from the Holocaust, did a great deal to preserve this siege mentality. After the establishment of the Jewish state in 1948, Arab countries tried actively to destroy it. First, Israel was invaded by five regular armies from Egypt, Transjordan, Syria, Iraq, and Lebanon. Until the peace treaty with Egypt, all the Arab states closed their borders, declared an embargo, pressed the world to stop relations with Israel, and maintained a state of war, refusing to recognize Israel and employing instead the rhetoric of the "liberation of Palestine" and the "liquidation of Zionist aggression." In its 50 years of existence, Israel has fought several major wars with Arab states in which many thousands of Israelis have been killed. In addition, Palestinian terrorist attacks against Jews, which have caused many civilian casualties, also boost siege beliefs (see Ben-Gurion, 1963; Eban, 1957; Meir, 1973).

Israeli society can, therefore, be characterized by societal siege beliefs, which are widespread and constitute a significant part of the Israeli ethos (see Arian, 1995; Liebman & Don-Yehiya, 1983). The popular song "The Whole World Is Against Us,"[1] composed in the late 1960s, is probably the most vivid and obvious expression of this:

The whole world is against us.
This is an ancient tale
Taught by our forefathers
To sing and dance to.
If the whole world is against us,
We don't give a damn
If the whole world is against us,
Let the whole world go to hell.

The analysis of the example of the Israeli Jewish society will be somewhat extended to illustrate the prevalence of societal beliefs of siege in an individual's repertoire and as expressed in various cultural, political, and educational channels.

Several studies and polls have established the prevalence of siege beliefs in Israeli Jewish society. For example, following the 1973 Yom Kippur war, respondents were asked what in their opinion was the attitude of the "nations of the world" regarding Israel. About 40% of all respondents felt that the nations of the world were always, or generally, against Israel, whereas only 5% of the sample were willing to make the opposite generalization (Liebman

& Don-Yehiya, 1983, p. 198). About 14 years later (January 1987), a survey revealed that 50% of respondents believed that "The whole world is against us"; 67% believed that "World criticism of Israeli policy stems mainly from anti-Semitism"; and 63% believed that "Israel is and will continue to be 'a people dwelling alone'." An important finding is that these beliefs are evenly distributed among the Jewish Israeli population, independent of socio-economic class, education, age, and even political ideology (Arian, 1989). Arian (1995) reported that the beliefs associated with siege mentality are quite stable, and surveys performed in 1990, 1991, and 1994 found similar percent-ages of agreement with the same statements.

Expressions of siege beliefs can be found in various forms in Israeli litera-ture. A literary critic, Ben-Ezer (1977), suggested that the motif of being under siege played a large part in shaping the literature written before the Six Day War in 1967, and even before 1948. According to Ben-Ezer, the es-tablishment of the State of Israel has not affected the feelings of nightmare, estrangement, and siege expressed by Israeli writers. Following victory in the 1967 war, such experiences of siege mentality briefly diminished, but the euphoria quickly disappeared, and the beliefs of siege re-emerged. Thus, for instance, Amos Oz, one of Israel's most popular writers, often expresses fears of nightmares. He feels that Israeli existence "is a piece of culture in a jungle, which surrounds us" (Ben-Ezer, 1968, p. 130). In his story, "The Jackal Coun-tries," he tells of a nightmarish hallucination:

> Many black, skinny people, rushing, falling like a collapse of stones and flowing swiftly in the lower plain. . . . Already they are near enough for you to distinguish their shape. A filthy mob, dark, skinny, lice- and flea-infested, defi-nitely smelly. Hunger and hatred distort their faces. Their eyes burn with mad-ness. . . . And suddenly you are also surrounded. Besieged. Standing motionless from fear. (Oz, 1976, p. 22)

Similarly, the popular satirist Ephraim Kishon has frequently referred to "our little country surrounded by enemies." In his story, "A Nation That Dwells Alone," Kishon (1988) wrote,

> This title was given us by Bilam while being interviewed in the paper "Num-bers" and till this very day we do not know if it was meant as a compliment or a curse. In any event, from then until today we have succeeded in preserving our special status as the only nation who does not have an ally for sure. (p. 55)

Also, Israeli films reflect the societal beliefs of siege. Recently, Ben-Shaul (1997), in an analysis of Israeli films made between 1930 and 1988, pointed out that siege mentality is one of their leading themes. The films depict a hostile world as a tragic reality. Ben-Shaul lists the different techniques used to achieve this sense: lighting that emphasizes closed spatial formation, unpredictable abrupt editing and unexpected camera movements, temporally circular structures, claustrophobically structured narratives, suspicious and violent interactions, and portrayal of isolated characters. All these characteristics indicate that Israeli films are greatly influenced by beliefs of siege, and then, in turn, they transmit the essence of these beliefs to the Israeli public.

The press in Israel, which is widely read, has a significant influence on the accessibility of ideas. Over the years, it has printed numerous references to the world's hostility toward the Jews and Israel. These beliefs are not limited to newspapers associated with a particular political position but rather are representative of a wide scope of political opinion, including the left-wing newspapers, *Davar* and *Al Hamishmar*. An article in the Labor party's newspaper *Davar* reads,

> Right and left joined together in order to inflame the old-new anti-Semitism: The cross-fire within which the Jewish People, Zionism and the State of Israel find themselves on both sides of Europe . . . shows that the illusions encouraged at the beginning of the Emancipation and which were proven false by the distorted metamorphoses of liberalism and socialism have been dashed . . . the anti-Semitic movement in all its anti-Zionist and anti-Israel revelations proves that its perpetrators wish to complete the "final solution" which Hitler initiated through the division of roles: The Arab nations will continue with physical genocide and the "enlightened" nations will conduct a spiritual genocide of survivors. (Gothelf, 1970)

Similar ideas were expressed by Shalom Rosenfeld (1980), a leading Israeli journalist and an editor of *Ma'ariv*:

> The hatred of Israel has always been the all powerful cement which connected the different nations and states, which in other areas not only did not share similar interests but were often contradictory and at odds with each other. . . . Let the historical philosophers and anthropologists search for the explanation of this remarkable phenomenon which has swept away the masses, coming from different traditions and cultures to a common ritual of hatred towards a nation and state whose name they can hardly pronounce . . . what preoccupies us primarily is the spiritual, political and security expressions which this international brotherly hatred has toward the existence of the State of Israel and the security of the masses of Jews in the Diaspora.

The public statements made by political leaders reflect a society's ethos. These statements not only help to maintain already existing beliefs but are also instrumental in socializing the younger generations (Liebman & Don-

Yehiya, 1983). In other words, leaders define situations for the public, who readily absorb and internalize them (Keis, 1975). A review of speeches made by political leaders reveals that, irrespective of their ideology or political affiliation, these beliefs are deeply embedded in their repertoire. Several examples will illustrate how political leaders express them.

The first Prime Minister of Israel, David Ben-Gurion, in an address made in 1953, spoke of the total and constant hostility of the world toward Israel:

> We took upon ourselves a mighty struggle with three focal points: A struggle with ourselves, with our Diaspora mentality . . . , a struggle with the nature of the land . . . , a struggle against forces of evil and hatred in the world, far and near, that did not understand and did not want to understand the uniqueness and the wondrous mission of our nation since we stepped onto the stage of history in ancient times until this very day. (Ben-Gurion, 1965, p. 11)

The third Prime Minister of Israel, Golda Meir, during a press conference in Washington, addressed columnist Stewart Alsop as follows: "And you, Mr. Alsop, you say that we have a Masada complex . . . it is true. We do have a Masada complex. We have a Pogrom complex. We have a Hitler complex" (*Newsweek,* March 13, 1973)[2]

At the Holocaust Memorial Ceremony in 1987, Yitzhak Rabin, then Minister of Defense, said, "In every generation they rise up to destroy us, and we must remember that this could happen to us in the future. We must therefore, as a state, be prepared" (*Ha'aretz,* April 27, 1987).

Yitzhak Shamir, Prime Minister in the 1980s and early '90s, frequently referred to "the world's hatred." In one speech, he said, "We have plenty of . . . 'friends' in the world who would like to see us dead, wounded, trampled, suppressed. And then it is possible to pity the wretched Jew, to commiserate with him" (*Newsweek,* January 25, 1988).

Prime Minister Benjamin Netanyahu, in the late 1990s, said,

> The complaints about the wall tunnel and the complaints about the rigid position of Israel in the peace talks are libel. It brings us back to unpleasant memories from the past when the Jews were attacked all the time with blood libels and were described as humanity's enemy. (*Ha'aretz,* October 10, 1996)

Schools, the major agent of socialization, play a principal role in transmitting societal beliefs of ethos. A study by Adar and Adler (1965), which analyzed the values taught in Israeli schools, found that school curricula were centrally preoccupied with issues concerning the country's relationship with other nations. The general outlook conveyed was of Israel's isolation among nations and the latter's hatred of Jews (Adar & Adler, 1965, p. 59). The investigators, moreover, found that teachers tended to further emphasize these motifs, even beyond the textbook's message. They tended to focus on anti-Semitism, isolation, persecutions, or pogroms and to present any help or positive attitude or action as resulting from ulterior motives.

Another study, which concentrated on the analysis of history schoolbooks, was done by Firer (1980). She found that books dealing with the history of Israel between 1900 and 1980 presented the relations between Israel and other nations as dominated by hatred toward Israel, glossing over other aspects of the contact. The expression, "The eternal hatred of the eternal people," expresses a frequent theme in the history textbooks. The hatred of Jews is regarded as permanent, although its expressions may change from time to time or from nation to nation. Periods in which Jews were not persecuted are seen as short, temporary reprieves that occur in preparation for next wave of pogroms. A recent analysis (Bar-Tal, 1998b) of all the textbooks in history, geography, Hebrew language, and civil studies, approved by the Ministry of Education in 1994, found that the theme of self-victimization had a prominent place. Especially in history books, this is the most dominant motif. Jews are presented as lonely victims in a hostile world, suffering from continuous and constant persecution and hatred.

This line of education, together with the previously reviewed examinations of Israeli literature and films, leaders' speeches, and journalists' commentaries, lays bare the mechanisms that maintain societal beliefs about siege. By such means, these beliefs are conserved among society members and transmitted to young generations, even though, since the establishment of Israel and the end of World War II, worldwide opinion has changed dramatically. The societal beliefs about siege clearly fulfill important functions in the life of a society. These functions will be considered in the next section.

⁂ THE FUNCTIONS OF SIEGE BELIEFS

Societal beliefs about siege fulfill several important functions, both for society members as individuals and for society as a whole. From the individual's perspective, much has been written about the functions of personal hostility toward other groups (e.g., Adorno, Frenkel-Brunswik, Levinson, & Sanford, 1950; Allport, 1954). I would like to focus only on two functions of siege mentality that do not necessarily entail pathological reactions. First, beliefs about siege permit society members to define the world in relatively simple, manageable terms. These beliefs are especially functional in equivocal situations in which individuals receive extensive, threatening information about dangers to their personal and societal existence. Siege beliefs facilitate management of cognitive ambiguities by dichotomizing the world into black and white solutions, for example, rejection of all other groups versus acceptance of one' own group. Recently, Kruglanski and Webster (1996) suggested that certain situations create a need for closure in the form of the desire to have some guiding knowledge on a given issue, as opposed to confusion and uncertainty. This need appears in situations of stress, overload of information, or pressure, characteristics typical of conflict. It is possible to assume that in this situation, society members experience an enhanced need to have validated knowledge. Siege beliefs, in this case, provide firm, parsimonious knowledge that sheds clear light on the situation, and therefore, they are easily adopted.

Second, in line with the previously described epistemic function, siege beliefs permit economic predictability by preparing society members for the worst their life may bring. Individuals have a need to live in a world whose future can be predicted to some extent. Unpredictable events may cause psychological negative reactions, especially if the events are harmful. Given, however, that some degree of unpredictability is unavoidable, individuals prefer to be surprised with positive experiences or events. In this sense, expectations of negative events prevent disappointment. Therefore, some individuals may prefer to form negative expectations rather than to experience disappointments. Siege beliefs imply a pessimistic worldview and do not allow disappointment. Nothing good can be expected from the rest of the world. The late Israeli leader, and one of the founders of Israel, Pinchas Sapir, expressed this function directly when he said, "If we don't believe [that our backs are against the wall], if we don't take into account the worst possibility, we will bring upon ourselves Holocaust because of our sightedness" (*Ha'aretz,* April 29, 1973).

On the societal level, siege beliefs fulfill several functions. First, they satisfy society's need for a firm social identity, differentiating this group from others. By positioning the society in conflict with the rest of the world, siege beliefs clearly demarcate the boundaries of the society, differentiating between "us" and "them"—in this case, all others. As Coser (1956) pointed out in his classic work about the function of conflicts, "group boundaries are established through conflict with the outside, so that a group defines itself by struggling with other groups" (p. 87). Siege beliefs probably facilitate the clearest boundary between a society and other groups. That boundary separates the society from the rest of the world, allowing the experience of "pure" identity and "unadulterated" culture. This function was directly and continuously exploited by the leaders of Albania and North Korea. Thus, for example, in 1984, the Albanian leader, Ramiz Alia, said, "we do not open our doors to reactionary decadent and cosmopolitan culture, etc., which poisons the consciousness of people and leads to their degeneration" (Biberaj, 1986, p. 5).

Second, societal beliefs concerning siege satisfy the need for solidarity and mobilization that every group has; Coser (1956), indeed, pointed out that conflict with other groups heightens the morale within the group and "leads to mobilization of the energies of group members and hence to increased cohesion of the group" (p. 95). As the siege beliefs imply threats to the society's well-being and even to its survival, they indicate a situation of emergency that requires uniting societal forces. Solidarity and unity are crucial for muting the threat. Of special importance is mobilization, because siege beliefs imply loneliness, which requires a series of actions for survival in the hostile world.

Third, siege beliefs indirectly answer the need for a sense of superiority. The belief that the rest of the world has negative intentions toward a society implies also that the other groups are evil and malevolent; it is, indeed, a common practice to delegate responsibility for conflict situations to other groups. As a result, the positive image of the ingroup is enhanced, and feelings of superiority are produced.

Fourth, siege beliefs help to satisfy basic needs for freedom of action and for self-reliance. A society that believes the world has negative intentions against it and does not trust other nations also feels less restricted by international norms and agreements that usually limit a nation's scope of action. These restrictions are based on moral considerations and come to prevent immoral and destructive behavior on the part of a society or a nation. But when a society holds siege beliefs, assuming that it is facing serious threats from other nations, it is likely not to feel bound by these norms and rules. The hostile world cannot serve as a positive reference group and, therefore, no longer constitutes a binding moral authority for the society. Survival, instead, is the overriding consideration. The society may thus use siege beliefs as a way to reject pressures from the international community and to justify taking free, unrestrained action. Finally, siege beliefs also satisfy needs for self-reliance, which usually function as a source of pride and self-esteem. Here, the belief is that the society cannot depend on others' assistance or help. Being alone among hostile others, it has to develop economic and political independence.

THE CONSEQUENCES OF SIEGE BELIEFS

Siege beliefs have affective and behavioral implications that can have serious consequences for the society as well as for the international community. Four attitudinal and behavioral outcomes will now be described. First, the threatened society with siege beliefs develops negative attitudes toward other societies. Second, the society becomes extremely sensitive to any information and cues transmitted by other societies that may indicate negative intentions. Third, the society develops internal mechanisms to cope with the threat by increasing pressure among society members toward conformity, unity, and mobilization. Finally, the society may take a course of action without consideration of international behavioral codes.

Negative Attitudes

Members of a society who believe that other nations have negative intentions toward them develop negative attitudes toward those nations, and these may be accompanied by feelings of xenophobia and chauvinism. These consequences are not surprising in view of certain findings in social psychology. Various social psychological theories suggest that beliefs about the negative intentions of another person, group, or groups may lead to negative attitudes and even negative behaviors toward that person, group, or groups. For example, cognitive consistency theories claim that there tends to be consistency between people's beliefs, attitudes, and behaviors (Abelson et al., 1968; Heider, 1958). Thus, beliefs with negative contents toward an object will tend to correlate with negative attitudes, too. Exchange theory suggests that individuals reciprocate with harm to perceived negative intentions (Blau, 1964). Theorists of aggression find that individuals react aggressively, when they perceive an intention to harm them (Berkowitz, 1969). This reaction is not unique to interpersonal relations; it is observed in intergroup relations as well (Lieberman, 1964). Negative actions from one group are met with negative reactions from the other group. The belief that other groups have negative intentions causes the threatened group to develop hostility toward these other groups. Moreover, because societal beliefs about siege imply threat to society members by other nations, these beliefs often lead to chauvinism, that is, blind and fanatical support of their own society with zealous rejection of the other societies (Shafer, 1972), and even to xenophobia, which indicates a complete rejection of strangers as such.

To illustrate, let us once more consider the case of Israel. As we have seen, those Israeli Jews who hold beliefs of siege view the nations of the world as evil, immoral, utilitarian, indifferent, and often brutal. These feelings have not been formed recently but are the outcome of a long history of anti-Semitism (Stein, 1978). The short history of Israel, and especially the years just preceding the foundation of the state, reinforced these feelings. An example of these negative attitudes, embedded in the description of the world, can be found in the following statement of the Likud party, published in *Ha'aretz,* November 14, 1975: "The central question facing us is how we in Israel and the Diaspora can stand against a world which is half tyrannical, evil and hostile and half democratic yet whose degenerated soul has been poisoned by the black liquid."

In the case of South Africa, the negative attitudes can be exemplified by the words of Prime Minister Botha, who viewed the isolation of South Africa as "a struggle between the powers of chaos, Marxism and destruction, on the one hand, and the powers of order, Christian civilization and the upliftment of people on the other" (Grundy, 1991, p. 102).

Sensitivity

Society members with siege beliefs feel threatened by outgroups and develop sensitivity to the information and cues coming from other societies. This sensitivity is based on lack of trust and the suspicion that society members feel toward other societies, which in their view have negative intentions. Such sensitivity is necessary to avoid being surprised by negative action from the other societies, which, given their evil intentions, may act harmfully at any time. Therefore, the society under siege has to be continuously prepared for harm. Every piece of information or cue must be scrutinized for indications of negative intentions.

Moreover, when siege beliefs are central, society members may be disposed to search for information that is consistent with these beliefs, while disregarding evidence that does not support them. Any ambiguous information may be interpreted as validating the siege beliefs, too. On the other hand, criticism or disapproval, even when conveyed in a constructive and friendly way, may be perceived as a demonstration of negative intentions. Society members may even unintentionally distort information to validate their siege beliefs. Also, social psychological studies have demonstrated that individuals may distort incoming information in times of stress so that it fits their beliefs (Lazarus, 1966). Here is George F. Kennan's (1947) observation regarding the behavior of the Soviet Union in this case:

> It is an undeniable privilege of every man to prove himself in the right of the thesis that the world is his enemy, for if he reiterates it frequently enough and makes it the background of his conduct, he is eventually to be right. (p. 569)

These tendencies are in line with social psychological research showing that in stress situations, individuals lower their threshold for what they will recognize and attend to as information indicating threat (Broadbent, 1971; Mackie, 1977).

This analysis can shed a light on suspicious, oversensitive, and mistrustful attitudes of the Soviet and Albanian governments when they were holding siege beliefs (see Kennan, 1947; Pollo & Puto, 1981). It also provides an explanation for the statement by the present North Korean leader, Kim Jong-il, who said on February 4, 1992, "The socialist-communist construction should accompany fierce struggles to oppose hostile elements and the imperialist.

As long as impure elements continue to collaborate with these imperialists and operate on the domestic scene" (Lee et al., 1993, p. 27).

Also, Israeli Jews developed basic mistrust toward other nations, which leads to special sensitivity. Arian, Talmud, and Hermann (1988) pointed out,

> The clear feeling of basic mistrust regarding the international environment is the basic feature of the foreign and security polity of Israel. There is a fundamental belief that in the final analysis the world will do nothing to protect Jews, as individuals, as a collectivity, as a state. (pp. 21-22)

Pressure Toward Conformity

When members of a group believe that other groups have negative intentions toward them, they prepare themselves for the worst possible events. At these times, cohesiveness and unity are needed to withstand the threat. To achieve these objectives, those who hold the beliefs most strongly exert pressure on others for conformity and unity. This pressure can take various forms, such as calls for unity and for patching up or concealing disagreement within the group, as well as threatening (and carrying out) negative sanctions against those who disagree within the group. Coser (1956) suggested, "Groups engaged in continued struggle with the outside tend to be intolerant within. They are unlikely to tolerate more than limited departures from the group unity" (p. 13).

Calls for unity are typically found in speeches by leaders who believe in the negative intentions of the rest of the world toward their group. During the Civil War, Lenin (1965) called on workers to "close their ranks more firmly than ever and set an example of organization and discipline in this struggle" (p. 33). Yitzhak Rabin, Israel's Prime Minister during the time of the U.N. resolution against Zionism, proposed that

> Israel and the entire Jewish people must learn a lesson from the latest resolutions by the General Assembly. The lesson is that we must all fight as one man for the aims we believe in for the sake of the Jewish people and the State of Israel. (*Ma'ariv,* November 11, 1975)

In Japan, General Araki, a minister of the army, issued a call for unity during the 1932 Manchurian crisis:

> Japan is at the present moment confronted with a crisis. She is like a small vessel which struggles with the tumultuous waves of a stormy ocean. In order to surmount the difficulties in the way, everybody, rich and poor, peasants and workers, young and old, men and women, all must unite for one purpose—to overcome the crisis. (Morris, 1963, p. 18)

In an attempt to heighten vigilance against possible external threats, sacrifice, unity, and patriotism became dominant societal themes in North Korea and Albania. This was accompanied by pressure to conform and use of collective discipline. North Korea, for example, practices Juche ideology, which involves the propagation of monolithic nationalistic-communistic party ideology behind which the people are expected to rally. In essence, Juche ideology is based on North Korean siege mentality: It emphasizes political independence and economic anarchy and discourages foreign transactions, trade, and investment (Yang, 1994).

When group members believe they are threatened by other groups, they may resort to (usually illicit) unaccepted means to ensure unity, to mobilize group members for struggle, and to facilitate acts that eliminate the threat. The need to avert the perceived threat in such times is considered enough to override the norms and rules that normally guide intragroup and intergroup relations.

It is in this perspective that Lenin's 1918 justification for the use of terror after the allied intervention should be seen:

> Everyone must give his life if necessary to defend Soviet power, to defend the interests of the working people, the exploited, the poor, to defend socialism . . . we shall fully and wholeheartedly support and carry out the ruthless punishment of the traitors. (Lenin, 1965, p. 541)

Later, on December 5, 1919, he explained that "the terror was forced on US by the terrorism of the Entente and by the terrorism of all powerful capitalism" (Lenin, 1965, pp. 66-67). Societal beliefs of siege have provided, and are still providing, an excuse to silence critics, punish opponents, and even eliminate them. These practices have been common in the Soviet Union, Albania, North Korea, South Africa, and Iraq.

Disregard of International Community Norms

When society members believe that other groups have negative intentions toward them, they may invoke drastic measures to prevent possible danger. Their actions may not be within the norms of the international community. A society that feels endangered may decide that its need to survive is so paramount that all means can be used; as a result, it may decide to take a course of action considered extreme and unacceptable by the international community. In this situation, society members may disregard any unfavorable reactions from these other groups, which they consider their adversaries. It is, thus, not surprising that Pruitt and Snyder (1969) consider perceived threat as one of the causes for war, and Lieberman (1964) noted that militant actions are more frequent under external threat. Indeed, many Israeli Jews feel that the goal of surviving is so important that all means are justified to ensure security. This has led to courses of action considered extreme and unacceptable by the international community.

Indeed, 64% of Jewish adults, in a national sample taken in June 1989, expressed a belief that "All means are allowed to secure the existence of the State of Israel." In the late 1940s, David Ben-Gurion expressed this feeling: "We don't care what the Gentiles are saying, but what the Jews are doing." This remark became a kind of slogan, restated by different leaders and recently even published as an advertisement in a leading newspaper (*Ha'aretz*, May 29, 1996).

In a statement following the Beirut massacre, the government announced, "No one will preach to us on ethics and dignity of human life" (*Yedioth Ahronoth*, September 20, 1982). The Minister of Energy, Yitzhak Berman, who resigned following the massacre, said in an interview:

> The premise on which the new policy was based was that Israel could simply ignore the reactions of the outside world, with the exception perhaps of the U.S., which should be treated with more caution. The underlying philosophy was: The goyim are against us anyhow, so it is immaterial what Israel does—the goyim will react negatively. (*Jerusalem Post*, October 4, 1982)

A similar idea was expressed by the Japanese army minister Araki, who declared in 1932, "The army should be prepared not only for military action but for solving economic, social and cultural problems pursuing in foreign policy an independent line founded on firm, sound and just premises" (Morris, 1963, p. 9). The attempts of North Korea, Iraq, and Iran to develop nuclear weapons as well as other means of mass destruction in breach of various international agreements can also be viewed in this light.

In line with the described view, a society with siege beliefs will try to be as independent of the world community as possible. Self-reliance frees the group from dependence on others who cannot be trusted. Thus, for example, in response to sanctions and boycotts, South African leadership developed a national strategy of self-sufficiency, militarized the society, deepened the involvement of the defense establishment in diverse aspects of civilian life, and increased the defense force and spending. As van Zyl Slabbert (1989) observed,

> Cut off from supply because of an international embargo as well as facing increasing diplomatic isolation, security planners turned to domestic resources to reshape the security system, firstly, in the area of armaments provision, and secondly, in terms of manpower. Politically this refocusing of the security system involved a massive propaganda campaign to sell the Total Onslaught. (p. 115)

Also, with its self-imposed isolation as a result of discord between North Korea and the Soviet Union and China, North Korea also practiced extreme self-reliance, falling back on domestic resources and developing national industries for this purpose. This tendency was accompanied by the minimization of trade and import, the need for which was diminished because of a dramatic decrease in aid from the Soviet Union and China (Savada, 1994). Similarly, Albanians have felt that they could not rely on other countries and therefore developed an ideology of self-reliance. Albania was probably the only state in the world that had a constitutional provision prohibiting its government from seeking foreign aid and credits, granting concessions to foreign corporations, or forming joint companies. Albania also minimized its relationship with foreign states and prevented any contact with foreigners. At the same time, Albania made every effort to preserve economic independence, political autonomy, reliance on internal manpower and resources, and implementation of strict savings (Biberaj, 1990; Marmullaku, 1975; Pollo & Puto, 1981).

The four consequences of siege mentality described here suggest that siege beliefs can have a serious effect on the attitudes and behaviors of the societies that hold them. These beliefs dictate a particular way of life, and in the cases we have looked at, they constitute the core beliefs of the societal ethos. It is possible, then, to characterize the societies of Albania and South Africa until several years ago, and of North Korea and Iraq today, as having an ethos of siege.

▓ NOTE

1. Lyrics by Yoram Tehar Lev reprinted by permission of Akum House (Society of Authors, Composers, and Music Publishers).

2. The notion of the Masada complex is one way of denoting a siege mentality; it derives its name from the historical event that took place in ancient Israel in the first century C.E., when a group of Jewish zealots took a last stand in the fortified outpost, Masada, after the failure of a Jewish rebellion against the occupying Roman empire. When the Romans were about to conquer the fortress, the defenders committed mass suicide to avoid falling into enemy hands. This event, as described in Chapter 5, was turned into a symbol of Jewish resistance and heroism, as well as loneliness in the face of a hostile world.

Societal Beliefs About Delegitimization

Societal beliefs do not only concern a person's own society. They may also consist of images of other groups or societies that the society members hold. These images reflect the nature of the society's intergroup relations and, thus, have relevance for the well-being of the society itself. They usually take the form of stereotypes, that is, beliefs about the characteristics of the other society (Bar-Tal, 1997a). Among the different categories of stereotypes, special meaning belongs to delegitimizing characteristics of the other group, especially when they are societal beliefs. In these cases, the delegitimizing societal beliefs have important implications for the society that holds them. They locate the society in a particular situation, which leads to a particular set of actions. They reveal characterizing knowledge about the delegitimized society as much as about the delegitimizing one, and they have far-reaching consequences for both societies. The present chapter describes this type of societal belief. First, it will define the nature of these beliefs; then, it will describe at length the experiences that underlie their formation; and finally, the functions of these societal beliefs will be presented.

THE NATURE OF DELEGITIMIZING BELIEFS

Delegitimizing beliefs are extremely negative stereotypes with clearly defined affective and behavioral implications. These extremely negative characteristics

AUTHOR'S NOTE: This chapter, although extensively rewritten, is based on a previously published article: Bar-Tal, D. (1990). Causes and consequences of delegitimization. *Journal of Social Issues, 46*(1), 65-81. It is used here with permission of that journal and its publisher, the Society for the Psychological Study of Social Issues.

are attributed to another group, with the purpose of excluding it from acceptable human groups and denying it humanity.

It is possible to classify delegitimizing beliefs into the following five categories:

Dehumanization. This involves labeling a group as inhuman, either by using references to subhuman categories, for example, "inferior" races and animals, or by referring to negatively valued superhuman creatures such as demons, monsters, and satans. In both cases, the members of the delegitimized group are depicted as possessing inhuman traits, so that by implication they are different from the human race. A classic example of dehumanizing delegitimization is the characterization of blacks by whites as an inferior race. Myrdal (1964) listed the beliefs that were then prevalent in southern U.S. white society:

1. The Negro people belong to a separate race from mankind.

2. The Negro race has an entirely different ancestry.

3. The Negro race is inferior in as many capacities as possible.

4. The Negro race has a place in the biological hierarchy somewhere between the White man and the anthropoids.

5. The Negro race is so different both in ancestry and in characteristics that all White people in America, in contradistinction to the Negroes, can be considered a homogeneous race.

6. The individuals in the Negro race are comparatively similar to one another and, in any case, all of them are definitely more akin to one another than to any White man. (pp. 103-104)

Dehumanization has been widely used throughout human history toward various groups. Examples are Christian beliefs regarding Jews, European beliefs about Indians, or Japanese beliefs about the Chinese.

Outcasting. Outcasting categorizes groups as violators of pivotal social norms. It includes such subcategories as murderers, thieves, psychopaths, or maniacs. These violators are usually excluded from society and often segregated in institutions. Israeli Jews and Palestinians provide a recent example of mutual delegitimization by means of outcasting. Israeli Jews have invested much effort in delegitimizing members and sympathizers of the Palestinian Liberation Organization by labeling them murderers and terrorists, whereas the Palestinians delegitimize Zionists as racists and terrorists (Bar-Tal, 1988).

Trait characterization. This involves the attribution of personality traits that are evaluated as extremely negative and unacceptable to a given society. Use of labels such as aggressors, idiots, or parasites exemplifies this type of delegitimization. For instance, Dr. Robert Ritter, who was head of the Racial

Hygiene and Population Biology Research Unit of the Ministry of Health under the Nazi regime in Germany, described the Gypsies in 1941 as being "unbalanced, characterless, unreliable, untrustworthy and idle, or unsteady and hot-tempered. In short, work-shy and asocial" (Kendrick & Puxon, 1972, p. 57).

Use of political labels. This is categorization into political groups that are considered totally unacceptable by the members of the delegitimizing society. The labels are mainly drawn from the repertoire of political goals, ideology, or values. Nazis, fascists, imperialists, colonialists, capitalists, and communists are examples of this type of delegitimization. Usually, these groups threaten the basic values of the delegitimizing society and are believed to endanger its well-being. The labeling of Americans as capitalists by the Russians and the labeling of Russians as communists by the Americans during the Cold War are examples of this type of delegitimization, and each case represented an evil to be kept out of the delegitimizing society. Communism (to Americans) and capitalism (to Russians) were perceived as threatening ideologies to the very existence of the respective social, economic, and political systems (see White, 1984).

Group comparison. In this type of categorization, the delegitimized group comes to serve as an instance of what is considered the essence of evil in a given society. Use of such categories as vandals or Huns is an example of this type of delegitimization. For example, during World War I, Americans labeled Germans *Huns,* and so a poster at the time read, "German agents are everywhere, eager to gather scraps of news about our men, our ships and our munitions. . . . Do not become a tool of the Hun by passing on the malicious, disheartening rumors which he so eagerly sows."

In sum, every society has in its cultural repertoire examples of other groups that serve as symbols of malice, evil, or wickedness. This is to say that the categories used for delegitimization are culture bound. What is considered extremely negative and unacceptable in one group does not necessarily have the same reputation in another one. For example, the category *Zionist* may be used as a delegitimizing category in Iran but not in Israel, where it is considered a positive category. However, some group categories are likely to be considered negative and unacceptable almost anywhere. Examples of these group categories may be thieves, savages, aggressors, or parasites.

Delegitimizing beliefs about another group, which include the described categories, have several unique characteristics that differentiate them from general stereotypic beliefs.

1. Delegitimizing beliefs are characterized by extremely negative, salient, and unique contents. Typical examples of such content categories were presented

above: despots, terrorists, imperialists, fascists, aggressors, enemies, carriers of infectious political and physical diseases, primitives, and savages.

2. Delegitimization implies inclusion of the delegitimized group in categories that are completely rejected by the norms and/or values of the delegitimizing society. Although many groups are negatively stereotyped or experience prejudice, they may continue to be considered part of the society (for example, Americans of Mexican origin in the United States or Jews in France). Delegitimization, in contrast, indicates that the delegitimized group is outside the boundaries of commonly accepted groups, and it is thus excluded from the society. The exclusion is often not temporary or conditional but permanent and persistent.

3. Delegitimizing beliefs are accompanied by intense negative emotions that derive from their extremely negative content. These emotions provide the direction and vigor for the delegitimizing beliefs. Individuals usually feel hatred, fear, aversion, anger, or disgust toward the delegitimized group.

4. Wide-scale delegitimization is usually regulated by social norms that maintain and encourage this process. Shared cultural delegitimization cannot easily flourish without institutionalized support. Indeed, delegitimization is sometimes enforced by political institutions or by legal code.

5. In addition to their unique cognitive and affective components, delegitimizing beliefs also come with attributed negative behaviors, potential or actual. That is, delegitimization indicates not only that the characteristics of the delegitimized group are extremely undesirable and absolutely unaccepted by the norms or values of the delegitimizing society but, more important, that this group can or does perform harmful behavior. Labels such as fascists, savages, or aggressors imply potential behavior, which may endanger the delegitimizing society or other societies.

6. Delegitimizing beliefs also have behavioral implications for the delegitimizing society. Because the delegitimized group does not deserve human treatment, it should be treated negatively, sometimes even to the extreme: for example, used for forced labor. These extreme actions are taken because the delegitimizing society feels an obligation to avert the danger to its values and norms and to protect its existence.

THE EXPERIENTIAL BASES OF DELEGITIMIZING BELIEFS

In most cases, societal beliefs are formed as a result of collective experiences in at least two types of extreme situations: in situations of severe conflict between two societies and in situations of extreme ethnocentrism. Each of these situations will now be elaborated.

Conflict Situation

Every intergroup conflict begins with the perception that a group's own goals are incompatible with the goals of another group (Bar-Tal, Kruglanski, & Klar, 1989; Pruitt & Rubin, 1986). Conflict is perceived when a group finds itself blocked because the attainment of a goal or goals is precluded by another group. This is a common, frequent, and inseparable component of intergroup relations. But of interest for the present analysis is the situation in which a society perceives the antagonistic goals of the outgroup as especially far-reaching, evil, and seriously threatening to its basic goals.

The particular nature of the threatening experiences lead society members to form societal beliefs concerning delegitimization to explain and manage the conflict. The perceived danger can be of an economic nature (e.g., the group may be left without raw materials for its industries), political (e.g., the political system is challenged), or military (e.g., the country or part of it is in danger of being conquered). Society members believe that the danger may be actualized and that the very core of their society is threatened. It should be noted that it does not matter here whether the beliefs are based on reality or imagination. What counts is the perception—this is what leads to action and reaction (see Bar-Tal et al., 1989; Pruitt, 1965). When a threat is perceived by society members, it is real for them (Cohen, 1979; Knorr, 1976).

The deligitimizing beliefs on the one hand explain why the other group threatens and, on the other hand, predict what the other group will do in the future. Delegitimization enables a fast, unequivocal, and simple way of understanding: The perception of high threat decreases ambiguity, narrows the range of considered alternatives, leads to antagonism, and raises the need for quick structuring and grasp of the situation (Bar-Tal, Kishon-Rubin, & Tabak, 1997; Holsti, 1971; Smock, 1955). Delegitimizing beliefs explain, for example, to Poles why German Nazis decided to occupy their country, or to Americans, during the Cold War, why the Soviet Union strove to dominate the world. A group branded as imperialist, satanic, or fascist can be perceived as a serious threat.

Moreover, once delegitimizing beliefs circulate, they increase the perception of threat by inference from the delegitimizing category. Thus, for example, use of such labels as aggressive, ruthless, devious, or oppressive indicates that the outgroup is capable of serious destruction, violence, or brutality, and therefore, a society's sense of security is further disrupted. In this way, the perception of severe threat and delegitimization feed each other in a vicious cycle.

The above analysis indicates that delegitimizing beliefs serve an important epistemic function of explaining the situation in which society finds itself and the behavior of the other group, as well as predicting what will happen next.

They illuminate reality as perceived by society members, providing a sense of meaningfulness to experiences and predictability to the future.

The conflict between the Americans and the Soviets, which reached a peak during the Cold War, provides an example of the formation of delegitimizing societal beliefs based on absolute negating goals of the two opposing societies. From the American perspective, the Soviet goals expressed in communism clashed fundamentally with their own system (see Chapter 7). Most Americans believed that the communist Soviets were in serious conflict with the United States, a conflict often presented as being of a zero-sum nature. Americans perceived the conflict as a struggle between good and evil and felt threatened by Soviet actions (e.g., Bialer, 1985; Free & Cantril, 1967; Frei, 1986; Welch, 1970).

On the basis of these perceptions, delegitimizing societal beliefs evolved and became part of the American ethos—and so, on the one hand, they served to explain the existing threat and, on the other hand, they strengthened the perception of threat. President Reagan expressed such delegitimizing beliefs in a direct way on March 8, 1983, when he said,

> They are the focus of evil in the modern world. [It is a mistake] to ignore the facts of history and the aggressive impulses of an evil empire, to simply call the arms race a giant misunderstanding and thereby remove yourself from the struggle between right and wrong, good and evil. (*New York Times,* March 9, 1983, p. 18)

Societal beliefs of delegitimization were directed especially toward Soviet communists but often were generalized to Russians, or Soviets, on the whole. First, the label *communists* itself became a delegitimization in the United States, implying that communists would try to overturn the norms and values of U.S. society—striving for dominance throughout the world with the commitment to destroy capitalism and democracy. Also, Russians or Soviets in general were delegitimized as being brutal, primitive, aggressive, sadistic, cold-blooded, ruthless, cruel, devious, oppressive, trouble makers without respect for human life or human rights, totalitarian, militaristic, deceptive, adventuristic, and offensive (Bialer, 1985; Bronfenbrenner, 1961; Buchanan & Cantril, 1953; Cohen, 1986; Frei, 1986; Stein, 1985; White, 1984).

Although serious conflicts involving far-reaching incompatibility usually end with direct violent confrontation or war, this is not necessarily the case. In spite of their severe conflict, the American and Soviet superpowers never did engage in direct warfare. Nevertheless, violent confrontation is the more prevalent outcome of a serious conflict that also leads to delegitimization through a perception of high threat. And the society that delegitimizes the outgroup with labels such as imperialists, fascists, or terrorists, which imply powerful threat and evil, is likely to act to prevent the danger. These acts by their nature cause harm to the outgroup. Depending on how delegitimized the outgroup is, the preventive measures will be accordingly severe. The denial of humanity, an inherent part of delegitimization, may lead to extreme acts of violence on the part of the delegitimizing group, especially when the motivating belief is a societal belief. Deportations, destruction, and mass killing of civil populations are not exceptional behaviors in these cases. These acts, in turn, further strengthen the delegitimizing beliefs, because the latter will now justify perpetrating acts that negate normative behavior. The greater the violence, the stronger the delegitimizing beliefs required. In addition, any violent acts performed by the delegitimized society in the confrontation reinforce the delegitimization, because they serve to explain the deviant or extreme behavior of this group.

Thus, the delegitimizing beliefs also serve an epistemic function by justifying aggressive behavior of the originating society as either preventive or reactive acts vis-à-vis the other group's actual or potential violence. That is, negative behavior, especially in the form of atrocities, needs justification. Individuals normally do not perform such behaviors, which violate basic universal norms of human treatment. Performing such behavior raises the need to understand why such behavior was done. Delegitimizing beliefs, fulfilling their epistemic function, supply the causal explanation for the inhumane behavior.

A current illustration of delegitimizing societal beliefs at work appears in Northern Ireland, a country torn by far-reaching conflict between a large Catholic minority that wants to unite Northern Ireland with the rest of the island as part of the Irish Republic and the Protestant majority, which is in political control of the region and aspires to be a part of Great Britain. These two positions were seen as irreconcilable, and the conflict led to violence that has claimed thousands of lives (Darby, 1983; Wichert, 1994).

Through the years, both societies have developed mutual negative stereotyping, including delegitimization (see Darby, 1976; Harris, 1972). Thus, for example, Cecil (1993) reports that Protestants view Catholics as "lazy, priest-ridden, untidy and potentially treacherous" (p. 152), whereas Catholics perceive Protestants as "bigoted, mean, and lacking in culture" (p. 152). Moreover, the enmity and violence are strengthened by mutual delegitimization. Both societies emphasize the terrorist nature of the other side. As an illustration, Hunter, Stringer, and Watson (1991) found that Catholic and Protestant respondents tended to attribute their own group's violence to external causes, whereas they ascribed the other group's violence to the delegitimized characteristics, using such labels as "psychopaths" or "bloodlusters."

The behavioral implications of societal beliefs concerning delegitimization are a separation between members of the two societies, very rare intermarriage, and little social mixing. Such differentiation is an addition and outcome to various antagonistic behaviors that each society exhibits toward the other. Intimidation to remove members of the other society who live in the midst of the enemy area is only one example. But the most cruel reflections of the delegitimization are the terrorist attacks on innocent civilians, murders of prominent society members, and bombings of civil properties (Darby, 1976; Wichert, 1994).

Not all conflicts begin with far-reaching incompatibility between goals of the parties involved. Conflicts may also begin and continue for a long period of time with low-key incompatibility, without involving a high level of threat. But these conflicts may spin out of control and escalate into violent confrontation. The deterioration may lead to mutual harm and violence. In this case, societal beliefs of delegitimization evolve on the basis of experienced violence, because a society needs an explanation for violent acts performed by members of the outgroup and a justification for the harm done by its own society members.

An example of a conflict that evolved more slowly into bloody and violent confrontation is the Iran-Iraq war, which ended in 1988 with heavy losses on both sides. The principal dispute between Iran and Iraq centered on the demarcation of a border on the Shatt al-Arab waterway and its administration, originating from a 1937 treaty. The conflict erupted at the end of 1959, as Iran began to demand a resolution to the disagreement. Through the years, the conflict between these two countries had been managed diplomatically, and only some minor confrontations occurred (see Pipes, 1983). But in September 1980, a war erupted that turned very quickly into one of the bloodiest confrontations since World War II, claiming hundreds of thousands of casualties, military as well as civilian.

During 8 years of war, both the Iranians and Iraqis formed societal beliefs of delegitimization to explain the brutality of the other side and to justify their own violent behavior. The *Daily Report of the Foreign Broadcast Information,* which reported radio speeches by and interviews with political and military leaders of both Iran and Iraq, offers a plethora of delegitimizing beliefs. In 1984, the Iranians, for example, called Iraqis Saddamist mercenaries, criminals, aggressive Ba'thist forces, Zionist protectors, terrorists, archsatans, imperialists, criminals, and reactionaries, describing their acts as inhuman and diabolical. For their part, the Iraqis branded Iranians as criminals, aggressors, a deceitful diabolic entity, neofascists, agents of Zionism, illiterates, and expansionists. Analyzing the political discourse in Iraq, Bengio (1998) points out that demonizing beliefs about Iranians became central societal beliefs during the conflict. Thus, for instance, Saddam Hussein, the Iraqi leader, said that Iraq must constantly keep an eye open on Iran, "where the treacherous, the heretical, and the bloodthirsty are found" (p. 145). One military commander reported in a publicized statement to Saddam, "We gladly inform you of the annihilation of thousands of harmful magi insects . . . We . . . will turn what is left of these harmful insects into food for the birds of the wilderness and the fish of the marshes" (Bengio, 1986, p. 475).

Ethnocentrism and Delegitimization

Societal beliefs concerning delegitimization do not only emerge in conflict situations. A society may also generate this type of belief as a result of ethnocentrism. Ethnocentrism, as defined originally by Sumner (1906), denotes the tendency to accept the ingroup and reject outgroups. Delegitimization can serve this tendency: Through it, society members see themselves as virtuous and superior, and the outgroup as contemptible and inferior (LeVine & Campbell, 1972). Conversely, the ethnocentric tendency to perceive another group as different and of inferior value can also be the basis for the formation of delegitimizing societal beliefs. But delegitimization is likely to occur only in extreme case of ethnocentrism, because it sharpens the intergroup differences to a maximum and totally excludes the delegitimized group from commonly accepted groups, implying a total inferiority of the delegitimized society. In fact, delegitimization does not just differentiate between groups by setting up definite boundaries; it also resorts to a denial of humanity.

The greater the differences between the two groups, the easier it is for each to delegitimize the other (Brewer, 1979). The salient differences clearly demarcate the intergroup boundary and allow simple identification of an outgroup member. The most obvious differences are in physical appearance. Thus, characteristics such as skin color, physiognomic features, hair color, body structure, or even dress allow unmistakable differentiation between groups. Indeed, this type of difference has most often served the purposes of differentiation and delegitimization throughout human history. Other cues, even invisible ones, are of course possible. People can be also differentiated and delegitimized on the basis of such intangible criteria as religion or ideology.

The identification of difference by itself does not lead necessarily to the formation of delegitimizing beliefs. Its combination with devaluation is a necessary condition for the formation of this type of belief. Devaluation constitutes the basis for ethnocentrism (Brewer & Campbell, 1976). It has been defined as society members' positive feelings and attributions for their own group combined with their feelings of antipathy toward the outgroup(s) (see the chapter by Levinson in Adorno et al., 1950).

The last necessary condition for the emergence of delegitimizing beliefs is the arousal of feelings of fear and contempt. Fear is elicited when the different and devalued group projects a threat or appears unapproachable and mysterious. As a response, the society members form delegitimizing beliefs. Feelings

of scorn and contempt often appear alongside feelings of fear. They are elicited when the outgroup is perceived as absolutely inferior. The inferiority is
inferred on the basis of cultural, economic, military, scientific, and political
achievements as judged according to ingroup criteria. The ingroup usually
evaluates these achievements on the basis of superficial cues, for example,
clothing, working tools, weapons, and households.

There are at least two causes for ethnocentric delegitimization: the desire
to make a complete differentiation between the society and the delegitimized
group to exclude it from human groups in general or the will to exploit the
delegitimized group. In most cases, these two reasons complement each other.

Delegitimizing beliefs become societal beliefs when they are widely held
by members of the society, underlie various institutionalized decisions, are
expressed in cultural products, are reflected in behaviors, and are sometimes
even fixed firmly in legal codes. In these cases, beliefs of delegitimization can
be said to characterize the delegitimizing society. Frequently, economic needs
dictate the nature of social categorization, and then, delegitimizing societal
beliefs are generated by the motivation to exploit another group. Here, the
delegitimizing beliefs serve again as a way to legitimize an abuse (although
not of the same kind as occurs in situations of war and conflict). Because the
delegitimized group is inhumane, harm is "allowed"; alternatively, the group
is presented as a threat and, therefore, to prevent the possible danger, certain
behaviors become legitimate. In turn, when subsequent harm is done, delegitimizing beliefs serve as its justification. They imply that the delegitimized
group deserves the inhumane treatment.

An example of an ethnocentric delegitimizing society is the white society
of the United States, which between the 17th and 19th centuries held societal
beliefs that delegitimized Native Americans (Indians) as part of its ethos. This
process began with the arrival in North America of European settlers, who
found about 2.5 million Native Americans already there, divided into numerous separate and autonomous tribes, each with its own highly developed culture and history. The whites quickly lumped these diverse peoples into the
single category, "Indians," and considered them inferior to (white) human
beings (Almaguer, 1994; Beuf, 1977).

Forbes (1964) provides several illustrations of this phenomenon by
reviewing early European texts on this issue. The following are some descriptions of American Indians:

> [They are] without religion or government, [having] nothing more than diverse
> superstitions and a type of democracy similar to that of ants. (p. 16)

> Indians are so free and live so like animals. (p. 16)

Viewed in the most favorable manner, these poor creatures are miserably brutish and degraded. (p. 16)

The indigenous population of America present man under many aspects, and society in various stages, from regular but limited civilization of Mexico and Peru, to savage life in it is most brutal state of abasement. (p. 17)

The Indians as a race are, of course, far inferior to White men in intellectual capacity. (p. 17)

Indians were viewed as a stumbling block to civilization; they were perceived as "agents of the devil" and were despised because they refused to change their way of life. These delegitimizing beliefs spread widely within the white society and led to institutionalized and official courses of action that drove the native population from its ancestral home, decimating tribe after tribe until the survivors were moved into reservations (Horsman, 1981; Sheehan, 1972). The beliefs in essence justified white people's territorial and economic expansion into the Indians' land. The Indian Removal Act of 1830 is fairly typical of the many laws that were based on delegitimizing beliefs. The U.S. government, believing Indians to be inherently inferior to whites, had no hesitation in legislating the removal of the Indians from their valuable ancestral lands to remote reservations (Beuf, 1977; Horsman, 1981).

Another salient example of how delegitimizing societal beliefs could be used as a rationalization of exploitation is the enslavement of blacks by whites in the United States. Here, these beliefs played a particularly important role and acted as perhaps the determinative justification for slavery, because it would otherwise be hard to explain how the moral, deeply religious, and gallant Southerners came to treat their fellow human beings so inhumanely. For the white society members in the U.S. South, delegitimizing beliefs served the epistemic needs of explaining and justifying exploitation, as well as of differentiating between themselves and the black people they exploited. As Myrdal (1964) noted,

It should be observed that in the pro-slave thinking of the ante-bellum South, the Southerners stuck to the American creed as far as Whites were concerned. ... In the precarious ideological situation—where the South wanted to defend a political and civic institution of one quality which showed increasingly great prospects for new land exploitation and commercial profit, but where they also wanted to retain the democratic creed of the nation—the race doctrine of biological inequality between Whites and Negroes offered the most convenient solution. (pp. 87-88)

Blacks, by being different in physical appearance and having different folkways and mores, a different religion, different languages, and a different culture, were the perfect target for exploitation. Their characteristics were not only immediately, obviously different but also greatly devalued; these were used for delegitimization. Blacks were perceived as primitive, savage, and inferior. As the preamble to South Carolina's legal code of 1712 declared, they had "barbarous, wild savage natures, and . . . [were] wholly unqualified to be governed by the laws, customs, and practices of this province." Thus, it is not surprising that records show that in the early 17th century, some American states had legally recognized black slavery (e.g., Maryland in 1640, Massachusetts in 1641, and Virginia in 1661). Stampp (1956) points out three beliefs that buttressed slavery: (a) the creator had designed the blacks for labor; (b) being intellectually inferior and having a different temperament, blacks were natural slaves of the white man; and (c) blacks were barbarians who needed to be subjected to rigid discipline and severe control. Enslavement, thus, was seen as natural and essential for the good of the blacks and for the preservation of white civilization (see also Bancroft, 1931; Sellers, 1950). Being thus considered inferior and subhuman, blacks were used as "property" to satisfy the economic needs of southerners (Genovese, 1966).

The delegitimization of blacks was so deep-rooted in the local ethos that even the Supreme Court in 1857 approvingly concluded that black slaves were "beings of an inferior order, and altogether unfit to associate with the White race, either in social or political relations; and so far inferior, that they had no rights which the White man was bound to respect" (Rothenberg, 1988, p. 9).

These societal beliefs of delegitimization were well nurtured by American tradition and habits. According to Wood (1970), they were based on two highly respected and unchallenged authorities. The first was the Holy Bible, which served as the staunchest bulwark of moral and historical claims about black inferiority. Probably the most explicit and certainly the most sweeping religious justification for the delegitimizing beliefs was the biblical episode in which Noah's son Ham's descendants, described as being black-skinned, were cursed to servitude under the descendants of Shem and Japheth, identified as white. The other basis for the delegitimizing beliefs was scientific, generated by the work of numerous anthropologists, ethnologists, phrenologists, and physicians (McKitrick, 1963; Stampp, 1956). For example, in the 19th century,

Dr. Samuel W. Cartwright of Louisiana argued that the visible difference in skin pigmentation is also extended to "the membranes, the muscles, the tendons, and . . . [to] all the fluids and secretions. Even the Negro's brain and nerves, the chyle and all the humors, are tinctured with a shade of the pervading darkness" and Dr. Josiah C. Nott of Mobile proposed that Negroes and Whites do not belong to the same species. (Stampp, 1956, p. 8)

One of the striking cases of ethnocentric delegitimization in the present century, whose tragic consequences are well-known, is that of the Jews by the Nazi rulers of Germany between 1933 and 1945 (see Bar-Tal, 1994, for an extensive analysis). Jews were perceived as different and devalued, arousing feelings of fear and contempt; as a result of the delegitimization, they were excluded, exploited, and murdered.

During the Nazi era, the German people grew to accept the belief that Jews were responsible for the alienation of humanity from the natural order and were the main obstacle to human redemption. Therefore, they were convinced that it was necessary to exclude Jews from the economic, political, societal, and cultural aspects of life and deny their humanity. The contents of the delegitimizing beliefs about Jews had a wide scope. They included all the previously presented ways of delegitimization. Jews were, for instance, presented as satanic, the incarnation of the destructive drive; Jews were devils, destroyers of civilization, parasites, demons, bacteria, vermin, and pests; they were responsible for the degeneration of mankind; they were international maggots and bedbugs, "spiders that slowly suck the people's blood at their pores," and inspirers and originators of dreadful catastrophes (Gordon, 1984; Noakes & Pridham, 1984). In addition, Jews were accused of starting World War I, causing Germany's war defeat, precipitating the Great Depression, polluting the Aryan race, exploiting the German people, performing criminal acts, and seeking world domination. They were also given political labels, viewed as promoters of such diverse evils as bolshevism, capitalism, democracy, and internationalism—all aimed at subverting Aryan racial superiority. All these and other delegitimizing beliefs became the daily diet of the German people during the Third Reich. Nazi propaganda was entirely preoccupied with the dissemination of delegitimizing beliefs. The press, films, lectures, literature, radio programs, art, and political speeches continuously and repeatedly expressed these beliefs (see, e.g., Mosse, 1966). The totalitarian Nazi regime used all means to delegitimize the Jews (Bramsted, 1965; Gordon, 1984). In a short time, the delegitimizing beliefs about Jews became a distinct and significant part of the German mass repertoire (Hamilton, 1982; Mosse, 1964). Moreover, these beliefs set the norm of social behavior during a 12-year period. That is, they implied a whole system of behaviors that the Germans practiced. Of special interest for the present analysis is the Nazis' success in turning their anti-Semitic beliefs into an important part of the definition of German groupness. Not only did these beliefs define the boundaries of the German people in accordance with racist ideology, but the Nazis also made special efforts to retain the German racial view (Mosse, 1978). A person who did not subscribe to these beliefs could not be considered German. Moreover, the delegitimization of Jews in Nazi Germany is one of the few cases in modern times in which delegitimization was legally enforced. Society members who violated the laws based on delegitimizing beliefs were arrested and even executed (Gordon, 1984; Wistrich, 1985).

There is little doubt that the distance between delegitimization of such scope as was the case with the Jews under Nazism and behavioral harm is very small. It is thus not surprising that between 1933 and 1945, Jews in Europe were subjected to exclusion, deportation, expropriation, expulsion, pogroms, mass killings, and ultimately genocide on an unprecedented scale, performed in a brutally systematic, well-organized way. During 6 years—from 1939 to 1945—about 6 million Jews perished as a consequence of starvation, deadly epidemics, mass executions, and systematic gassing (Bauer, 1982; Dawidowicz, 1975; Wistrich, 1985). Finally, there is little doubt that as they carried out these terrible actions, Germans could justify them only by means of delegitimizing beliefs, which, by the dynamics we already described, first led to the atrocities and later further reinforced this type of behavior.

A final example of societal beliefs of delegitimization based on ethnocentrism is that of the Afrikaner society in South Africa, which established apartheid. The term *apartheid,* which came into common use in South African political language after World War II, implied the segregation of races in their own geographical areas. Within this system, the societal beliefs of delegitimization held by the (white) Afrikaner society as part of its ethos referred to Afrikaners' absolute superiority and the need to safeguard their political and economic supremacy over the black majority. The blacks were presented and treated as primitive, inferior, savage, and backward (Cornevin, 1980; Lever, 1978). An official government publication put it quite unambiguously: "The White nation is culturally, economically, and politically the most advanced group in the country. . . . By contrast, the various Black nations may be generally described as developing peoples" (*South Africa,* 1978, p. 209).

The authority for these beliefs came mainly from the Holy Scriptures, the source used by members of the Afrikaner society, most of whom belonged to one of the three Dutch Reformed Churches. This racist theology was widely preached and served to justify decisions taken by the political elite (Cornevin, 1980). In addition, the Afrikaner society based its delegitimizing beliefs on "scientific" evidence from genetics, anthropology, or comparative psychology as to the inferiority of the black race—this type of evidence, which had been popular in 18th and 19th centuries, was still possible to find in the second half of the 20th century. For example, as late as 1969, a scientific journal, *The Mankind Quarterly,* maintained that "the inability of the Negro African in mathematics is due to the underdevelopment of his frontal lobes" (Cornevin, 1980, p. 31).

The laws of apartheid in South Africa restricted blacks' voting, residency in certain areas, political activity, fulfillment of official roles, professional occupations, trade union membership, and so on. Marital and extramarital relations between blacks and whites were forbidden (Lever, 1978). In effect, these delegitimizing beliefs served as the justification for exploitation, conquest, and territorial expansion.

▨ THE FUNCTIONS OF DELEGITIMIZING BELIEFS

The above analysis of delegitimizing societal beliefs and the illustrations given reveal—among other things—the epistemic function of these beliefs. Because individuals have a profound need to understand the non-normative behaviors either of members of other societies or of their own, these beliefs fulfill a central need. Because human beings internalize moral norms to prevent them from harming fellow human beings, rationales are needed for deviant, negative behavior. Beliefs of delegitimization provide these needed rationales. These beliefs come to explain and justify extremely negative behavior toward others.

In addition to this epistemic function, delegitimizing beliefs help people differentiate between groups and experience feelings of superiority; they also enhance group uniformity. Each of these functions will be further elaborated.

First, groups by definition differentiate themselves from other groups by demarcating the boundaries of membership (Tajfel & Turner, 1979). As elaborated above, delegitimizing beliefs sharpen intergroup differences to an extreme, because they totally exclude the delegitimized group from the society of groups. Such beliefs indicate that there exists and should continue to exist a clear difference between the two groups: Individuals in the delegitimized group cannot also be members of the delegitimizing group's social category. In this respect, these beliefs provide a criterion for the discrimination between the two groups, because the delegitimized group serves as a negative group reference. Such differentiation often takes the form of the legal prohibition of intermarriages or other associations, as happened in Germany during the Nazi regime with regard to non-Aryan groups or in South Africa with regard to blacks. As long as clear-cut boundaries are maintained, delegitimization continues; breaking down social boundaries is a crucial condition for creating a reversal process, whereby delegitimization can be restrained.

A second function of delegitimizing beliefs is to create a sense of superiority that the group tries to maintain in relation with the other group. Groups compete with each other and, through comparison, strive to view themselves as more successful, victorious, developed, or more moral and humane. Delegitimizing beliefs provide solid grounds for superiority by lowering the value of the other group drastically.

The function of delegitimizing beliefs is also to nourish and maintain a sense of uniformity, something indispensable for a society's existence. Members of an enduring society are likely to display at least some central beliefs that indicate their homogeneity. Lack of societal uniformity and, by definition, unity may cause low cohesiveness and may even result in societal disintegration. To avoid such processes, societies often apply pressure on their members to exhibit uniform beliefs, attitudes, and behaviors. The pressure to maintain unity, or specifically uniformity, is particularly strong in situations of threat. Delegitimizing beliefs imply that the delegitimized group has characteristics that threaten the delegitimizing group. Labels such as murderers, imperialists, or Nazis indicate danger and threat. Society members, then, are called on to unite behind the uniform beliefs and behaviors to avert the danger.

In addition, once delegitimizing beliefs circulate, the agreement that the delegitimized group deserves negative attitudes and behaviors becomes confirmed, and thus, the possibility of considering alternative beliefs diminishes. The delegitimizing group applies pressure on its members to adopt the delegitimizing beliefs and invokes sanctions against individuals who attempt to provide information inconsistent with or alternative to the delegitimizing beliefs. Because members of the delegitimizing group, like most people, seek positive rewards and avoid negative sanctions, they tend to conform to the group's pressure. The Nazi regime in Germany stands as an example of how extreme pressure can be applied to maintain group uniformity vis-à-vis various delegitimized groups. The Nazis delegitimized various ethnic, political, and social groups within the societal system and then used means of extreme terror to uphold the delegitimization and to unite the Germans into a homogeneous society (Allen, 1965; Bracher, 1971).

9

The Ethos of a Society

The conceptual framework of this book includes two key concepts: societal beliefs and ethos. After an extensive elaboration of the concept societal beliefs, this chapter is dedicated to the analysis of the concept ethos.

The discussed concept, societal beliefs, refers to a particular belief or set of beliefs in a particular theme that is prevalent in a society and is considered characteristic of it. A society has many more than one societal belief, and even many more than one set of these beliefs organized in a theme, because societal beliefs cover various domains of societal life, and societies form many themes of societal beliefs. But each society has only some societal beliefs, or themes, that provide the dominant characteristic or characteristics. The configuration of these particular beliefs constitutes a societal ethos. The concept of ethos is important for characterizing a society because no two societies have the same ethos. The concept ethos, thus, serves the important function of describing the totality of particular societal beliefs that distinguish a particular society.

THE CONCEPT OF ETHOS

Ethos is not a new concept in the social sciences. It has been in use throughout the last century, although there is no agreement with regard to the definition of the concept, and it has been used with different meanings. From the start, the Greek word *ethos,* which was derived from the word *ethics,* was an amorphic concept without formal definition. Ethos was originally and rather vaguely used to denote norms and behaviors of undefined social roots. *The Oxford English Dictionary* (1989) defines the Greek word ethos as "the characteristic spirit, prevalent tone of sentiment, of a people, or community."

One of the first sociologists to use the concept of ethos was Max Weber (1958). In his seminal work, *The Protestant Ethic and the Spirit of Capitalism,* first published in 1904, Weber discussed the religious beliefs of ascetic

Protestantism, which in his view constitute an ethos. In his conception, ethos, which Weber used alternatively with the term *spirit,* characterizes common values and norms of a group of people in a particular economic system. In his analysis of the Western capitalist ethos, Weber described people who work incessantly for profit, are driven by self-imposed motivation, manifest a sense of responsibility toward their work, and work hard to the best of their ability. The ideal type of capitalist "gets nothing out of his wealth for himself, except the irrational sense of having done a job well" (Weber, 1958, p. 71). Weber quotes from the writings of Benjamin Franklin to illustrate the basic beliefs underlying the capitalist ethos—for example, "time is money," "credit is money," "money is of a prolific, generating nature," "the good paymaster is lord of another man's purse." These beliefs reflect the capitalist ethos of honesty, punctuality, industry, frugality, self-reliance, self-discipline, hard work as an end in itself, saving, and devotion to one's task.

In Weber's analysis, the capitalist ethos is underlined by two beliefs that are central to Protestantism: vocation and predestination. Martin Luther's conception of a calling or vocation referred to the particular role that God has "called" every human being to fill. As such, the notion gave a moral justification to worldly activity: The belief stresses the pursuit of one's vocation, one's calling, as a way to serve God. This idea encourages hard work. Along with this came a belief in predestination, which states that God has destined every individual for heaven or for hell; there is nothing people can do to change this destiny. Such a harsh doctrine, Weber reasoned, would produce a feeling of inner loneliness and despair in those who believed in it. To cope with this feeling, the clergy made two suggestions: (a) It is one's duty to consider oneself saved and (b) one might gain self-confidence in one's heavenly destination through worldly activity. Protestants could bolster their conviction of salvation through good works, self-control, and purposeful activity. Thus, in Weber's terms, ethos is not tantamount to organizational structure. It refers to what people think and is reflected in how they behave in the system.

Following the introduction of the concept ethos by Weber, a number of social scientists used it to describe different characteristics of a society. For example, Sumner (1906) considered ethos a totality of characteristic traits of society members. Kluckhohn (1943) referred to it as principles of the covert culture. Bateson (1958) used the term ethos to describe the collective emotional emphases of a culture, as expressed via sentiments and attitudes. Ossowska (1973) and Epstein (1978) viewed ethos as describing values that underlie particular cultural behavior.

Through the years, the term ethos has been increasingly used by social scientists and historians to describe the moral, religious, political, ideological, and attitudinal characteristics of a group (Kurczewska, 1977). What all the uses have in common is their attempt to elucidate the unique features of a society that differentiate it from other societies. This is the basic problem for social scientists: how to characterize societies. However, few of them have provided an elaborate analysis of its meaning. Ethos, thus, became a useful— but vaguely defined—concept to characterize a group or a society. The present conception characterizes a society on the basis of its societal beliefs. This approach will be extended now.

THE PRESENT CONCEPTION OF ETHOS

According to the present view, ethos consists of dominant societal beliefs as its basic units. Ethos, here, is holistic in the sense that it refers to society as a whole; it is similar to the concept *personality* as used by psychologists to describe the total characteristics of an individual or the concept *climate* used to describe the total characteristics of an organizational environment.

The concept of ethos refers to the particular configuration of central societal beliefs as they appear in different societies. These societal beliefs are of far greater importance than other societal beliefs. They provide the key characteristics of a society in a holistic way, expressed in a coherent ethos. This holistic perspective allows an understanding that cannot be achieved when the societal beliefs are described separately. The combination of particularly dominant societal beliefs, in a particular structure, yields a comprehensive picture that is unique for a given society. As indicated, although different societies may share a particular societal belief or even a few societal beliefs, no two societies ever have an identical ethos. The contents of particular societal beliefs constituting the ethos differ from society to society.

With regard to the characteristic of centrality, on the individual level, a societal belief is considered central when it is highly prominent in the personal cognitive system and is frequently used in a wide range of the individual's evaluations, decisions, judgments, and behaviors because of its relevance (Bar-Tal, Raviv, & Freund, 1994). That is, individuals often consider their most central beliefs and take them into account in making inferences or behavioral decisions. Individuals hold central beliefs as anchors of their belief system, where they function as the basis for other beliefs. Such central beliefs are frequently held with high confidence, and those who hold them try to avoid uncertainties and ambiguities that may undermine their validity (see Petty & Krosnick, 1995). Empirical research has, indeed, found confirmation for all these assumptions in that central beliefs are held with high confidence (e.g., Bar-Tal et al., 1994), are extensively linked to other beliefs (Judd & Krosnick, 1989; Sherif & Cantril, 1947), and are relatively stable and resistant to persuasion (Eagly & Chaiken, 1995).

Beyond the individual level, central societal beliefs of the ethos also manifest themselves in society, where their centrality is expressed by the frequency, multiplicity, and extensiveness with which they appear in societal channels of communication. Frequency indicates that central societal beliefs are often communicated. Multiplicity indicates that they are communicated through a variety of channels: interpersonal, societal, educational, political, and cultural. Specifically, as indicated, societal beliefs are discussed by society members in their face-to-face interactions; some of them appear in school textbooks, because society members try to inculcate them in new generations; they are expressed in books, films, theatrical plays, and other cultural products as important themes; they are discussed in media and used by leaders in their speeches. Extensiveness indicates not only that they are frequently presented but also that much space and time is devoted to their presentation. Thus, for example, books devote much space to them, and leaders may devote a large part of their speeches to their transmission.

Societies do not exist without an ethos that gives meaning to societal life for society members. Ethos provides the shared mental basis for society membership. The knowledge of an ethos enables us to understand the society's present and past concerns as well as its future aspirations, how they are similar among the society's members and how they differ from those held by members of other societies. Ethos, thus, is the basis for a common societal view of the world and one of the foundations of societal life. Society members need basic shared views to experience a sense of belonging and identification, as well as to lead an integrative and coordinated life as one entity. In this respect, ethos provides the connection between the individual and society. Individuals who develop an identity as society members also acquire the beliefs of the ethos. It is, thus, not surprising that the society makes a special effort to impart the societal beliefs of its ethos to society members, along with social identity. As a result, the societal beliefs of the ethos are shared to a great extent by society members, and the extent of their sharing can be viewed as one indicator of societal integration and cohesiveness.

The ethos reduces various abstract concepts into beliefs that concern and are relevant to every member of a society. It gives meaning and predictability to societal life and provides a coherent picture of societal institutions, the society's structure, history, visions, concerns, and course of actions. For Tannenbaum (1945), who focuses on past experiences only, ethos is "any unwritten summary—of all the efforts, strivings, success and failures of the past that makes the present what it is" (p. 343). In the present extended conception, ethos provides the dominant narrative of the society; when society members acquire it, their worldview will be constructed according to this narrative. As a result, they see their societal world through the prism of the ethos, and this is a unique view, unlike that of other societies. Ethos, thus, is both a conceptual framework to view a society and a theory that drives the world's perception of the society members.

The notion of ethos assumes that beliefs that guide the behavior of any society are not just random but represent a coherent and systematic pattern of knowledge. Based on this assumption, ethos offers a balanced picture of rational choices based on this knowledge. Ethos implies that the coordinated behavior of the society's members, the decisions of its leaders, the structure of the society, and its functioning are all based on coherent and comprehensive beliefs that justify and motivate society members to act in the society and accept the system. Ethos provides legitimacy to the societal order and fosters integration among society members. Ethos thus serves as a crucial mechanism for organizing a collective of individuals as a society.

Although it is important to study societal beliefs separately, because they often have direct and particular implications for specific societal behaviors, the study of their wholeness, the ethos, enables a more complete understanding of a society. The investigation of the configuration of dominant societal beliefs allows us to elucidate the structure of ethos. Societies may have one or several dominant themes of beliefs that become the main characteristics of an ethos. In these cases, the dominant societal beliefs affect the contents of other societal beliefs and have a determining influence on the attitudes and behaviors of society members. Thus, for example, a society can have an ethos constructed around dominant societal beliefs concerning democracy or communism or capitalism or Islam. But a society might be characterized by two or more opposing dominant societal beliefs, which may eventually lead to a clash of one ethos with another. Extreme examples are Russian society before the 1917 Bolshevik Revolution and Spanish society before the beginning of the domestic war in 1936. In both societies, the severe contradiction between two ethoses led to the outbreak of bloody civil wars. In each society, ethos can be seen as a kind of societal ideology that provides the society's identity and is the portion of the belief system that interprets and evaluates

> the nature of the collectivity and of the situation in which it is placed, the processes by which it has developed to its given state, the goals to which its members are collectively oriented and their relation to the future course of events. (Parsons, 1951, p. 349)

After elaborating on the meaning of ethos, two detailed examples are provided. These examples are accompanied by two studies that used the term ethos but did not try to develop this concept. The first one concerns the American ethos, and the study was done by McClosky and Zaller (1984). The second presents the conflictual ethos of the Israeli society (Bar-Tal, 1998c). The present analysis locates the two cases within the conceptual framework discussed here, as examples of how societal beliefs of ethos can be empirically investigated. Each example will now be described.

⁗ THE AMERICAN ETHOS

Herbert McClosky and John Zaller (1984) studied the American ethos. They proposed that "two major traditions of belief, capitalism and democracy, have dominated the life of the American nation from its inception" (p. l), and thus, both capitalism and democracy, according to them, are values (i.e., beliefs) of the American ethos. They proposed that the ethos of democracy rests on the beliefs (i.e, societal beliefs) that all people are equal and should enjoy equal opportunities. People should have the equal right to share their own governance by ruling either by themselves or through elected leaders. Also, people should consent to the rules, which must avoid being arbitrary. They must obey the laws, but the people who enforce the laws must be accountable to the people. In addition, the democratic ethos includes societal beliefs about respect for freedom of speech, press, assembly, and worship.

With regard to the ethos of capitalism, McClosky and Zaller (1984) suggest that it includes societal beliefs about the desirability of private ownership of the means of production, the pursuit of profit by self-interested entrepreneurs, and the right to unlimited gain through economic effort. In addition, the ethos includes societal beliefs emphasizing competition among producers, a substantial measure of laissez-faire, market determination of production and distribution, economic rewards, personal achievement, and hard work.

According to McClosky and Zaller (1984), the societal beliefs of capitalism and democracy evolved in American society over many years to become "major constituents of the American civic culture." Members of American society, including opinion leaders, hold these beliefs, which lead to particular goals, norms, and means: They underlie many of the society's political policies and practices.

To study the prevalence of the societal beliefs reflecting the American ethos of capitalism and democracy, McClosky and Zaller (1984) used a series of surveys administered to national cross-sectional samples and to members of the political elite. The researchers used different items and questions expressing societal beliefs of capitalism and democracy, to which the respondents were asked to give their answers. Of special importance was the Opinion and Values of Americans questionnaire, which consisted of 267 items that covered a wide scope of opinions and attitudes on matters of public interest, including 28 items on capitalism and 44 items on democracy. "Public ownership of large industry would be a good/bad idea," "The profit system: teaches people the value of hard work and success / brings out the worst in human nature," and "The free enterprise system: survives by keeping the poor down / gives everyone a fair chance" are examples of items measuring beliefs about capitalism. "The employment of radicals by newspapers and TV: is their right as Americans / should be forbidden," "Our laws should aim to: enforce the community's standards of right and wrong / protect a citizen's rights to live by any moral standard he chooses" and "Efforts to make everyone as equal as possible should be: increased/decreased" are examples of items assessing beliefs of democracy.

The results of this large-scale study indicate that members of American society share beliefs of the American ethos to a large extent and consider them important characteristics of their society. Specifically, they support the ideas of liberty and equality, as well as capitalistic values. But the researchers also point to a conflict between the societal beliefs about capitalism and democracy held by society members. The conflict is manifested in disagreements about the extent of business regulation, the size of workers' salaries, and the extent of power granted to labor unions. As McClosky and Zaller observed,

> While most Americans favor a competitive, private economy in which the most enterprising and industrious individuals receive the greatest income, they also want a democratic society, in which everyone can earn a decent living and has an equal chance to realize his or her full human potential. (p. 292)

These two desires stand in conflict, and the results of the study show that the democratic beliefs are more deeply rooted than the capitalistic beliefs, as expressed in the percentage of elite members and young people who hold them. McClosky and Zaller concluded,

> Conflicts between capitalism and democracy remain a recurrent feature of American life: when these conflicts surface, they are likely to be resolved in ways predominantly favorable to the democratic tradition; and some type of welfare capitalism is the institutional form this resolution is likely to take. (p. 302)

THE CONFLICTUAL ETHOS OF THE JEWISH ISRAELI SOCIETY

The Jewish Israeli ethos, as an ethos of conflict, emerged as a result of the powerful Jewish collective experience of living under conditions of intractable conflict. Intractable conflict has been defined as persisting for a long time (at least a generation), being perceived as irreconcilable, and being violent; it evokes existential and basic needs or values and constantly preoccupies members of a society (Bar-Tal, 1998c). Moreover, the constantly involved parties have a vested interest in the conflict's continuation, and the conflict is of a zero-sum nature. Intractable conflict is exhausting, demanding, stressful, painful, and costly—both in human and material terms. It requires that society members adapt to these conditions, both in their individual and social lives. My basic thesis suggests that a society engaged in intractable conflict develops a particular ethos that is functional for successful coping with the situation.

The intractable Israeli-Arab conflict developed regarding the contested territory known over the last centuries as Palestine, which two national movements claimed as their homeland. For more than 70 years, Palestinian nationalism and Zionism, the Jewish national movement, clashed recurrently over the right to self-determination, statehood, and justice. The conflict, however, is not only territorial and political but also involves deep contradictions in religious and cultural interests.

For a long time, the conflict seemed irreconcilable and was perceived as being total. Also, the Israeli-Arab conflict has been violent almost from its beginning, and this violence has played a central role in the life of the society and the lives of individuals. In view of these collective prolonged experiences, an ethos of intractable conflict developed in the Jewish society in Israel.

Societal Beliefs of the Israeli Jewish Ethos of Conflict

I would like to propose that during the intractable conflict with the Arabs in the late 1940s and the 1950s, 1960s, and 1970s, the Israeli Jewish ethos consisted of the following themes of societal beliefs about (a) the justness of the Israeli Jewish cause (goals), (b) security, (c) positive self-image, (d) the delegitimization of Arabs, (e) Jewish victimization, (f) patriotism, (g) unity, and (h) peace (Bar-Tal, 1998c). These societal beliefs were nourished during the years of intractable conflict, although not all of them originated in that period. Some of them—societal beliefs about self-victimization or about positive self-image—had been part of a long Jewish tradition. Each will be described in brief.

The justness of Israel's cause (goals). Beliefs about the justness of the Israeli cause not only outline goals and establish their justice, they also provide the rationale for the eruption of conflict. First of all, beliefs in the justness of one's own cause assume the supreme and existential importance of that cause. Accordingly, failure to achieve these goals will be perceived to threaten the very existence of the society. Second, such beliefs justify the society's goals and their importance. These reasons can be of different kinds and are drawn from different sources such as history, nationalism, theology, culture, and so on.

The return of the Jews to Israel after 2,000 years of exile to establish their own state in Palestine was inspired by the nationalist ideology of Zionism. This ideology provided Jews with goals and their justifications (Avineri, 1981; Vital, 1982), and it also served as a basis for the formation of other societal beliefs referring to self-image, the image of other nations, patriotism, and unity. On the basis of this ideology, beliefs evolved that characterized the new-born state. But at the same time, the Zionist ideology led to direct confrontation with those Arabs who considered the same land as their homeland and had similar national aspirations. The particular circumstances under which the Israeli-Arab conflict developed required appropriate societal beliefs to enable successful coping (Cohen, 1989). Israeli Jewish beliefs about the justness of Israeli goals were especially crucial: historical, theological, national, existential, political, societal, and cultural reasons were adduced for this purpose (Avineri, 1981; Halpern, 1961). Among them can be found references to the fact that the Jewish nation was formed in the land of ancient Israel; that for long periods of the Jews' ancient history, the land of Israel was their homeland; that during their exile, Jews maintained close spiritual as well as physical relations with the land of Israel, continuously aspiring to return to it; and that the repeated experience of anti-Semitism in exile proved the need for the secure existence of the Jewish people in their old homeland.

Security. As intractable conflict involves violent clashes, including military actions and terrorist attacks, it is necessary to assure security in the widest sense of the word: Military, political, economic, societal, cultural, and educational resources all have to be deployed for this aim. This is the case with the Middle East conflict—both personal and national security has become one of the most central preoccupations of Israeli Jews (see Chapter 6 for elaboration). This concern has turned Israeli Jewish society into a "nation in arms," whose members live in a situation that has been labeled "dormant war" (Yaniv, 1993). As a result, it is generally assumed that Israel has the right and duty to cope with threats by means of the country's own armed might without relying on foreign military help (Horowitz, 1993). Security beliefs have served as the major input for the legitimization, justification, and rationalization of decisions made and actions taken in the society (Bar-Tal et al., 1998; Ben-Eliezer, 1995; Kimmerling, 1993; Perlmutter, 1969).

Self-image. Another theme of societal beliefs in the Israeli Jewish ethos pertains to a positive self-image. The difficult demands of coping with intractable conflict, the need for mobilization, the violence, and especially the perpetration of aggressive acts—sometimes immoral and even atrocious—all these require the forceful maintenance of a positive self-image. For this purpose, Israeli Jewish society has engaged in self-praise, self-glorification, and self-justification. The societal beliefs present Jews in the positive light of a tradition that views Jewish culture and religion as the roots of Western civilization, having superior morality (Hazani, 1993). Superimposed on this is the newer image of Israelis as the "new Jews" (Hofman, 1970). Their attributes relate to courage, heroism, persistence, self-reliance, determination, intelligence, initiative, morality, fairness, and humanness (Hofman, 1970; Liebman & Don-Yehiya, 1983). These beliefs add up to a self-image that is then contrasted to that of the Arabs, to differentiate between them in the Jews' favor.

The delegitimization of Arabs. It has been postulated in Chapter 8 that societies in intractable conflict form societal beliefs that delegitimize the adversary. In the Israeli-Arab conflict, too, from early on, the encounter between Jews, initially coming mostly from Europe, and the Arabs who were living in Palestine brought about negative stereotyping (Lustick, 1982). Arabs were labeled as primitive, uncivilized, savage, and/or backward (e.g., Benyamini, 1981; Cohen, 1985). With time, after the state of Israel was established and as the conflict deepened and became violent, Arabs came also to be perceived as killers, a bloodthirsty mob, rioters, treacherous, untrustworthy, cruel, and wicked. In addition, Arabs were blamed for the continuation of the conflict and for the eruption of all the wars and military activities; they were presented as intransigent, refusing a peaceful resolution of the conflict (Ben-Gurion, 1963; Harkabi, 1977; Landau, 1971).

Jewish victimization. A society in intractable conflict believes that it is being victimized by the opponent. This theme of societal beliefs is formed in the course of a long period of violence, as a result of the society's losses and damage sustained. Beliefs about the justness of the society's goals, positive self-image, and the delegimization of the adversary feed into and buttress this theme. In the case of Israel, the contents of beliefs about victimization portrayed, on the one hand, the tremendous suffering of the Israeli side in the conflict and, on the other hand, the Arab's evil intentions, their intransigence, cruelty, cowardice, maliciousness, and dishonesty as characteristics, as well as the violence and viciousness of their acts. The traditional Jewish ethos, in which Jews are seen as victims in a hostile world, functioned as a foundation to the current sense of victimization (Bar-Tal & Antebi, 1992; Liebman, 1978; Stein, 1978; and Chapter 7 in the present book). The concerted attempts of the Arab states to annihilate Israel during the first 30 years of its existence, the Arab embargo on Israeli trade, and terrorist attacks on Israeli and non-Israeli

Jews were all perceived by Israeli Jews as unequivocal evidence of their victimization. In this frame of reference, all four major wars, in 1948, 1956, 1967, and 1973, and numerous military clashes are perceived as self-defensive actions.

Patriotism. Patriotic beliefs are essential during intractable conflict because the society needs cohesiveness, loyalty, commitment, mobilization, and even sacrifice from its members. It is, thus, not surprising that the Israeli society made a special effort to impart societal beliefs associated with patriotism as part of its ethos. These beliefs propagated patriotism by directly praising citizens' love of country, loyalty, and sacrifice through the glorification of patriotic models. These patriotic models come three spheres. Ancient Hebrew heroes who defended the country against enemies and fought for the independence of the Jewish nation are honored; for example, Yehuda Maccabee, who freed Israel from Greek occupation; the defenders of Masada, who rebelled against the Romans and committed suicide to avoid falling into enemy hands; and Bar Kochba who led an (unsuccessful) rebellion against the Romans. From the early history of modern Israel, the first pioneers who left Europe and came to rebuild the old homeland are especially venerated. They led harsh lives, trying to cultivate the land and defend themselves against a hostile environment. Finally, the military history of modern Israel provided exemplars through the fighters who heroically defended the newly established country and the battles in which they fought (e.g., Liebman & Don-Yehiya, 1983; Zerubavel, 1995).

Israeli Jews were asked to suffer the burdens of economic hardship, the military service, and human loss. All types of volunteerism were strongly encouraged, and the term *to go on a "people's mission"* was often used to describe special or voluntary service in the security forces, in a kibbutz, or in border regions.

Unity. More than usual, a society involved in intractable conflict has to be united. Societal beliefs of unity focus on the importance of setting aside all internal conflicts, controversies, and disagreements to unite the society in the face of external threat. In this vein, Israeli society developed societal beliefs that aimed to foster unity, to build a sense of belonging and solidarity, and to demarcate the line of consensus. This was done by stressing the common heritage and religion—and by minimizing ethnic differences—among Jews coming from different parts of the world. The so-called consensus pertained especially to societal beliefs relevant to the Israeli-Arab conflict and particularly to societal beliefs about the justness of Israel's goals and about security (Lahav,

1993; Negbi, 1985). To maintain unity, sanctions were applied to those who expressed opinions or exhibited behaviors that did not come within this accepted consensus (Smooha, 1978).

Peace. Engaged in intractable conflict, Israeli society also developed societal beliefs about peace as part of the ethos of conflict. In times of conflict, a light at the end of the tunnel is needed, and beliefs about peace fulfill this role. Societal beliefs about peace provide hope and optimism by referring to the ultimate goal that Israeli society yearns for. This had the additional advantage of presenting society members as peace-loving and peace-seeking, a universally appreciated characteristic, thus contributing, too, to Israelis' positive self-image. On a concrete level, Israeli Jews presented themselves as being ready to negotiate and achieve peace, while Arabs were portrayed as rejecting any peaceful resolution of the conflict and even refusing to have direct contact with Jews.

In sum, it is assumed that the societal beliefs of an ethos of conflict appear in high intensity, are widespread, and appear interrelated in their totality during periods of intractable conflicts. In the case of the Israeli society, the ethos of intractable conflict dominated the Israeli repertoire at least during the first 25 years of the state independence.

Empirical Evidence: Analyses of School Books

To flesh out the above description of societal beliefs in Israel during intractable conflict, findings of studies that analyzed Israeli school textbooks used between the 1950s and 1970s will be presented. First of all, however, it should be pointed out that school textbooks, in general, provide an excellent illustration of institutionalized societal beliefs, especially in democratic societies. They express a society's ethos as it tries to inculcate it in new generations (Apple, 1979; Bourdieu, 1973). In the words of Luke (1988), school textbooks "act as the interface between the officially state-adopted and sanctioned knowledge of the culture and the learner. Like all texts, school textbooks remain potentially agents of mass enlightenment and/or social control" (p. 69). School books are used by the entire young generation in the society, because school attendance is mandatory; the knowledge imparted through them is usually presented and perceived as objective, truthful, and factual. The dominant themes of a society's ethos appear in the various contents of different subject matters but especially in language, history, geography, and social sciences.

School books in Israel follow the curricula developed by the Ministry of Education and Culture, which outlines the didactic, scholastic, and societal objectives to be achieved (Eden, 1971). The ministry has to approve these books. Their contents, thus, reflect the beliefs that the dominant part of society tries to impart to its members. The following review will mainly look at four major studies that analyzed school textbooks in three subject areas—history, geography, and Hebrew—that were used in the first two decades of the existence of Israel, at the height of the intractable conflict with the Arabs.

The first study was done by Firer (1985), who content-analyzed 142 history textbooks used in Jewish schools in Israel; the second study was performed by Bar-Gal (1993), who analyzed 200 geography textbooks; the third study was carried out by Bezalel (1989), who investigated Zionist values in elementary school readers; and the fourth study was done by Zohar (1972), who examined Arab stereotypes in elementary school readers. The first three studies pointed out that during the intractable conflict with Arabs in the 1950s, 1960s, and 1970s, school books were used to serve the national needs by imparting contents that present the themes of an ethos of conflict. The books focused on justifications for the Jewish people's claim to the land, while at the same time discrediting any parallel Arab claims. The same books delegitimized Arabs, denied the existence of the Palestinian national movement, and even refused to recognize a Palestinian entity. Arabs were stereotyped as primitive, apathetic, unproductive, hostile to Jews, violent, and impulsive. Zohar (1972) found use of such delegitimizing labels as robbers, wicked ones, bloodthirsty mob, killers, gangs, or rioters. These descriptions were in sharp contrast to an uncritically positive image of the Jewish people. In all the books, Jewish Israelis were presented as victims, and together with this image, they were described with such labels as moral, courageous, modern, or industrious. Within this framework, the books made special efforts to glorify the pioneers who came to resettle in the homeland as models of patriotism. They were presented as having heroic traits as they rebelled against their historic oppression and left to conquer the old Eretz Israel. In their new homeland, the pioneers struggled with immense difficulties: the virgin land, deadly swamps, the Arabs, the hostile colonial authorities. By sheer will power and their readiness for self-sacrifice, the pioneers overcame these difficulties, holding a gun in one hand and a plough in the other, while under their feet stretched green fields and fertile orchards and in front of their eyes the Jewish nation was being renewed on its historical land as it existed during the First and Second Temple (Firer, 1985).

In sum, it is evident that the Israeli educational system powerfully inculcated the societal beliefs it assumed functional for successful coping with the Israeli-Arab conflict. During the climax of the conflict, this amounted to a form of indoctrination. The specific nature of the conflict, the foundation of the new state, and the attempt to form a new Israeli nation made it almost natural for socialization to take such a direction. The described societal beliefs of the Israeli ethos were transmitted through more than the educational channels of school textbooks just described. Every societal, political, and cultural mechanism and institution was recruited to impart these beliefs of the ethos (see, e.g., Bar-Tal, 1988; Ben-Ezer, 1977; Ben-Shaul, 1997; Caspi & Limor, 1992; Cohen, 1985; Gertz, 1995; Liebman & Don-Yehiya, 1983; Urian, 1997; Zerubavel, 1995).

10 /////~

Societal Beliefs and Ethos: Contribution to Societal Psychology

As we come to the end of the book, it is time to summarize the presented conception of societal beliefs and ethos and locate it within a disciplinary perspective. The second task provides an opportunity to evaluate the state of the art of social psychology to consider the place of the present contribution in this discipline and propose a development of societal psychology that can serve as a framework for social psychological work focused on societies. In other words, the last part of this chapter will examine how the promises made by the founding fathers of social psychology have been realized and will introduce the readers to societal psychology, which tries to fulfill these promises.

🎞 THE CONTRIBUTION OF THE PRESENT BOOK

The conceptual framework presented in this book introduces a particular category of shared beliefs, societal beliefs, which play an important role in a society's life. Karl Mannheim (1952), the founder of the sociology of knowledge, realized decades ago that the thought of individuals is marked by the social system of which they are part: "A large part of thinking and knowing cannot be correctly understood, as long as its connection with existence or with the social implications of human life are not taken into account" (p. 241). According to this line of thought, societal beliefs are first of all societal phenomenon, which should be studied as societal product produced via societal processes.

The concept of societal belief provides a connction between individual beliefs and the beliefs that characterize the social system of which individuals are members. It has a number of derivations, but first of all, it redirects the attention of social psychologists to the concept of belief. Beliefs can be studied in isolation or as they interrelate with social systems. They can also be characterized from the individual and group perspective in terms of their centrality, or the degree of confidence with which they are held, and they can be discussed in terms of the functions they fulfill for both individuals and societies.

Individuals form beliefs. They infer, expect, define, make assumptions, criticize, form opinions and impressions, make attributions, plan, explain, justify, reason, and so on. They formulate beliefs at varying levels of concreteness, generality, confidence, and centrality. These diverse cognitive processes necessarily occur within a social context, because even interpersonal dialogue is based on familiarity with social others. But of special importance are social contexts that derive from membership in significant groups. The beliefs held by society members are influenced greatly by the collective of which they are part. Individuals are born into societies; from the earliest days of their life, they are imbued with beliefs that are shared by society members. Society members acquire many of their beliefs in the course of social interaction and social influence, storing them in their minds, but the framing and consequences of these beliefs have a social nature. Many of these beliefs have meaning only in the societal context and serve as a basis for societal functioning. They not only appear in the verbal communication of society members but also are expressed through tangible products. Society members write about them and reflect them in different cultural creations. On their basis, as much as on the basis of stored beliefs, it is possible to learn about groups and societies.

On the basis of this general framework that connects between individuals and the societal system, a number of specific postulates can be derived.

Societies develop a unique set of beliefs. As they go through their particular experiences, societies form their own knowledge consisting of societal beliefs, which although held by individual society members, make sense when viewed as a characteristic of the society as a whole. These societal beliefs are unique, as they are based in the society's particular collective experiences. They play a crucial role in establishing commonality among individuals, and they contribute in forming people's identity as society members.

In addition, societal beliefs provide members a meaningful view of their society. Societal beliefs give answers to basic questions of society members: Who are they? What unites them? What are their present concerns? Why are they as they are? Where are they going? Why did they follow a particular course of action in the past? And why do they act in a particular way at present? Societal existence requires that these questions be answered.

Acquired societal beliefs play a further role in the formation of new societal knowledge, because there is continuous reciprocal interaction between societal beliefs and new collective experiences of the society. On the one hand, the new collective experiences serve as a source for the formation of new societal beliefs, and on the other hand, the already accumulated societal beliefs serve as a prism through which the new experiences are understood and new beliefs are formed. Societal beliefs allow, thus, a firm construction of societal reality in spite of the fact that their contents often concern ambiguous social events, abstract concepts, and information that in most cases is not observed at firsthand or experienced.

In the present conception, of special importance are particular societal beliefs that give a coherent and comprehensible orientation to the society. The totality of dominant societal beliefs constitutes the ethos of the society. That is, the contents of these central societal beliefs concern different themes; although a study of them separately can illuminate a particular part of the puzzle, there is a need to look at the whole—the ethos. This conception of ethos is based on a Gestalt principle and suggests that the sum of central societal beliefs is more meaningful for describing and understanding the society than the mere addition of its parts. Ethos provides the most basic societal foundation—that is, the coherent narrative that indicates societies are not accidental associations but well-structured and coordinated collectives with deep-rooted and well-defined beliefs. Ethos serves as one of the bases that give meaning to social identity. It indicates the particular characteristic of the society and allows differentiation from other societies.

Membership in a society implies sharing certain beliefs. If societies are characterized by a set of societal beliefs and an ethos, then membership in societies requires holding these beliefs. Sharing societal beliefs is one of the conditions of being society members, because these beliefs are one of the elements that makes a society. Sharing beliefs, in general, and sharing societal beliefs, in particular, is an important human social phenomenon because it operates on the basis of a commonality of ideas that serve as a basis for common understanding and communication. Society members acquire these beliefs, and their acquisition, especially beliefs of the ethos, is an indication of society membership.

On the individual level, sharing beliefs strengthens confidence in the perceived reality and provides a strong sense of similarity to and identification with other society members, while on the societal level, it increases cohesiveness, perception of society's uniqueness, mutual liking, and strong group identity. Also, shared societal beliefs enable members to feel that they have the power to influence their leaders; to society's leaders, shared beliefs offer the requisite strength to pursue their policies.

Societal functioning includes dissemination and maintenance of societal beliefs. The processes of disseminating and maintaining societal beliefs are at the core of societal functioning, because a society cannot exist without societal beliefs. Therefore, societies make special efforts to impart societal beliefs to new members and maintain them among the veterans. This is done in various ways, beginning with interpersonal influence and ending with well-planned, systematic, societal indoctrination. In this exercise of social influence, society uses various institutions and channels of communication. Educational systems, cultural institutions, and mass media are the most salient examples of mechanisms.

Society members actively negotiate the meaning of societal beliefs. Society members are not passively stimulated, influenced, or persuaded. They are active human beings who process information, evaluate it, make inferences and judgments, select the knowledge that suits them, argue, oppose, struggle for their ideas, and try to persuade other society members of the rightness of their beliefs. Hence, the formation, dissemination, and maintenance of societal beliefs is a continuous process of negotiation in which societal beliefs are formed and changed.

Societal beliefs have an important influence on societal behavior. Coordinated behaviors of society members always have an epistemic basis. This type of behavior never begins automatically or instinctively; its initiation is always based on some kind of rationale that precedes the society members' engagement. In most cases, society members need a rationale and justification for their societal behaviors to take part in coordinated societal activities. Thus, even orders or commands for societal action are accompanied by explanations. In this role, societal beliefs, and especially societal beliefs of the ethos, are often used as a rationale for societal behaviors, because society members share them and consider them truthful.

   In addition to the outlined postulates, the present contribution demonstrates the complexity of examining the two fundamental questions regarding the relation between the individual and society: How does a collective of individuals become a society? How do individuals function as society members? Comprehensive answers to these questions require an interdisciplinary approach because they touch on different aspects of societal behavior and require different perspectives. Accordingly, the present volume suggests a conceptual framework that is formulated principally on the basis of the knowledge that has accumulated in social psychology, but at the same time, it draws ideas and observations from other disciplines of social sciences.

Such an interdisciplinary approach requires reliance on various types of supportive observations; experiments, observational studies, surveys, and content analyses were used. In addition, some of the conceptual postulates are supported by description of cases taken from the history of different societies and from the analysis of their present situation. Both ways of collecting evidence, through formal methods and through cases, are subjected to the principles of logical implication and, in effect, reflect the same processes of knowledge acquisition (Feyerabend, 1976; Kruglanski, 1989; Kuhn, 1962; Popper, 1972; Weimer, 1979). They have, thus, the same logical validity but differ in the extent of their acceptance by the norms of the various disciplines.

In sum, the present work demonstrates that social psychology has much relevance to the study of social macro systems and that it can benefit by being open to absorb accumulated knowledge in other disciplines of social sciences. Social psychology accumulated impressive knowledge about individuals, their mental structures, and their activities, but this line of work needs to be transformed to a societal context if it is to be relevant to explaining life of individuals as society members. Knowledge of various social science disciplines can be useful in such transformation. Such themes as societal institutions, norms and values, processes of influence, or communication networks should be integrated with analysis of individuals' behavior as society members. The integration permits a more complete, coherent, and comprehensible picture of social behavior in a society. The present conception, therefore, combines the micro and macro levels of analysis. It recognizes that individuals are the ones that form societal beliefs; that society members as individuals absorb these beliefs, process them, and store them in their minds; that they ascribe to them first of all meaning but also confidence and centrality; that they behave on their basis. But, at the same time, I recognize that these processes are not carried out in a vacuum but in a societal context. Individuals are part of a complex social system that has institutions, structures, processes, networks of communication, and special characteristics. They identify with the system and feel committed to its existence. At least part of their "self" functions on the basis of their social identity. Therefore, these beliefs can only be understood in the framework of the particular social system of which they are an integral part.

Finally, this volume encourages and even urges the study of the contents of shared beliefs to reveal the preoccupations and the concerns of society members. It exposes the constructed reality of the society, which provides the basis for its functioning. The mapping of societal beliefs is a necessary condition for understanding the structure and the dynamics of the specific society: It allows us to assess the respective centrality of societal beliefs and to predict the direction of possible societal action. It also indicates the norms, values, and goals of the society. Ultimately, studying the contents of societal beliefs leads to a description of the ethos of the society, which provides an important basis for drawing societal boundaries and societal identity.

A society's beliefs and its ethos, although held by society members and expressed by them, constitute an essential and functional societal system that exists beyond the particular individuals and provides the basis for a society's existence and functioning. This assumption is in line with one of the founding fathers of modern social psychology, who wrote, observing the relationship between individuals and groups,

> Group facts must have their foundation in individuals; group consciousness, group purpose, and group values have an existence, and in them alone. But they cease to be "merely" individual facts by virtue of their reference to others. It follows that a group process is neither the sum of individual activity, nor a fact added to the activities of individuals. (Asch, 1952, p. 252)

The present volume can be considered a contribution to social psychology, or preferably to societal psychology, which slowly emerges as a reaction to the dominant individualistic orientation of social psychology. The contribution implies that social psychology cannot escape from dealing with larger societal systems if it desires to be *social* in the broad meaning of the term and to be relevant to real problems that preoccupy people in their social life.

The founders of social psychology believed that it should locate the study of groups, societies, nations, and crowds, and their influence on individual behavior as one of its main focuses (e.g., Asch, 1952; Durkheim, 1953; Freud, 1960; Lewin, 1936, 1947; McDougall, 1920; Sherif, 1936; Tarde, 1969; Wundt, 1916). But although social psychology has enjoyed spectacular development in recent decades, it is, in a certain respect, an "unfulfilled promise." As a basis for this claim, I will first describe the foundations of social psychology and then outline the direction of its present mainstream.

THE UNFULFILLED PROMISE OF SOCIAL PSYCHOLOGY

Foundations of Early Social Psychology

When psychology emerged as a differentiated and recognized discipline at the beginning of the 20th century, one of its preoccupations was with topics and issues that, years later, came to be considered as falling in the realm of social psychology. These issues included behavior of a crowd (LeBon,

1895/1968), collective action (Bekhterev, 1921), social institutions (Judd, 1926), formation of groups (Tarde, 1969), and collective religious experiences (James, 1902). In addition, as indicated in Chapter 2, the study of shared beliefs was one of the central areas of interest in psychology in the first few decades of the 20th century. Wundt's *Völkerpsychologie,* Durkheim's *Collective Representations,* McDougall's *Group Mind,* and Freud's *Massenpsychologie* all testify to this interest in collective thinking and shared thoughts that characterized early psychology.

A century ago, Durkheim argued for the establishment of a special branch of sociology, which he called social psychology, dedicated to the study of "the laws of collective ideation." At that time, there was every reason to believe that this discipline would be distinct from individual psychology, because it would be devoted to investigate, for example, "mythical themes, popular legends and traditions, and languages, the ways in which social representations attract and exclude one another, how they fuse together or become distinct, etc." (Durkheim in Lukes, 1973, p. 8). Years later, a renowned psychologist, William McDougall (1908), who published one of the first two textbooks in social psychology, argued that social psychology cannot disregard the fact that society is made up of individual members. Membership in a society is an important part of social life, and it influences the way group members behave, because societies play a role in shaping the mental activities of their members (McDougall, 1920). In his view,

> Any psychology that recognizes these facts and attempts to display the reciprocal influences of the individual and the society in which he plays his part may be called social psychology. Collective or group psychology is, then, a part of this larger field. It has to study the mental life of societies of all kinds; and such understanding of the group life as it can achieve has then to be used by social psychology in rendering more concrete and complete our understanding of the individual life. (p. 8)

McDougall's book, *The Group Mind,* published in two editions in 1920 and 1939, devoted considerable attention to the analysis of the macro system, for example, the nation. Two parts of the book, "The National Mind and Character" and "The Development of National Mind and Character," discuss the national life as collective life recognizing that

> Just, then, as the nation, as a certain group, has an existence different from (though not separable from) the existence of the individuals, so the national character implies that particular combination of mental forces of which the national life is the external manifestation. (McDougall, 1939, p. 107)

Foundations of
Modern Social Psychology

The founding fathers of modern social psychology, Kurt Lewin, Muzafer Sherif, and Solomon Asch, were influenced by the Gestaltist approach (especially Lewin and Asch). They suggested that the whole possesses properties that are more than the mere sum of the individual parts of which it is made up. They applied this principle to the investigation of groups in general (i.e., small groups and large social systems), proposing that groups have important properties that cannot be explained in terms of the characteristics of the individuals that constitute the group. Therefore, the founders were convinced that the study of groups as such should be the essential endeavor of social psychology. In their opinion, this direction of study would cover a wide range of topics, such as conformity to group decisions, intergroup conflict, cooperation, formation of group norms, cohesiveness, and leadership. Moreover, in their view, an understanding of individual behavior depends on the elucidation of the social forces acting in the group, influencing individuals' behaviors.

In line with this view, in the 1930s, 1940s and early 1950s, social psychologists considered the study of macro societal context as part of the endeavor of social psychology. During these years, for example, Hadley Cantril (1941), a productive early social psychologist, was interested in a wide range of social movements, from the mob gathered to perform a lynching through the rise of Nazism to the Townsend movement. His research questions concerned such issues as people's motivation to join social movements, mob behavior, beliefs of people acting in social movements, or the needs that social movements satisfy. Another example of early deep interest in a social context is work by Newcomb (1943), who studied the influence of a social setting (e.g., college) on the beliefs and attitudes of students and found that students changed their conservative ideology during their study in a liberal college: They discarded the conservative beliefs and attitudes with which they began their study in favor of the more left-wing beliefs and attitudes that were prevalent at the college.

This line of interest was clearly reflected in the contents of social psychology textbooks. For example, the textbook, *Social Psychology,* published by Newcomb in 1950, included 9 chapters out of 17 devoted to groups and societies, with titles such as Social Norms and Common Attitudes, Effects Upon Individuals of Membership in Groups, Culture and Personality, Multiple Group Membership, and more. Similarly, at least half of the chapters in the textbook by Hartley and Hartley (1959) are devoted to similar topics on the assumption that "the social psychologist examines the individual functioning as a unit in society . . . as a unit of an organized social field rather than an abstraction implicitly independent of social fields" (p. 3).

Nevertheless, social psychology, which was supposed to link sociology and psychology and create a collaborative field for both disciplines (Farr, 1996), gravitated toward a psychological, individualistic-cognitive orientation. This was a result of the move of the social-psychological center from Europe to North America following the rise of Nazism in Germany. The new orientation, which still dominates social psychology today, reflects the individualistic ethos of American society and the cognitive dominance of psychology (Farr, 1996; Pepitone, 1997; Sampson, 1977). The individualistic ethos that prevails in the United States was an especially influential force in the development of psychology; as Farr (1989) noted, "the individual is such a powerful and pervasive representation within American culture that, truly, it would be surprising if this particular representation had not affected the way in which psychology had developed, there, as a science" (p. 161).

The Mainstream of Modern Social Psychology

American social psychology, which since World War II has largely dictated the discipline's scope of interest and the main directions of research, has not changed much in the last 35 years. Although it has extended its topics, developing remarkable research techniques and advanced statistical tests, it remains in essence mostly cognitive and individualistic in outlook, relying on experimentation as its main research method and using college students as its main research population. Social psychology, as it has developed, is considerably skewed toward psychological science as opposed to social science (see Cartwright, 1979; Morgan & Schwalbe, 1990; Pepitone, 1986; Stryker, 1989). Its topics of interest are drawn mostly from the personal system: cognitive, motivational, affective, emotional, and evaluative. The dominant paradigm of social psychological research puts the individual in artificial situations, often in isolation from other people. It removes individuals from their natural social systems, which play a determinative role in their lives.

As for the cognitive slant of current social psychology, in the last 25 years, the main thrust of social psychology has been the study of social cognition, whose roots are derived from the information-processing perspective in cognitive psychology. Research in social cognition began in the early 1970s with the study of attribution, that is, the explanations people provide for their own and other people's behaviors. Since then, the scope of social cognition has greatly widened: It now includes the study of the structures, processes, and contents of individual cognition, including the effects of motivation, and their relations to affect, emotion, and behavior (e.g., Wyer & Srull, 1984, 1994). The *Annual Review of Psychology* reveals the following specific research questions as representative: How is information organized and stored in memory? How does information processing link information stored in memory with current activities in the social environment? How does ongoing experience modify the content and structure of stored information? How do goals and motivations influence cognitive processes? Are cognitive biases inevitable, or can people judge accurately? (Fiske, 1993; Schneider, 1991; Sherman, Judd, & Park, 1989). These research questions indicate, as Levine et al. (1993) have noted, either that social psychologists have borrowed from cognitive research pertaining to individuals, applying these ideas to social contents, or that they are interested in problems of a purely cognitive nature.

Criticism

This situation continues in spite of occasional waves of criticism and calls for more relevance, more emphasis on the social nature of human behavior, more socially meaningful research, and more work on social contexts (e.g., Armistead, 1974; Bar-Tal & Bar-Tal, 1988; Elms, 1975; Israel & Tajfel, 1972; McGuire, 1973; Pepitone, 1997; Rijsman & Stroebe, 1989; Ring, 1967; Smith, 1972, 1978).

In one of the first books about social cognition, Simon (1976) noted that social psychologists tend to disregard the social nature of cognition, retreating to the "social psychology of one." Very recently, Brewer (1997) observed that

> Over the years, the process of legitimizing social psychology as a sub-field of the discipline of psychology has led us to focus almost exclusively on the cognitive, motivational, and affective *underpinnings* of social behavior— treating these individual level processes as the building blocks of social processes. This emphasis has had the unintended consequence of colonializing social psychology. (p. 54)

The individualistic orientation of social psychology has undermined the study of small groups, as Moreland and Hogg (1993) noted:

> Social psychology's continuing obsession with social cognition may also explain why so little of the work done on small groups is published in our major journals. Social processes are assumed to arise within the individual, reflecting his or her encoding, processing, and retrieval of information about the self and others. (p. 2)

In view of this development, it is not surprising that Levine and Moreland (1990), reviewing small group research, pointed out that groups are alive and well—but elsewhere. Research in small groups is done by other disciplines, particularly by organizational psychology (see also Sanna & Parks, 1997).

The Work of Tajfel and Moscovici

Although mainstream American social psychology has remained mostly individualistically oriented as the study of social cognition, there have been important alternative developments through the years, especially in Europe. Henry Tajfel, who together with Serge Moscovici has had a formative influence on the re-emergence of a European social psychology following World War II, proposed that the

> task of social psychology is the study of social situations in which the long-lasting or temporary identifications with some groups, and differentiation from others, bring about a large variety of forms of collective behavior which can range from a carnival organized by an ethnic minority to deep rumblings capable of shaking up a whole social system. (Tajfel, 1984, p. 712)

Together with his European collaborators, Tajfel developed social identity theory (Tajfel, 1978, 1981; Turner & Tajfel, 1986), extended years later by self-categorization theory (Turner, 1991, 1999; Turner et al., 1987).

While Tajfel was formulating his concept of social identity, Serge Moscovici (1973, 1981, 1988) was conceptualizing the theory of social representations, which tried to understand structures, functions, and contents of complex shared social knowledge used by collectives. He also contributed to the definition of the social influence process by arguing that minorities also exert influences on the majority group by creating conflict, which eventually leads to innovation (Moscovici, 1976; Mugny, 1982). Despite the importance of these developments, the major emphasis and research paradigm of social psychology, however, did not change. The great majority of social psychologists are ready to accept research about small groups as part of social psychology, but they view the study of larger systems as being beyond its scope. Pepitone (1976, 1997), therefore, criticized social psychology for adhering to a fundamental paradigm that neglects macro social structure and culture, both theoretically and empirically.

> The failure to conceive individuals as embedded in socioeconomic environments, as role players in organizational structures, as positioned in multiple communication channels and networks, and as members of cultural groups, has discouraged theoretical accounts and representations of human social behavior that accurately map what is observed in the real world as people know it. (Pepitone, 1997, p. 253)

The Missing Perspective

Individuals are not only members of small groups such as families, school classes, or work teams; they also participate in macro systems such as urban or rural communities, ethnic groups, nations, or religious communities. This membership is often very meaningful for individuals. Social psychology cannot disregard this fact: that its subjects' view of the world is, at least partly, shared with other members of the social system, that much of this worldview is acquired in the social system, that this worldview is constantly negotiated in the social system, and that this common worldview is a basis for communication and coordinated behaviors in the social system. This is to say that neither contents of beliefs nor the process of their acquisition can be separated from the societal context. As Damon (1991) has noted,

> All cognition is embedded in historical, cultural, and social-relational contexts. In this sociocultural application, cognition is seen to be spawned by social interaction and communication. In use, it is seen to be widely distributed across individuals and collectives. (p. 385)

For many individuals, membership in various social systems shapes their reality. It even sometimes determines every aspect of their daily life, with individuals' thoughts, affects, attitudes, values, beliefs, and behaviors rooted in the group membership. For orthodox Jews or fundamentalist Muslims, for members of extremist political groups, or for guerrilla fighters for national independence, their group is the most important and determinative factor in their lives. But even if the above examples are extreme, still, we find that for most individuals, group membership influences to a considerable degree their beliefs, attitudes, and behaviors. It is of special importance for social psychology to take account of the fact that the personal self and social self are not separate entities: Shared knowledge becomes personal knowledge, and individuals continuously negotiate with their social environment the meaning of their worldview.

Concepts such as public issues, public opinions, shared beliefs, a myth, social value, or collective memory do not exist separately from social systems and the individuals who are its parts. As members of social systems, individuals are subjects of social influence, which is a core social process together with social interaction. Through the processes of interaction and influence, group members continuously form, modify, and change their attitudes, beliefs, values, and patterns of behaviors. Their personal repertoire at least partially reflects the characteristics of the social system of which they are members. Individuals are concerned daily with numerous issues, ideas, or problems that have meaning only in the context of their membership in various groups: They worry about unemployment, follow the government policy of the president, demonstrate against various government decisions, are happy to be the majority, support the grievances of minorities or disseminate them, and so on. In most cases, the boundaries between life as an individual and life as a society member are blurred.

In view of the societal nature of human beings' lives, there is a great need for social psychology to focus on the societal context of which individuals are part. Social psychology, as a study of human social behavior, has a bearing not only on the understanding of individual, interpersonal, or small group behavior but also on the explanation of functioning of larger social systems such as societies or nations. Individuals think, feel, and act as society members, and therefore, understanding how social systems function also requires an analysis that relates society members and the societal system as, for example, What kind of shared beliefs in a society are of importance to social systems? What functions do they fulfill? How are they formed and disseminated? What are the societal consequences of the shared beliefs? All of these questions were dealt with in the present book. But social psychology, being closed in its present individualistic orientation, cannot change; therefore, there is a need to develop, as an addition, *societal psychology,* which can contribute a social-psychological perspective to the study of a wide range of social problems in a society.

Societal psychology can fulfill the promise of early social psychologists by directing attention to the societal and cultural contexts in which individuals live and by examining the reciprocal influence between these contexts and individuals. As a subdiscipline of social psychology, it can integrate the psychological knowledge of social psychology with knowledge of other social sciences, because the exclusive preoccupation with the psychological perspective of social psychology is insufficient, if we want to examine the social foundations of human behavior.

THE PROMISE OF SOCIETAL PSYCHOLOGY

Assumptions of Societal Psychology

The emergence of societal psychology can be an extremely meaningful development in social psychology. It might redirect the attention of social psychologists to macro analysis, taking the particular perspective of social psychology. Societal psychology should not forget the valuable knowledge accumulated by individual social psychology; on the contrary, it should capitalize on it. But it should place this knowledge in a societal framework, focusing on the psychological conditions and processes that form and maintain social systems and on the sociocultural contexts in which individuals act as group members.

Societal psychology can provide a new paradigm for the study of social behavior, which will incorporate the large social systems of which individuals are a part. Societal psychology can bridge between the individual and societal levels—the micro and macro levels—taking into account that society members as individuals think, feel, and act but do so frequently within a societal context. Moreover, it should be recognized that society members not only are influenced by the society of which they are part but also shape the nature of their society. Societies do not exist in isolation from society members, but the meaning of the society can only be understood when the cognitive-affective repertoire of the society members is taken into account. Society members change their societies, as they change their beliefs, attitudes, values, and patterns of behaviors. There is a continuous interaction and reciprocal influence between society members' repertoires, on the one hand, and societal institutions, structures, culture, and other societal characteristics, on the other.

The new paradigm will make it possible not only to look at the individuals in their social environment and to deal with real life issues, but also to use a variety of research methods and different ways of studying societal problems. The new paradigm will release social psychologists from principal reliance on experimentation. Societal psychology will naturally extend the legitimate scope of research methods to include observation, surveys, and content analysis. It may also open the door for qualitative methods, which social psychologists are usually reluctant to tolerate. And this, in turn, may pave the way to the kind of interdisciplinary collaboration that is necessary in any serious attempt to study societal issues. By their nature, societal issues are multifaceted and complex, requiring examination from various perspectives. For this reason, being part of interdisciplinary teams can benefit social psychologists, enabling them to learn new approaches, concepts, theories, and research methods.

The attempt to found societal psychology is not novel. Of special note is a book titled *Societal Psychology* (Himmelveit & Gaskell, 1990), which touches on various issues of societal psychology, discussing its meaning and scope and providing concrete examples of its contents. In the opening chapter, Himmelweit (1990) states the need to develop the subdiscipline of societal psychology within social psychology: "Societal psychology emphasizes the all-embracing force of the social, institutional, and cultural environments, and with it the study of social phenomena in their own right as they affect and are affected by the members of the particular society" (p. 17).

She urged social psychologists to return to a much more broadly defined discipline, as envisioned by Kurt Lewin, which includes attention to societal issues. Among the guiding principles for the newly defined discipline,

Himmelweit includes the following requirements: to study the sociocultural context in which individuals live, as an antecedent to human behavior and also as an outcome of human action; to develop dynamic conceptual frameworks and models based on theoretical pluralism; to maintain a historical perspective; to develop an interdisciplinary approach that combines theoretical and applied research; to adopt a multilevel system approach that combines micro and macro levels of research; and to extend the range of research tools and recognize the pluralism in the values underlying social research.

In spite of the fact that societal psychology has not been established as yet and the mainstream of social psychology has remained narrowly defined, there are social psychologists who are actually addressing issues that would fall into the domain of societal psychology. They do so in various academic departments, for example, the social sciences, business, management, social work, law, education, or medicine, as well as in numerous organizations and agencies that deal with societal problems. This work continues the long and rich tradition of research on societal issues such as discrimination, poverty, war prevention, lasting peace, drug use and abuse, unemployment, economic crisis, conflicts (interpersonal and intergroup), cults, legal issues, psychological foundations of health and health care, and so on. But this line of research is usually carried out by social psychologists beyond the "legitimate" stream of social psychology. A reflection of this state can be exemplified in the fact that whereas the mainstream of social psychology has more than a dozen journals (some of them organs of professional organizations) that focus mainly on individualistic-cognitive social psychology with some emphasis on interpersonal interaction and small-group behavior, very few social psychological journals focus on social psychological issues of a society. Therefore, at present, social psychologists studying societal problems publish their work in journals of other disciplines and participate in their professional meetings.

Many of those working on societal issues view themselves as social psychologists and would like to continue doing so. Many do not want to be part of other disciplines. They would like to extend the knowledge of social psychology by looking at people in their real-life settings and systems and studying their social behavior.

In the present definition of the scope of social psychology, there is not much place for such work. Rarely is there openness to explore macro issues studied on the basis of sociopsychological knowledge, because these studies are often based on different research paradigms, different lines of thinking, or interdisciplinary approaches. This closedness of social psychology is surprising in view of the great interest of social scientists in social psychological knowledge. Experts in political science, business, management, public policy, and other disciplines follow developments in social psychology closely and continuously borrow its concepts, theories, conceptual developments, or models to apply to the analysis of their topics of interest. The most salient example of this is the work of Amos Tversky and Daniel Kahneman, which has become the accepted model of individual decision-making processes (e.g., Quattrone & Tversky, 1988; Simonson, 1992; Simonson & Tversky, 1992; Tversky & Kahneman, 1991).

Contributions to Societal Psychology

Even though social psychology has generally avoided the macro study of social behavior, a number of social psychologists have contributed to a better understanding of societal issues by using social psychological knowledge in their analysis. The next section will review some of this work. One example of a contribution to societal psychology is the work of Michael Billig during the last two decades. In one of his early studies, he analyzed fascism in general and the National Front (a British fascist party) in particular from a social psychological perspective (Billig, 1978). On a general psychological level, Billig suggested that there is no single fascist personality and that there is a contradiction between the authoritarian personality of fascists and fascist practices. Whereas fascist ideology preaches respect for law and discipline, fascist behavior often stands in shrill contrast to these principles. In Billig's view, fascism should be studied by examining the correspondence between fascist systems of beliefs and the structure of fascist propaganda. In-depth interviews with a small sample of National Front members revealed respect for authority and a tendency to uncontrolled violence. Through content analysis of National Front propaganda, Billig showed that this political movement is perpetuating long-established anti-Semitic traditions.

In his most recent work, Billig (1995) directed attention to the social phenomenon of *banal nationalism,* which refers to the everyday life and normal habits that enable the established nations of the West to maintain their national framework. In his view, nationalism requires a discursive, ideological consciousness, that is, one in which national identities and national homelands appear "natural" as moral orders. He provides several examples of how banal nationalism works by analyzing, for instance, the speeches of politicians who typically reproduce the clichés of nationhood and the tendency of newspapers to address their readers as members of the nation. These and other cues constantly and continuously remind people that they are part of a nation differentiated from other groups.

Another important contribution to societal psychology is by Ervin Staub, a social psychologist, who has addressed one of the most fundamental questions: How can human beings torture and murder each other and even perform genocide? In his book *The Roots of Evil: The Origins of Genocide and Other Group Violence,* Staub (1989) analyzes the historical cases of the Nazi Holocaust, the Turkish genocide of the Armenians, the Cambodian genocide, and the mass killings in Argentina. Drawing on social psychological knowledge as well as on other knowledge accumulated in other social sciences, he focused on the personal, societal, and cultural factors that foster extreme mistreatment of other people. According to Staub, under extremely difficult life conditions, when people live under authoritarian or totalitarian systems in which an ethnocentric-nationalistic ideology is fostered, people derive their basic motivations by devaluing other groups, scapegoating, joining authoritative groups, and adopting nationalist ideology. These developments give rise to the motivation to harm other groups and diminish inhibitions against such acts. The emergence of mass killing is dependent on the cultural norms of the society (for example, the history of discrimination in the society), the passivity of the bystanders, the degree to which the victims have been devalued, and the availability of justification for mass murder.

Another research in societal psychology was the study by Reykowski and his collaborators (Reykowski, 1995, 1996) investigating images of democracy and the functioning of democratic institutions. Reykowski posited that the functioning of democratic institutions depends on the normative beliefs that members of a society hold regarding the nature of democracy and on their cognitive and communicative abilities, that is, their political competence. He focused on such research questions as how ordinary people conceptualize democracy and whether it is possible to observe systematic differences. What kind of socioeconomic and cultural factors are associated with individual differential conceptualizations of democracy? Is the conceptualization of democracy related to political problem solving? Is there a relationship between the conceptualization of democracy and the functioning of democratic institutions? To answer these research questions, Reykowski and his associates developed a scale to assess the conceptualization of democracy and a questionnaire that measured political problem solving. In addition, the political behavior of city council members, who also participated in the study, was observed during regular committee meetings of the city council. The authors administered the questionnaires to various groups of adults differing with regard to age, level of education, economic status, political involvement, gender, and profession. Four different beliefs about democracy were detected among the respondents about democracy as a system that cares for ordinary people, involves political institutions, guarantees some basic human and political rights, and is supposed to realize some ideological values. These beliefs were related to various demographic and cultural variables: for example, people with higher levels of education tended to view democracy in terms of its institutions and values, whereas people with lower levels of education tended to view it as a system caring for ordinary citizens. The results also showed that the way they construe democracy seem to have some bearing on the way people approach political conflicts. Thus, respondents who viewed democracy in terms of a "social" dimension and those who did not have a clear idea of what democracy is were less likely to become involved in macro-level political conflicts but, at the same time, were more prone to employ contentious strategies in dealing with opponents. Finally, the results showed that the city council members participating in the study adopted mostly an institutional or axiological view of democracy. They differed in the way they functioned in meetings, but these differences were unrelated to their different construals of democracy.

Sidanius and Pratto (1999) presented an integrative theory of intergroup relations entitled social dominance theory, which they supported by an impressive set of data. The theory suggests that most forms of socially based oppression such as racism, sexism, nationalism, or religious intolerance are manifestations of the same basic psycho-social-institutional mechanism associated with the apparent human predisposition to form and maintain society-based hierarchical systems. The theory suggests that all societies that produce a surplus also form hierarchical systems in which groups are socially constructed on the basis of such cues as race, social class, gender, religion, geographical location, ethnic origin, and so on. In the hierarchical structure, groups found at the top are called dominant, and those at the bottom are called subordinate. The dominant groups tend to develop mechanisms to produce and maintain society-based hierarchy. These mechanisms consist of social ideology, defined social roles, and institutional decision making, all of which result in individual and institutional discrimination. Of special importance are shared beliefs (legitimizing myths), which provide moral and/or intellectual legitimacy to the hierarchical system. Racism or sexism are examples of these beliefs. In a series of empirical studies, a scale of social dominance orientation, which measures the desire to make one's own ingroup superior to and dominant over other relevant and comparable outgroups, was constructed. Use of this scale yielded attitudinal and behavioral correlates of dominance orientation. In addition, a different line of research observed institutional practices that maintain the hierarchical order. Such practices tend to be engaged in by individuals who have a dominance orientation. The studies showed how these practices perpetuate discrimination in the societal system. One example is the criminal justice system, which discriminates among society members on the basis of their race. The social dominance theory relates personality characteristics, individual behavior, shared social ideology, and institutional systems to integrate the individual level and societal level of analysis. It thus draws heavily on social and personality psychology, social-evolutionary theory, neoclassical elitism theory, political psychology, and sociology.

Recently, some stimulating social psychological contributions to the understanding of the problem of ethnic and national identity have appeared. Worchel (1999) has written a book that explores why ethnic identity is important to people and why ethnicity is so often the cause of intergroup violence and conflict. He suggests that the desire for personal value and social order creates the need for ethnic identity, and this is reflected in people's identification with their ethnic group. Ethnic identity is the most basic, because it is established at birth. Nevertheless, individuals may be ethnic mongrels, and identification with an ethnic group depends on physical traits, ethnicity of the father, the characteristics of the ethnic group, institutional demands, the personal advantage of identifying with a particular group, personal conditions, and the existence of other ethnic groups. Worchel proposes that once an individual identifies with an ethnic group, the social forces of that group operate to invite increasing loyalty and solidarity. These forces, in his opinion, set the stage for intergroup conflict, which is usually instigated by factors such as proximity, similarity, competition for scarce resources, and strangeness of the outgroup. According to Worchel, conflict between groups facilitates maintenance of group identity, allows the drawing of distinct boundaries, and leads to the homogeneous perception of the outgroup as dangerous and threatening.

As indicated, the present book is an additional contribution to societal psychology. This study of shared societal beliefs sheds light on society members' behavior, the interactive relationship between them and the society, and societal functioning. This was done by using accumulated social psychological knowledge with the support of social sciences–relevant knowledge. By writing and publishing this book, I hope not only to present ideas about shared societal beliefs, but also to stimulate the interest of social psychologists to take a wider perspective in their orientation and extend the interest in developing societal psychology. This move is done not as an alternative to social psychology but as an extension and addition that make the social concept more meaningful and fulfill the promise of the founding fathers of social psychology.

References

Abelson, R. P. (1986). Beliefs are like possessions. *Journal for the Theory of Social Behavior, 16,* 223-250.

Abelson, R. P. (1988). Conviction. *American Psychologist, 43,* 267-275.

Abelson, R. P., Aronson, E., McGuire, W. J., Newcomb, T. M., Rosenberg, M. J., & Tannenbaum, P. H. (Eds.). (1968). *Theories of cognitive consistency: A sourcebook.* Chicago: Rand McNally.

Abelson, R. P., & Prentice, D. A. (1989). Beliefs as possessions: A functional perspective. In A. R. Pratkanis, S. J. Breckler, & A. G. Greenwald (Eds.), *Attitude structure and function* (pp. 361-381). Hillsdale, NJ: Lawrence Erlbaum.

Aberle, D. F., Cohen, A. K., Davis, A. K., Levy, M. J., & Sutton, F. X. (1950). The functional prerequisite of a society. *Ethics, 60,* 100-111.

Adar, L., & Adler, C. (1965). *Education for values in school for immigrants' children.* Jerusalem: The Hebrew University and Ministry of Education and Culture. (Hebrew)

Adorno, T. W., Frenkel-Brunswik, E., Levinson, D. J., & Sanford, R. N. (1950). *The authoritarian personality.* New York: Harper.

Allen, W. S. (1965). *The Nazi seizure of power: The experience of a single German town, 1930-1935.* Chicago: Quadrangle Books.

Allport, F. H. (1920). *Social psychology.* Boston: Houghton-Mifflin.

Allport, G. W. (1954). *The nature of prejudice.* Reading, MA: Addison-Wesley.

Allport, G. W. (1985). The historical background of social psychology. In G. Lindzey & E. Aronson (Eds.), *Handbook of social psychology* (3rd ed., Vol. 1, pp. 1-46). New York: Random House.

Almaguer, T. (1994). *Racial fault lines: The historical origins of white supremacy in California.* Berkeley: University of California Press.

Almond, G. A. (1960). *The American people and foreign policy.* New York: Frederick A. Praeger.

Anderson, B. (1991). *Imagined communities: Reflections on the origin and spread of nationalism* (rev. ed.). London: Verso.

Apple, M. W. (1979). *Ideology and curriculum.* London: Routledge & Kegan Paul.

171

Arian, A. (1989). A people apart: Coping with national security problems in Israel. *Journal of Conflict Resolution, 33,* 605-631.

Arian, A. (1995). *Security threatened: Surveying Israeli opinion on peace and war.* Cambridge, UK: Cambridge University Press.

Arian, A., Talmud, I., & Hermann, T. (1988). *National security and public opinion in Israel.* Boulder, CO: Westview.

Armistead, N. (Ed.). (1974). *Reconstructing social psychology.* Harmondsworth, UK: Penguin.

Asch, S. E. (1952). *Social psychology.* New York: Prentice Hall.

Ashkenazy, D. (Ed.). (1994). *The military in service of society and democracy: The challenge of the dual role military.* Westport, CT: Greenwood.

Ashmore, R. D., & DelBoca, F. K. (1981). Conceptual approaches to stereotypes and stereotyping. In D. L. Hamilton (Ed.), *Cognitive processes in stereotyping and intergroup behavior* (pp. 1-35). Hillsdale, NJ: Lawrence Erlbaum.

Avineri, S. (1981). *The making of modern Zionism: The intellectual origins of the Jewish State.* London: Weidenfeld & Nicolson.

Aycoberry, P. (1981). *The Nazi question.* New York: Pantheon.

Bancroft, F. (1931). *Slave-trading in the old South.* Baltimore, MD: J. H. Furst.

Bar-Gal, Y. (1993). *Homeland and geography in a hundred years of Zionist education.* Tel Aviv: Am Oved. (Hebrew)

Barghoorn, F. C. (1956). *Soviet Russian nationalism.* New York: Oxford University Press.

Barnhart, M. A. (1987). *Japan prepares for total war: The search for economic security, 1919-1941.* Ithaca, NY: Cornell University Press.

Bar-Tal, D. (1988). Delegitimizing relations between Israeli Jews and Palestinians: A social psychological analysis. In J. Hofman (Ed.), *Arab-Jewish relations in Israel: A quest in human understanding* (pp. 217-248). Bristol, IN: Wyndham Hall Press.

Bar-Tal, D. (1990a). *Group beliefs: A conception for analyzing group structure, processes, and behavior.* New York: Springer-Verlag.

Bar-Tal, D. (1990b). Israel-Palestinian conflict: A cognitive analysis. *International Journal of Intercultural Relations, 14,* 7-29.

Bar-Tal, D. (1994). Delegitimization of the Jews in Germany, 1933-1945: A case of group beliefs. In C. Kulke & G. Lederer (Eds.), *Der gewohnliche Antisemitisus* (pp. 51-69). New York: Centaurus.

Bar-Tal, D. (1997a). Formation and change of ethnic and national stereotype: An integrative model. *International Journal of Intercultural Relations, 21,* 491-523.

Bar-Tal, D. (1997b). The monopolization of patriotism. In D. Bar-Tal & E. Staub (Eds.), *Patriotism in the lives of individuals and nations* (pp. 246-270). Chicago: Nelson-Hall.

Bar-Tal, D. (1998a). Group beliefs as an expression of social identity. In S. Worchel, J. F. Morales, D. Paez, & J. C. Deschamps (Eds.), *Social identity: International perspective* (pp. 93-113). Thousand Oaks, CA: Sage.

Bar-Tal, D. (1998b). The rocky road toward peace: Beliefs on conflict in Israeli textbooks. *Journal of Peace Research, 35,* 723-742.

Bar-Tal, D. (1998c). Societal beliefs in times of intractable conflict: The Israeli case. *International Journal of Conflict Management, 9,* 22-50.

Bar-Tal, D., & Antebi, D. (1992). Beliefs about negative intentions of the world: A study of the Israeli siege mentality. *Political Psychology, 13,* 633-645.

Bar-Tal, D., & Bar-Tal, Y. (1988). A new perspective for social psychology. In D. Bar-Tal & A. W. Kruglanski (Eds.), *The social psychology of knowledge* (pp. 83-108). Cambridge, UK: Cambridge University Press.

Bar-Tal, D., & Jacobson, D. (1998). The elusive concept and pursuit of security. In D. Bar-Tal, D. Jacobson, & A. Klieman (Eds.), *Security concerns: Insights from the Israeli experience.* Stamford, CT: JAI.

Bar-Tal, D., Jacobson, D., & Klieman, A. (Eds.). (1998). *Security concerns: Insights from the Israeli experience.* Stamford, CT: JAI.

Bar-Tal, D., & Kruglanski, A. W. (1988). The social psychology of knowledge: Its scope and meaning. In D. Bar-Tal & A. W. Kruglanski (Eds.), *The social psychology of knowledge* (pp. 1-14). Cambridge, UK: Cambridge University Press.

Bar-Tal, D., Kruglanski, A. W., & Klar, Y. (1989). Conflict termination: An epistemological analysis of international cases. *Political Psychology, 10,* 233-255.

Bar-Tal, D., Raviv, A., & Freund, T. (1994). An anatomy of political beliefs: A study of their centrality, confidence, contents, and epistemic authority. *Journal of Applied Social Psychology, 24,* 849-872.

Bar-Tal, D., Raviv, A., & Raviv, A. (1991). The concept of epistemic authority in the process of political knowledge acquisition. *Representative Research in Social Psychology, 19,* 107-120.

Bar-Tal, D., Raviv, A., Raviv, A., & Brosh, M. E. (1991). Perception of epistemic authority and attribution for its choice as a function of knowledge area and age. *European Journal of Social Psychology, 21,* 477-492.

Bar-Tal, D., & Raviv, A., Rosen, M., & Bruker, N. (1999). *Consequences of sharing beliefs.* Manuscript submitted for publication.

Bar-Tal, D., & Saxe, L. (1990). Acquisition of political knowledge: A social psychological analysis. In O. Ichilov (Ed.), *Political socialization, citizenship education, and democracy* (pp. 116-133). New York: Teachers College Press.

Bar-Tal, D., & Zafran, A. (2000). *Measuring the ethos of intractable conflict in Israel: The effects of personal variables.* Manuscript in preparation.

Bar-Tal, Y., Kishon-Rabin, L., & Tabak, N. (1997). The effect of need and ability to achieve cognitive structuring on cognitive structuring. *Journal of Personality and Social Psychology, 73,* 1158-1176.

Bateson, G. (1958). *Naven* (2nd ed.). Stanford, CA: Stanford University Press.

Bauer, Y. (1982). *A history of the holocaust.* New York: F. Watts.

Baynes, N. H. (Ed.). (1969). *The speeches of Adolf Hitler: April 1922-August 1939* (Vol. 1). New York: Howard Fertig.

Bekhterev, V. W. (1921). *Collective reflexology* (E. Lockwood, Trans., L. H. Strickland, Ed.) Petrograd: Kolos.

Bem, D. J. (1967). Self-perception: An alternative interpretation of cognitive dissonance phenomena. *Psychological Review, 74,* 183-200.

Bem, D. J. (1970). *Beliefs, attitudes, and human affairs.* Belmont, CA: Brooks/Cole.

Bem, D. J. (1972). Self-perception theory. In L. Berkowitz (Ed.), *Advances in experimental social psychology* (Vol. 6, pp. 1-62). New York: Academic Press.

Ben-Amos, A. (1997). The uses of the past: Patriotism between history and memory. In D. Bar-Tal & E. Staub (Eds.), *Patriotism in the lives of individuals and nations* (pp. 129-148). Chicago: Nelson-Hall.

Ben-Dor, G. (1998). Responding to threat—The dynamics of the Arab-Israel conflict. In D. Bar-Tal, D. Jacobson, & A. Klieman (Eds.), *Security concerns: Insights from the Israeli experience* (pp. 113-138). Greenwich, CT: JAI.

Benedict, R. (1967). *The chrysanthemum and the sword.* Cleveland, OH: Meridian Books.

Ben-Eliezer, U. (1995). A nation-in-arms: State, nation, and militarism in Israel in Israel's first years. *Comparative Studies in Society and History, 37,* 264-285.

Ben-Ezer, E. (1968, Summer). Breaking out and besieged: Studies in young Israeli's literature. *Keshet,* No. 4, pp. 126-160. (Hebrew)

Ben-Ezer, E. (1977). War and siege in the Israeli literature (1967-1976). *Iton 1977 Lesifrut Veletarbut,* Issue No. 1, pp. 5-6, Issue No. 3, pp. 14-15. (Hebrew)

Bengio, O. (1986). Iraq. In H. Shaked & D. Dishon (Eds.), *Middle East contemporary survey* (Vol. 8, pp. 465-496). Tel Aviv: Tel Aviv University.

Bengio, O. (1998). *Saddam's word.* New York: Oxford University Press.

Ben-Gurion, D. (1963). *Israel: Years of challenge.* Tel Aviv: Massadah. (Hebrew)

Ben-Gurion, D. (1965). *Things as they are.* Tel Aviv: Am Hasefer. (Hebrew)

Ben-Shaul, N. (1997). *Mythical expressions of siege in Israeli films.* Lewiston, NY: Edisin Mellen.

Benyamini, K. (1981). Israeli youth and the image of the Arab. *Jerusalem Quarterly, 20,* 87-95.

Ben-Yehuda, N. (1995). *The Masada myth: Collective memory and myth making in Israel.* Madison: University of Wisconsin Press.

Berger, P. (1969). *The sacred canopy.* Garden City, NY: Doubleday.

Berger, P., & Luckmann, T. (1967). *The social construction of reality.* Harmondsworth, UK: Penguin.

Berkowitz, L. (1968). Social motivation. In G. Lindzey & E. Aronson (Eds.), *The handbook of social psychology* (2nd ed., Vol. 3, pp. 50-135) Reading, MA: Addison-Wesley.

Berkowitz, L. (1969). *Aggression: A social psychological analysis.* New York: McGraw-Hill.

Berry, J. W. (1997). Immigration, acculturation, and adaptation. *Applied Psychology: An International Review, 46,* 5-68.

Bettenhausen, K. L., & Murnighan, J. K. (1985). The emergence of norms in competitive decision-making groups. *Administrative Science Quarterly, 30,* 350-372.

Beuf, A. (1977). *Red children in white America.* Philadelphia: University of Pennsylvania Press.

Bezalel, Y. (1989). *Changes in Zionist values as reflected in elementary school literature and language readers from the late fifties to the mid eighties.* Thesis for the MA degree, Ben Gurion University of the Negev, Beer Sheva, Israel.

Bialer, S. (1985). The psychology of U.S.-Soviet relations. *Political Psychology, 6*, 263-273.

Biberaj, E. (1986). *Albania between East and West* (Conflict studies No. 190). London: Institute for the Study of Conflict.

Biberaj, E. (1990). *Albania: A socialist maverick.* Boulder, CO: Westview.

Billig, M. (1978). *Fascists: A social psychological view of the national front.* London: Academic Press.

Billig, M. (1982). *Ideology and social psychology: Extremism, moderation, and contradiction.* Oxford, UK: Basil Blackwell.

Billig, M. (1995). *Banal nationalism.* London: Sage.

Blank, T. (1997, July). *Authoritarianism, anomie, and self-concept: Can they explain nationalism and patriotism? Empirical results with German data.* Paper presented at the Annual Scientific Meeting of the International Society of Political Psychology, Krakow, Poland.

Blau, P. M. (1964). *Exchange and power in social life.* New York: John Wiley.

Borhek, J. T., & Curtis, R. F. (1975). *A sociology of belief.* New York: John Wiley.

Boster, J. S. (1991). The information economy model applied to biological similarity judgment. In L. B. Resnick, J. M. Levine, & S. D. Teasley (Eds.), *Perspectives on socially shared cognition* (pp. 203-225). Washington, DC: American Psychological Association.

Bourdieu, P. (1973). Cultural reproduction and social reproduction. In R. Brown (Ed.), *Knowledge, education, and cultural change* (pp. 71-112). London: Tavistock.

Bourdieu, P., & Paseron, J. C. (1990). *Reproduction in education, society, and culture.* London: Sage.

Boyce, D. B. (1995). *Nationalism in Ireland.* London: Routledge.

Bracher, K. D. (1971). *The German dictatorship.* London: Weidenfeld & Nicholson.

Bramsted, E. K. (1965). *Goebbels and National Socialist propaganda 1925-1945.* East Lansing: Michigan State University Press.

Bransford, J. D. (1979). *Human cognition: Learning, understanding, and remembering.* Belmont, CA: Wadsworth.

Brewer, M. B. (1979). Ingroup bias in the minimal intergroup situation: A cognitive motivational analysis. *Psychological Bulletin, 86*, 308-324.

Brewer, M. B. (1991). The social self: On being the same and different at the same time. *Personality and Social Psychology Bulletin, 17*, 475-482.

Brewer, M. B. (1997). On the social origins of human nature. In C. McGarty & S. A. Haslam (Eds.), *The message of social psychology: Perspectives on mind in society* (pp. 54-62). Cambridge, MA: Blackwell.

Brewer, M. B., & Campbell, D. T. (1976). *Ethnocentrism and intergroup attitudes: East African evidence.* New York: Halsted.

Broadbent, D. E. (1971). *Decision and stress.* London: Academic Press.

Bronfenbrenner, U. (1961). The mirror image in Soviet-American relations: A social psychologist's report. *Journal of Social Issues, 27*(3), 45-56.

Brown, D. (1966). *Against the world.* Garden City, NJ: Doubleday.

Brubaker, R. (1992). *Citizenship and nationhood in France and Germany.* Cambridge, MA: Harvard University Press.

Brzezinski, Z. (1957). *The permanent purge: Politics in Soviet totalitarianism.* Cambridge, MA: Harvard University Press.

Buchanan, W., & Cantril, H. (1953). *How nations see each other.* Westport, CT: Greenwood.

Bullock, A. (1962). *Hitler: A study in tyranny.* Harmondsworth, UK: Penguin.

Burr, V. (1995). *An introduction to social constructionism.* London: Routledge.

Byrne, D. (1961). Interpersonal attraction and attitude similarity. *Journal of Abnormal and Social Psychology, 62,* 713-715.

Byrne, D. (1971). *The attraction paradigm.* New York: Academic Press.

Campbell, D. T. (1958). Common fate, similarity, and other indices of the status of aggregates of persons as social entities. *Behavioral Science, 3,* 14-25.

Cancian, F. (1975). *What are norms?* New York: Cambridge University Press.

Cantril, H. (1941). *The psychology of social movements.* New York: John Wiley.

Carmines, E. G., & Merriman, W. R., Jr. (1993). The changing American dilemma: Liberal values and racial policies. In P. M. Siderman, P. E. Tetlock, & E. G. Carmines (Eds.), *Prejudice, politics, and American dilemma* (pp. 237-255). Stanford, CA: Stanford University Press.

Cartwright, D. (1979). Contemporary social psychology in historical perspective. *Social Psychology Quarterly, 42,* 82-93.

Cartwright, D., & Zander, A. (Eds.). (1968). *Group dynamics: Research and theory* (3rd ed.). New York: Harper & Row.

Caspi, D., & Limor, Y. (1992). *The mediators: The mass media in Israel 1948-1990.* Tel Aviv: Am Oved. (Hebrew)

Cecil, R. (1993). The marching season in Northern Ireland: An expression of politico-religious identity. In S. MacDonald (Ed.), *Inside European identities* (pp. 146-166). Providence, RI: Berg.

Clark, H. H., & Marshall, C. R. (1981). Definite reference and mutual knowledge. In A. K. Joshi, B. L. Webber, & I. A. Sag (Eds.), *Elements of discourse understanding* (pp. 10-63). Cambridge, UK: Cambridge University Press.

Cohen, A. (1985). *An ugly face in the mirror: National stereotypes in Hebrew children's literature.* Tel Aviv: Reshafim. (Hebrew)

Cohen, E. (1989). The changing legitimations of the state of Israel. *Studies in Contemporary Jewry, 5,* 148-165.

Cohen, R. (1979). *Threat perception in international crisis.* Madison: University of Wisconsin Press.

Cohen, S. F. (1986). *Sovieticus: American perceptions and Soviet realities.* New York: Norton.

Cole, M. (1991). Conclusion. In L. B. Resnick, J. M. Levine, & S. D. Teasley (Eds.), *Perspectives on socially shared cognition* (pp. 398-417). Washington, DC: American Psychological Association.

Coleman, L. (1941). What is American? A study of alleged American traits. *Social Forces, 19,* 492-510.

Connerton, P. (1989). *How societies remember.* Cambridge, UK: Cambridge University Press.

Converse, P. E. (1964). The nature of belief systems in mass publics. In D. E. Apter (Ed.), *Ideology and discontent* (pp. 106-261). New York: Free Press.

Cordesman, A. H., & Hashim, A. S. (1997). *Iraq: Sanctions and beyond.* Boulder, CO: Westview.

Cornevin, M. (1980). *Apartheid: Power and historical falsification.* Paris: UNESCO.

Coser, L. A. (1956). *The functions of social conflict.* New York: Free Press.

Costa, N. J. (1995). *Albania: A European enigma.* New York: Columbia University Press.

Crowne, D. P., & Marlowe, D. (1964). *The approval motive: Studies in evaluative dependence.* New York: John Wiley.

Crutchfield, R. S. (1955). Conformity and character. *American Psychologist, 10,* 191-198.

Curt, M. (1946). *The roots of American loyalty.* New York: Columbia University Press.

Curtis, M. (1979). *Totalitarianism.* New Brunswick, NJ: Transaction Books.

Cushman, D., & Whiting, G. C. (1972). An approach to communication theory: Toward consensus on rules. *Journal of Communication, 22,* 217-238.

D'Andrade, B. G. (1981). The cultural part of cognition. *Cognitive Science, 5,* 179-195.

D'Andrade, B. G. (1984). Cultural meaning systems. In R. A. Shweder & R. A. LeVine (Eds.), *Culture theory* (pp. 88-119). Cambridge, UK: Cambridge University Press.

Daft, R. L., & Weick, K. E. (1984). Toward a model of organization as interpretive systems. *Academy of Management Review, 9,* 284-295.

Damon, W. (1991). Problems of direction in socially shared cognition. In L. B. Resnick, J. M. Levine, & S. D. Feasley (Eds.), *Perspectives on socially shared cognition* (pp. 384-397). Washington, DC: American Psychological Association.

Darby, J. (1976). *Conflict in Northern Ireland: The development of a polarized community.* New York: Harper & Row.

Darby, J. (Ed.). (1983). *Northern Ireland: The background of the conflict.* Belfast: Appletree Press.

Dawe, A. (1970). The two sociologies. *British Journal of Sociology, 21,* 207-218.

Dawidowicz, L. S. (1975). *The war against the Jews. 1933-1945.* New York: Holt, Rinehart & Winston.

Dawson, R. E., & Prewitt, K. (1969). *Political socialization.* Boston: Little, Brown.

Deutsch, M. (1968). The effects of cooperation and competition upon group process. In D. Cartwright & A. Lander (Eds.), *Group dynamics* (3rd ed., pp. 461-482). New York: Harper & Row.

Doob, L. W. (1964). *Patriotism and nationalism: Their psychological foundations.* New Haven, CT: Yale University Press.

Dougherty, J. W. D. (Ed.). (1985). *Directions in cognitive anthropology.* Urbana: University of Illinois Press.

Durkheim, E. (1898). Representations indiviuelles et representations collectives. *Revue de metaphysique, 6,* 274-302. (Reprinted in D. F. Pocock, Trans., *Sociology and philosophy,* New York: Free Press, 1953).

Durkheim, E. (1933). *The division of labor in society.* New York: Macmillan.

Durkheim, E. (1951). *Suicide.* Glencoe, IL: Free Press.

Durkheim, E. (1953). *Sociology and philosophy.* London: Cohen & West.

Dziewanowski, M. K. (1977). *Poland in the twentieth century.* New York: Columbia University Press.

Eagly, A. H., & Chaiken, S. (1993). *The psychology of attitudes.* Fort Worth, TX: Harcourt Brace Jovanovich.

Eagly, A. H., & Chaiken, S. (1995). Attitude strength, attitude structure, and resistance to change. In R. E. Petty & J. A. Krosnick (Eds.), *Attitude strength: Antecedents and consequences* (pp. 413-432). Mahwah, NJ: Lawrence Erlbaum.

Eban, A. (1957). *Voice of Israel.* New York: Horizon Press.

Eban, A. (1984). *Heritage: Civilization and the Jews.* London: Weidenfeld & Nicolson.

Edelstein, A. S. (1982). *Comparative communication research.* Beverly Hills, CA: Sage.

Eden, S. (1971). *On the new curricula.* Jerusalem: Maalot. (Hebrew)

Edwards, A. L. (1957). *The social desirability variable in personality assessment and research.* New York: Dryden Press.

Eisenstadt, S. N. (1954). *The absorption of immigrants.* London: Routledge & Kegan Paul.

Elms, A. C. (1975). The crisis of confidence in social psychology. *American Psychologist, 30,* 967-976.

Elon, A. (1971). *The Israelis.* London: Weidenfeld & Nicolson.

Epstein, A. L. (1978). *Ethos and identity.* London: Tavistock.

Erikson, R. S., Luttberg, N. R., & Tedin, K. L. (1980). *American public opinion: Its origin, content, and impact* (2nd ed.). New York: John Wiley.

Farr, P. M. (1996). *The roots of modern social psychology 1982-1954.* Oxford, UK: Blackwell.

Farr, R. (1989). The social and collective nature of representations. In J. P. Forgas & J. M. Innes (Eds.), *Recent advances in social psychology: An international perspective* (pp. 157-166). Amsterdam: North-Holland.

Festinger, L. (1950). Informal social communication. *Psychological Review, 57,* 271-282.

Festinger, L. (1954). A theory of social comparison process. *Human Relations, 7,* 117-140.

Festinger, L., Gerard, H., Hymovitch, B., Kelley, H. H., & Raven, B. (1952). The influence process in the presence of extreme deviates. *Human Relations, 5,* 327-346.

Feyerabend, P. (1976). *Against method.* New York: Humanities Press.

Firer, R. (1980). *Consciousness and knowledge: Influence of the Zionistic values on the Hebrew schoolbooks of the history of the Israeli people in Eretz Israel in the years 1900-1980.* Doctoral dissertation, The Hebrew University, Jerusalem. (Hebrew)

Firer, R. (1985). *The agents of Zionist education.* Tel Aviv: Sifriyat Poalim. (Hebrew)

Fishbein, M., & Ajzen, I. (1975). *Belief, attitude, intention, and behavior: An intro-duction to theory and research.* Reading, MA: Addison-Wesley.

Fisher, L. (1951). *The Soviets in world affairs.* Princeton, NJ: Princeton University Press.

Fiske, A. P. (1991). *Structures of social life.* New York: Free Press.

Fiske, S. T. (1993). Social cognition and social perception. *Annual Review of Psychology, 44,* 155-194.

Fiske, S. T., & Taylor, S. E. (1991). *Social cognition* (2nd ed.). New York: McGraw-Hill.

Flenley, P. (1996). From Soviet to Russian identity: The origins of contemporary Russian nationalism and national identity. In B. Jenkins & S. A. Sofos (Eds.), *Nation and identity in contemporary Europe* (pp. 223-250). London: Routledge.

Forbes, J. D. (1964). *The Indian in America's past.* Englewood Cliffs, NJ: Prentice Hall.

Forsyth, D. R. (1980). The functions of attributions. *Social Psychology Quarterly, 43,* 184-189.

Fraser, C., & Gaskell, G. (Eds.). (1990). *The social psychology of widespread beliefs.* Oxford, UK: Clarendon.

Free, L. A., & Cantril, H. (1967). *The political beliefs of Americans—A study of a public opinion.* New Brunswick, NJ: Rutgers University Press.

Frei, D. (1986). *Perceived images: U.S. and Soviet assumptions and perceptions in disarmament.* Totowa, NJ: Rowman & Allanheld.

Frei, N. (1993). *National Socialist rule in Germany.* Oxford, UK: Blackwell.

Freud, S. (1960). *Group psychology and the analysis of the ego.* New York: Bantam Books.

Fulbrook, M. (1994). Aspects of society and identity in the new Germany. *Daedalus, 123*(1), 211-234.

Gallup, G. H. (1972). *The Gallup Poll: Public opinion 1935-1971* (Vol. 1-3). New York: Random House.

Gallup, G. H. (1978). *The Gallup Poll: Public opinion 1972-1977* (Vol. 1-2). Wilmington, DE: Scholarly Resources.

Gamson, W. A. (1988). A constructionist approach to mass media and public opinion. *Symbolic Interaction, 11,* 161-174.

Gardner, R. C. (1993). Stereotypes as consensual beliefs. In M. P. Zanna & J. M. Olson (Eds.), *The psychology of prejudice: The Ontario symposium* (Vol. 7, pp. 1-31). Hillsdale, NJ: Lawrence Erlbaum.

Geertz, C. (1973). *The interpretation of cultures.* New York: Basic Books.

Gelman, R., Massey, C. M., & McManus, M. (1991). Characterizing supporting environments for cognitive development: Lessons from children in a museum. In L. B. Resnick, J. M. Levine, & S. D. Teasley (Eds.), *Perspectives on socially shared cognition* (pp. 226-256). Washington, DC: American Psychological Association.

Genovese, E. (1966). *The political economy of slavery: Studies in the economy and society of the slave South.* New York: Random House.

Gerard, H. B. (1954). The anchorage of opinions in face-to-face groups. *Human Relations, 7,* 313-325.

Gergen, K. J. (1985). The social constructionist movement in modern psychology. *American Psychologist, 40,* 266-275.

Gergen, K. J. (1994). *Toward transformation in social knowledge* (2nd ed.). London: Sage.

Gertz, N. (1984). The few against the many. *The Jerusalem Quarterly, 30,* 94-104.

Gertz, N. (1995). *Captive of a dream: National myths in Israeli culture.* Tel Aviv: Am Oved. (Hebrew)

Gertz, N. (1998). From destruction to redemption: Israeli literature and cinema 1960-1990. In D. Bar-Tal, D. Jacobson, & A. Klieman (Eds.), *Security concerns: Insights from the Israeli experience* (pp. 193-214). Greenwich, CT: JAI.

Giddens, A. (1984). *The constitution of society.* Berkeley: University of California Press.

Ginossar, P., & Bareli, A. (Eds.). (1996). *Zionism: A contemporary controversy.* Beer Sheva, Israel: Ben Gurion University of the Negev Press. (Hebrew)

Gitelman, Z. (1982). *Becoming Israelis: Political resocialization of Soviet and American immigrants.* New York: Praeger.

Gitlin, T. (1995). *The twilight of the common dream.* New York: Metropolitan.

Gordon, S. (1984). *Hitler, Germans, and the "Jewish Question."* Princeton, NJ: Princeton University Press.

Gothelf, Y. (1970, March 13). Old and new anti-Semitism. *Davar.* (Hebrew)

Gozman, L. (1997). Russian patriotism: Forward to the past. In D. Bar-Tal & E. Staub (Eds.), *Patriotism in the lives of individuals and nations* (pp. 293-326). Chicago: Nelson-Hall.

Greenberg, M. S. (1963). *The effect of social support for one's beliefs on two techniques of attitude change.* Doctoral dissertation, University of Houston.

Greenfeld, L. (1992). *Nationalism: Five roads to modernity.* Cambridge, UK: Harvard University Press.

Greenstein, F. I. (1965). *Children and politics.* New Haven, CT: Yale University Press.

Gregor, A. J. (1979). *Italian fascism and developmental dictatorship.* Princeton, NJ: Princeton University Press.

Griswold, W. (1994). *Cultures and societies in a changing world.* Thousands Oaks, CA: Pine Forge Press.

Grosser, D. (Ed.). (1992). *German unification: The unexpected challenge.* Oxford, UK: Berg.

Grosser, P. E., & Halperin, E. G. (1979). *Anti-semitism. The causes and effect of a prejudice.* Secaucus, NY: Citadel.

Grundy, K. W. (1991). *South Africa: Domestic crisis and global challenge.* Boulder, CO: Westview.

Guzzo, R. A., Yost, P. R., Campbell, R. J., & Shea, G. P. (1993). Potency in groups: Articulating a construct. *British Journal of Social Psychology, 32,* 87-106.

Halbwachs, M. (1992). *On collective memory.* Chicago: University of Chicago Press.

Hall, R. G., Varca, P. E., & Fisher, T. D. (1986). The effect of reference groups, opinion polls, and attitude polarization on attitude formation and change. *Political Psychology, 7,* 309-321.

Halperin, S. W. (1964). *Mussolini and Italian fascism.* Princeton, NJ: D. Van Nostrand.

Halpern, D. (1961). *The idea of the Jewish state.* Cambridge, MA: Harvard University Press.

Hamilton, R. F. (1982). *Who voted for Hitler?* Princeton, NJ: Princeton University Press.

Hardin, C. D., & Higgins, E. T. (1996). Shared reality: How social verification makes the subjective objective. In R. M. Sorrentino & E. T. Higgins (Eds.), *Handbook of motivation and cognition* (Vol. 3, pp. 28-84). New York: Guilford.

Harkabi, Y. (1977). *Arab strategies and Israel's response.* New York: Free Press.

Harris, N. (1968). *Beliefs in society.* London: C. A. Walts.

Harris, R. (1972). *Prejudice and tolerance in Ulster: A study of neighbors and strangers in a border community.* Manchester, UK: Manchester University Press.

Hartley, E. L., & Hartley, R. E. (1959). *Fundamentals of social psychology.* New York: Knopf.

Haslam, S. A. (1996). Stereotyping and social influence: Foundations of stereotype sharedness. In R. Spears, P. J. Oakes, N. Ellemers, & S. A. Haslam (Eds.), *The social psychology of stereotyping and group life* (pp. 119-143). Oxford, UK: Blackwell.

Haslam, S. A., McGarty, C., & Turner, J. C. (1996). Salient group membership and persuasion: The role of social identity in the validation of beliefs. In J. L. Nye & A. M. Brower (Eds.), *What's social about social cognition? Research on socially shared cognition in small groups* (pp. 29-56). Thousands Oaks, CA: Sage.

Haslam, S. A., Oakes, P. J., Turner, J. C., & McGarty, C. (1996). Social identity, self-categorization, and the perceived homogeneity of ingroups and outgroups: The interaction between social motivation and cognition. In R. M. Sorrentino & E. T. Higgins (Eds.), *Handbook of motivation and cognition* (Vol. 3, pp. 182-221). New York: Guilford.

Haslam, S. A., Turner, J. C., Oakes, P. J., McGarty, C., & Reynolds, K. J. (1998). The group as a basis for emergent stereotypic consensus. In W. Stroebe & M. Hewstone (Eds.), *European review of social psychology* (Vol. 8, pp. 203-239). New York: John Wiley.

Hatano, G., & Inagaki, K. (1991). Sharing cognition through collectve comprehension activity. In L. B. Resnick, J. M. Levine, & S. D. Teasley (Eds.), *Perspectives on socially shared cognition* (pp. 331-348). Washington, DC: American Psychological Association.

Hayes, C. J. H. (1974). *France: A nation of patriots.* New York: Octagon Books.

Hazani, M. (1993). Netzah Yisrael, symbolic immortality, and the Israeli-Palestinian conflict. In K. S. Larsen (Ed.), *Conflict and social psychology,* (pp. 57-70). London: Sage.

Heider, F. (1958). *The psychology of interpersonal relations.* New York: John Wiley.

Henry, J. (1963). *Culture against man.* New York: Random House.

Herek, G. M. (1986). The instrumentality of attitudes: Toward a neofunctional theory. *Journal of Social Issues, 42*(2), 99-114.

Herrmann, R. K. (1985). American perceptions of Soviet foreign policy: Reconsidering three competing perspectives. *Political Psychology, 6,* 375-411.

Herrmann, R. K. (1986). The power of perceptions in foreign-policy decision making: Do views of the Soviet Union determine the policy choices of American leaders. *American Journal of Political Science, 30,* 841-875.

Herzlich, C. (1973). *Health and illness: A social psychological analysis.* London: Academic Press.

Hess, R. D., & Torney, J. V. (1967). *The development of political attitudes in children.* Chicago: Aldine.

Hewstone, M., Jaspars, J., & Lalljee, M. (1982). Social representations, social attribution, and social identity. The intergroup images of "public" and "comprehensive" schoolboys. *European Journal of Social Psychology, 12,* 241-269.

Higgins, E. T. (1996). Shared reality in the self-system: The social nature of self-regulation. In W. Stroebe & M. Hewstone (Eds.), *European review of social psychology* (Vol. 7, pp. 1-30). Chichester, UK: Wiley.

Higgins, E. T., & Kruglanski, A. W. (Eds.). (1996). *Social psychology: Handbook of basic principles.* New York: Guilford.

Hildebrand, K. (1991). *The third reich.* London: Routledge.

Himmelweit, H. T. (1990). Societal psychology: Implications and scope. In H. T. Himmelweit & G. Gaskell (Eds.), *Societal psychology* (pp. 17-45). Newbury Park, CA: Sage.

Himmelweit, H. T., & Gaskell, G. (Eds.). (1990). *Societal psychology.* Newbury Park, CA: Sage.

Hinsz, V. B., Tindale, R. S., & Vollrath, D. A. (1997). The emerging conceptualization of groups as information processors. *Psychological Bulletin, 121,* 43-64.

Hirshberg, M. S. (1993). The self-perpetuating national self-image: Cognitive biases in perceptions of international interventions. *Political Psychology, 14,* 77-98.

Hoebel, E. A. (1960). The nature of culture. In H. L. Shapiro (Ed.), *Man, culture, and society* (pp. 168-181). New York: Oxford University Press.

Hofman, J. E. (1970). The meaning of being a Jew in Israel. An analysis of ethnic identity. *Journal of Personality and Social Psychology, 15,* 196-202.

Hogg, M. A., & Abrams, D. (1988). *Social identifications: A social psychology of intergroup relations and group processes.* London: Routledge.

Hogg, M. A., & Abrams, D. (1993). Towards a single-process uncertainty-reduction model of social motivation in groups. In M. A. Hogg & D. Abrams (Eds.), *Group motivation: Social psychological perspectives* (pp. 173-190). New York: Harvester Wheatsheaf.

Hogg, M. A., Hardie, E. A., & Reynolds, K. J. (1995). Prototypical similarity, self-categorization, and depersonalized attraction: A perspective on group cohesiveness. *European Journal of Social Psychology, 25,* 159-177.

Hogg, M. A., & Mullin, B. A. (1999). Joining groups to reduce uncertainty: Subjective uncertainty reduction and group identification. In D. Abrams & M. A. Hogg (Eds.), *Social identity and social cognition* (pp. 249-279). Oxford, UK: Blackwell.

Hogg, M. A., & Turner, J. C. (1987). Social identity and conformity: A theory of referent information influence. In W. Doise & S. Moscovici (Eds.), *Current issues in European social psychology* (Vol. 2, pp. 139-182). Cambridge, UK: Cambridge University Press.

Holsti, O. R. (1971). Crisis, stress, and decision-making. *International Social Science Journal, 23,* 53-67.

Holsti, O. R., & Rosenau, J. N. (1984). *American leadership in world affairs.* Boston: Allen & Unwin.

Holsti, O. R., & Rosenau, J. N. (1986). Consensus lost: Consensus regained? Foreign policy beliefs of American leaders (1976-1980). *International Studies Quarterly, 30,* 375-409.

Horowitz, D. (1984). Israeli perception of national security (1948-1972). In B. Neuberger (Ed.), *Diplomacy and confrontation: Selected issues in Israel's foreign relations, 1948-1978* (pp. 104-148). Tel Aviv: Everyman's University. (Hebrew)

Horowitz, D. (1993). The Israeli concept of security. In A. Yaniv (Ed.), *National security and democracy in Israel* (pp. 11-53). Boulder, CO: Lynne Rienner.

Horsman, R. (1981). *Race and manifest destiny: The origins of American racial Anglo-Saxonism.* Cambridge, UK: Harvard University Press.

Hunt, L. (1984). *Politics, culture, and class in the French Revolution.* Berkeley: University of California Press.

Hunter, J. A., Stringer, M., & Watson, R. P. (1991). Ingroup violence and intergroup attributions. *British Journal of Social Psychology, 30,* 261-266.

Ichilov, O. (Ed.). (1990). *Political socialization, citizenship education, and democracy.* New York: Teachers College Press.

Inbar, E., & Goldberg, G. (1990). Is Israel's political elite becoming more hawkish? *International Journal, 45,* 631-660.

Inglehart, R. (1990). *Culture shift in advanced industrial society.* Princeton, NJ: Princeton University Press.

Iniguez, L., Valencia, J., & Vazquez, F. (1997). The construction of remembering and forgetfulness: Memories and histories of the Spanish civil war. In J. W. Pennebaker, D. Paez, & B. Rime (Eds.), *Collective memory of political events: Social psychological perspectives* (pp. 237-252). Mahwah, NJ: Lawrence Erlbaum.

Inkeles, A., & Bauer, R. A. (1959). *The Soviet citizen: Daily life in a totalitarian society.* Cambridge, MA: Harvard University Press.

Innami, I. (1992). Determinants of the quality of group decisions and the effects of the consensual conflict resolution. *Academy of Management Best Papers Proceedings,* pp. 217-221.

Ishida, T. (1989). *Japanese political culture: Change and continuity.* New Brunswick, NJ: Transaction.

Israel, J., & Tajfel, H. (Eds.). (1972). *The context of social psychology: A critical assessment.* London: Academic Press.

Jacobs, R., & Campbell, D. T. (1961). The perpetuation of an arbitrary tradition through several generations of a laboratory microculture. *Journal of Abnormal and Social Psychology, 62,* 649-658.

James, W. (1902). *The varieties of religious experience: A study in human nature.* New York: Longmans, Green.

Janis, I. L. (1982). *Groupthink: Psychological studies of policy decisions and fiascoes* (2nd ed.). Boston: Houghton Mifflin.

Jarymowicz, M. (1991). The self-distinctive traits as personal identity attributes. *Cahiers de Psychologie Cognitive, 11,* 679-695.

Jarymowicz, M. (1998). The self-we-others schemata: Distinctness and social identifications. In S. Worchel, J. F. Morales, D. Paez, & J. C. Deschamps (Eds.), *Social identity: International perspectives.* Thousand Oaks, CA: Sage.

Jennings, M. K., & Niemi, R. G. (1974). *The political character of adolescence: The influence of families and schools.* Princeton: Princeton University Press.

Jessop, B. (1974). *Traditionalism and conservatism and British political culture.* London: George Allen & Unwin.

Jodelet, D. (1991). *Madness and social representations: Living with the mad in one French community.* Berkeley: University of California Press.

Johnson, G. R. (1989). The role of kin recognition mechanisms in patriotic socialization: Further reflections. *Politics and the Life Sciences, 8,* 62-69.

Johnson, G. R. (1997). The evolutionary roots of patriotism. In D. Bar-Tal & E. Staub (Eds.), *Patriotism in the lives of individuals and nations* (pp. 45-90). Chicago: Nelson-Hall.

Jones, E. E. (1985). Major developments during the five decades of social psychology. In G. Lindzey & E. Aronson (Eds.), *Handbook of social psychology* (3rd ed., Vol. 1, pp. 47-107). New York: Random House.

Judd, C. H. (1926). *The psychology of social institutions.* New York: Macmillan.

Judd, C. M., & Krosnick, J. A. (1989). The structural bases of consistency among political attitudes: Effects of political expertise and attitude importance. In A. R. Pratkanis, S. J. Breckler, & A. G. Greenwald (Eds.), *Attitude structure and function* (pp. 99-128). Hillsdale, NJ: Lawrence Erlbaum.

Jung, C. G. (1959). *The collected works of C. G. Jung: The archetypes and the collective unconscious* (Vol. 9). New York: Pantheon.

Kammen, M. (1991). *Mystic chords of memory: The transformation of tradition in American culture.* New York: Knopf.

Kashti, Y. (1997). Patriotism as identity and action. In D. Bar-Tal & E. Staub (Eds.), *Patriotism in the lives of individuals and nations* (pp. 213-228). Chicago, IL: Nelson-Hall.

Katz, D. (1960). The functional approach to the study of attitudes. *Public Opinion Quarterly, 24,* 163-204.

Keis, N. (1975, September). The influence of public policy on public opinion—Israel 1967-1974. *State Government and International Relations,* No. 8, pp. 33-53. (Hebrew)

Kelley, H. H. (1968). Two functions of reference groups. In H. H. Hyman & E. Singer (Eds.), *Readings in reference group theory and research* (pp. 77-83). New York: Free Press.

Kelly, G. (1955). *The psychology of personal constructs.* New York: Norton.

Kendrick, D., & Puxon, G. (1972). *The destiny of Europe's gypsies.* London: Sussex University Press.

Kennan, G. (1947). The source of Soviet conduct. *Foreign Affairs, 25,* 566-582.

Kennan, G. F. (1960). *Russia and the West under Lenin and Stalin.* Boston: Little, Brown.

Kimmerling, B. (1993). Patterns of militarism in Israel. *Archives Europeenes de Sociologie, 34,* 196-223.

Kishon, E. (1988). *The journey book.* Tel Aviv: Sifriyat Maariv. (Hebrew)

Klare, M. T., & Thomas, D. C. (Eds.). (1991). *World security: Trends and challenges at century's end.* New York: St. Martin's.

Klimoski, R., & Mohammed, S. (1994). Team mental model: Construct or metaphor. *Journal of Management, 20,* 403-437.

Kluckhohn, C. (1943). Covert culture and administrative problems. *American Anthropologist, 45,* 213-229.

Knorr, K. (1976). Threat perception. In K. Knorr (Ed.), *Historical dimensions of national security problems* (pp. 78-119). Lawrence: University of Kansas Press.

Kogan, N. (1983). *Political history of Italy: The postwar years.* New York: Thomas Y. Cromwell.

Kohn, H. (1956). *Nationalism and liberty: The Swiss example.* London: Allen & Unwin.

Krauss, R. M., & Fussell, S. R. (1991). Constructing shared communicative environments. In L. B. Resnick, J. M. Levine, & S. D. Teasly (Eds.), *Perspectives on socially shared cognition* (pp. 172-200). Washington, DC: American Psychological Association.

Kruglanski, A. W. (1989). *Lay epistemics and human knowledge.* New York: Plenum.

Kruglanski, A. W., & Webster, D. M. (1996). Motivated closing of the mind: "Seizing" and "freezing." *Psychological Review, 103,* 263-283.

Krystal, H. (Ed.). (1968). *Massive psychic trauma.* New York: International Universities Press.

Krystufek, Z. (1981). *The Soviet regime in Czechoslovakia.* New York: Columbia University Press.

Kuhn, T. S. (1962). *The structure of scientific revolution.* Chicago: Chicago University Press.

Kurczewska, J. (1977). A study of ethos as history of ideas. *Polish Sociological Bulletin, 3-4,* 105-111.

Lahav, D. (1993). The press and national security. In A. Yaniv (Ed.), *National security and democracy* (pp. 173-195). Boulder, CO: Lynne Rienner.

Landau, J. J. (1971). *Israel and the Arabs.* Jerusalem: Israel Communication.

Lane, R. E. (1973). Patterns of political beliefs. In J. N. Knutson (Ed.), *Handbook of political psychology* (pp. 83-116). San Francisco: Jossey-Bass.

Larson, J. R., & Christensen, C. (1993). Groups as problem-solving units: Toward a new meaning of social cognition. *British Journal of Social Psychology, 32,* 5-30.

Lazarus, R. S. (1966). *Psychological stress and the coping process.* New York: McGraw-Hill.

Le Bon, G. (1968). *The crowd: A study of the popular mind* (2nd ed.). Dunwoody, GA: Norman S. Berg. (Original work published 1895)

Lee, I. S., Park, J. U., & Rhee, B. J. (1993). *North Korea: After collapse of socialist camp.* Seoul: Naewoe Press.

LeGloanes, A. M. (1994). On German identity. *Daedalus, 123*(1), 129-148.

Legum, C., & Legum, H. (1964). *South Africa: Crisis for the West.* London: Pall Mall Press.

Lenin, V. I. (1965). *Collected work* (Vols. 27 and 28). Moscow: Progress Publishers.

Lever, H. (1978). *South African society.* Johannesburg: Jonathan Ball.

Levine, J. M., Bogart, L. M., & Zdaniuk, B. (1996). Impact of anticipated group membership on cognition. In R. M. Sorentino & E. T. Higgins (Eds.), *Handbook of motivation and cognition* (Vol. 3, pp. 531-569). New York: Guilford.

Levine, J. M., & Moreland, R. L. (1990). Progress in small group research. *Annual Review of Psychology, 41,* 585-634.

Levine, J. M., & Moreland, R. L. (1991). Culture and socialization in work groups. In L. B. Resnick, J. M. Levine, & S. D. Teasley (Eds.), *Perspectives on socially shared cognition* (pp. 257-279). Washington, DC: American Psychological Association.

Levine, J. M., & Moreland, R. L. (1994). Group socialization: Theory and research. In W. Stroebe & M. Hewstone (Eds.), *European review of social psychology* (Vol. 5, pp. 305-336). Chichester, UK: Wiley.

Levine, J. M., Resnick, L. B., & Higgins, E. T. (1993). Social foundations of cognition. *Annual Review of Psychology, 44,* 585-612.

LeVine, R. A., & Campbell, D. T. (1972). *Ethnocentrism: Theories of conflict, attitudes, and group behavior.* New York: John Wiley.

Levinson, D. J. (1964). Idea systems in the individual and in society. In G. K. Zollschan & W. Hirsch (Eds.), *Explorations in social change* (pp. 297-318). New York: Houghton Mifflin.

Levy, S. (1988, March 25). Ingrained Israeli attitudes to the areas. *The Jerusalem Post.*

Levy, S., Levinsohn, H., & Katz, E. (1993). *Beliefs, observances and social interaction among Israeli Jews.* Jerusalem: The Louis Guttman Israel Institute of Applied Social Research.

Lewin, K. (1936). *Principles of topological psychology.* New York: McGraw-Hill.

Lewin, K. (1947). Frontiers in group dynamics. *Human Relations, 1,* 5-41.

Lewin, K. (1948). *Resolving social conflicts.* New York: Harper & Row.

Lewin, K. (1951). *Field theory in social science.* New York: Harper.

Lieberman, E. J. (1964). Threat and assurance in the conduct of conflict. In R. Fisher (Ed.), *International conflict and behavioral science* (pp. 110-122). New York: Basic Books.

Liebman, C. (1978). Myth, tradition, and values in Israeli society. *Midstream, 24,* 44-53.

Liebman, C. S., & Don-Yehiya, E. (1983). *Civil religion in Israel: Traditional Judaism and political culture in the Jewish state.* Berkeley: University of California Press.

Lincoln, B. (1989). *Discourse and the construction of society: Comparative studies of myth, ritual, and classification.* New York: Oxford University Press.

Lira, E. (1997). Remembering: Passing back through the heart. In J. W. Pennebaker, D. Paez, & B. Rime (Eds.), *Collective memory of political events: Social psychological perspectives* (pp. 223-235). Mahwah, NJ: Lawrence Erlbaum.

Lott, A. J., & Lott, B. E. (1965). Group cohesiveness as interpersonal attraction: A review of relationships with antecedent and consequent variables. *Psychological Bulletin, 64,* 259-309.

Luke, A. (1988). *Literacy, textbooks, and ideology.* London: Falmer.

Lukes, S. (1973). *Emile Durkheim: His life and work.* London: Allen Lane—The Penguin Press.

Lustick, I. (1982). *Arabs in the Jewish State.* Austin: University of Texas Press.

Mackie, R. R. (Ed.). (1977). *Vigilance: Theory, operational performance, and physiological correlates.* New York: Plenum.

Mannheim, K. (1952). *Ideology and utopia.* New York: Harcourt, Brace.

Markus, H., & Zajonc, R. B. (1985). The cognitive perspective in social psychology. In G. Lindzey & E. Aronson (Eds.), *Handbook of social psychology* (3rd ed., Vol. 1, pp. 137-230). New York: Random House.

Marmullaku, R. (1975). *Albania and the Albanians.* London: C. Hurst.

Martindale, D. A. (1960). *American social structure: Historical antecedents and contemporary analysis.* New York: Appleton-Century-Crafts.

Maslow, A. H. (1970). *Motivation and personality* (2nd ed.). New York: Harper & Row.

McClelland, D. C. (1961). *The achieving society.* New York: Free Press.

McClosky, H., & Zaller, J. (1984). *The American ethos: Public attitudes toward capitalism and democracy.* Cambridge, MA: Harvard University Press.

McDougall, W. (1908). *An introduction to social psychology.* London: Methuen.

McDougall, W. (1920). *The group mind.* New York: G. P. Putnam.

McDougall, W. (1939). *The group mind* (2nd ed.). Cambridge, UK: Cambridge University Press.

McGuire, W. J. (1964). Inducing resistance to persuasion: Some contemporary approaches. In L. Berkowitz (Ed.), *Advances in experimental social psychology* (Vol. 1, pp. 191-220). New York: Academic Press.

McGuire, W. J. (1973). The Yin and Yang of progress in social psychology. *Journal of Personality and Social Psychology, 26,* 446-456.

McGuire, W. J. (1986). The vicissitudes of attitudes and similar representational constructs in 20th century psychology. *European Journal of Social Psychology, 16,* 89-130.

McKitrick, E. L. (Ed.). (1963). *Slavery defended: The views of the old South.* Englewood Cliffs, NJ: Prentice Hall.

Mead, G. H. (1934). *Mind, self, and society.* Chicago: University of Chicago Press.

Mead, G. H. (1956). *The social psychology of George Herbert Mead.* Chicago: University of Chicago Press.

Medin, T. (1990). *Cuba: The shaping of revolutionary consciousness.* Boulder, CO: Lynne Rienner.

Meir, G. (1973). *A land of our own.* New York: G. P. Putnam.

Merton, R. K. (1957). *Social theory and social structure.* New York: Free Press.

Mesa-Lago, C. (1976). Social security stratification and inequality in Mexico. In J. W. Wilkie, M. C. Meyer, & E. M. deWilkie (Eds.), *Contemporary Mexico* (pp. 238-255). Berkeley: University of California Press.

Metcalf, D., & Richardson, R. (1986). Labour. In M. J. Artis (Ed.), *Prest and Coppock's The UK economy: A manual of applied economics* (pp. 266-332). London: Weidenfeld & Nicolson.

Mitchell, R. (1986). Team building by disclosure of internal frames of reference. *The Journal of Applied Behavioral Science, 22,* 15-28.

Moreland, R. L., Argote, L., & Krishman, R. (1996). Socially shared cognition at work: Transactive memory and group performance. In J. L. Nye & A. M. Brower (Eds.), *What's social about social cognition? Research on socially shared cognition in small groups* (pp. 57-84). Thousands Oaks, CA: Sage.

Moreland, R. L., & Hogg, M. A. (1993). Theoretical perspectives on social processes in small groups. *British Journal of Social Psychology, 32,* 1-4.

Morgan, D. L., & Schwalbe, M. L. (1990). Mind and self in society: Linking social structure and social cognition. *Social Psychology Quarterly, 53,* 148-164.

Morley, J. W. (Ed.). (1974). *Japan's foreign policy 1868-1941.* New York: Columbia University Press.

Morris, I. (Ed.). (1963). *Japan 1931-1945: Militarism, fascism, Japanism.* Boston: D. C. Heath.

Morrow, O. (1995). Church and religion in the Ulster crisis. In S. Dunn (Ed.), *Facets of the conflict in northern Ireland* (pp. 151-167). New York: St. Martin's.

Morse, A. D. (1968). *While six millions died.* New York: Aced.

Moscovici, S. (1973). Foreword. In C. Herzlich, *Health and illness: A social psychological analysis.* London: Academic Press.

Moscovici, S. (1976). *Social influence and social change.* New York: Academic Press.

Moscovici, S. (1981). On social representation. In J. P. Forgas (Ed.), *Social cognition: Perspectives on everyday understanding* (p. 181-209). London: Academic Press.

Moscovici, S. (1982). The coming era of representation. In J. P. Codol & J. P. Leyens (Eds.), *Cognitive analysis of social behavior* (pp. 115-150). The Hague: Nijhoff.

Moscovici, S. (1984). The phenomenon of social representations. In R. M. Farr & S. Moscovici (Eds.), *Social representations* (pp. 3-69). Cambridge, UK: Cambridge University Press.

Moscovici, S. (1988). Notes towards a description of social representations. *European Journal of Social Psychology, 18,* 211-250.

Moscovici, S. (1993). Introductory address. *Papers on Social Representations, 2,* 160-170.

Mosse, G. L. (1964). *The crisis of German ideology.* New York: Grosset & Dunlap.

Mosse, G. L. (1966). *Nazi culture: Intellectual, cultural, and social life in the Third Reich.* New York: Grosset & Dunlap.

Mosse, G. L. (1978). *Toward the final solution: A history of European racism.* New York: Howard Fertig.

Mugny, G. (1982). *The power of minorities.* London: Academic Press.

Murdock, G. P. (1960). How culture changes. In H. L. Shapiro (Ed.), *Man, culture, and society* (pp. 247-260). New York: Oxford University Press.

Myrdal, G. (1964). *An American dilemma.* New York: McGraw-Hill.

Negbi, N. (1985). *Paper tiger: The struggle for a press freedom in Israel.* Tel Aviv: Sifriyat Hapoalim. (Hebrew)

Neuman, W. R., Just, M. R., & Crigler, A. N. (1992). *Common knowledge.* Chicago: The University of Chicago Press.

Newcomb, T. M. (1943). *Personality and social change.* New York: Holt, Rinehart & Winston.

Newcomb, T. M. (1961). *The acquaintance process.* New York: Holt.

Noakes, J., & Pridham, G. (Eds.). (1984). *Nazism 1919-1945: A documentary reader* (Vols. 2 and 3). Exeter, UK: University of Exeter.

Nordland, R. (1999, April 12). Vengeance of a victim race. *Newsweek,* pp. 35-36.

Nye, J. L., & Brower, A. M. (Eds.) (1996). *What's social about social cognition? Research on socially shared cognition in small groups.* Thousands Oaks, CA: Sage.

Nye, J. S., & Lynn-Jones, S. M. (1988). International security studies: A report of a conference on the state of the field. *International Security, 12,* 5-27.

O'Malley, P. (1990). *The uncivil wars: Ireland today.* Boston: Beacon.

Orasanu, J., & Salas, E. (1993). Team decision making in complex environments. In G. A. Klein, J. Rasanu, J. Calderwood, & C. E. Zsambok (Eds.), *Decision making in action: Models and methods* (pp. 327-345). Norwood, NJ: Ablex.

Ossowska, M. (1973). *The knight's ethos and its forms.* Warsaw, Poland: Panstwowe Wydawnictwo Naukowe. (Polish)

Ostrom, T. M. (1984). The sovereignty of social cognition. In R. S. Wyer, Jr., & T. K. Srull (Eds.), *Handbook of social cognition* (Vol. 1, pp. 1-38). Hillsdale, NJ: Lawrence Erlbaum.

Ostrom, T. M. (1994). Foreword. In R. S. Wyer, Jr., & T. K. Srull (Eds.), *Handbook of social cognition* (2nd ed., Vol. 1, pp. vii-xii). Hillsdale, NJ: Lawrence Erlbaum.

Oxford English Dictionary (Vol. 5, 2nd ed.). (1989). Oxford, UK: Clarendon Press.

Oz, A. (1976). *Where the jackals howl.* Tel Aviv: Am Oved. (Hebrew)

Page, F. (1915). *An anthology of patriotic prose.* London: Oxford University Press.

Parsons, T. (1951). *The social system.* Glencoe, IL: Free Press.

Pepitone, A. (1976). Toward a normative and comparative biocultural social psychology. *Journal of Personality and Social Psychology, 34,* 641-653.

Pepitone, A. (1986). Culture and the cognitive paradigm in social psychology. *Australian Journal of Psychology, 38,* 245-256.

Pepitone, A. (1997). Nonmaterial beliefs: Theory and research in cultural social psychology. In G. McGarty & S. A. Haslam (Eds.), *The message of social psychology* (pp. 252-267). Cambridge, MA: Blackwell.

Perez-Diaz, V. M. (1993). *The return of civil society: The emergence of democratic Spain.* Cambridge, MA: Harvard University Press.

Perlmutter, A. (1969). *Military and politics in Israel.* London: Frank Cass.

Perret-Clermont, A. N., Perret, J. F., & Bell, N. (1991). The social construction of meaning and cognitive activity in elementary school children. In L. B. Resnick, J. M. Levine, & S. D. Teasley (Eds.), *Perspectives on socially shared cognition* (pp. 41-62). Washington, DC: American Psychological Association.

Petty, R. E., & Krosnick, J. A. (Eds.). (1995). *Attitude strength: Antecedents and consequences.* Mahwah, NJ: Lawrence Erlbaum.

Pick, O., & Critchley, J. (1974). *Collective security.* London: Macmillan.

Pipes, D. (1983). A border adrift: Origins of conflict. In S. Tahir-Kheli & S. Ayubi (Eds.), *The Iran-Iraq war: New weapons, old conflicts* (pp. 3-25). New York: Praeger.

Poliakov, L. (1974). *The history of anti-Semitism.* (Vols. 1 and 2). London: Routledge & Kegan Paul.

Pollo, S., & Puto, A. (1981). *The history of Albania.* London: Routledge & Kegan Paul.

Pomfret, J. (1999, September 27). A communist ideology wanes, China searches for new beliefs. *Herald Tribune,* p. 1.

Ponomaryov, B., Gromyko, A., & Uhvostov, N. (1969). *History of Soviet foreign policy 1917-1945.* Moscow: Progress Publishers.

Popper, K. R. (1972). *Objective knowledge.* Oxford, UK: Oxford University Press.

Popper, M. (1998). The IDF as a socializing agent. In D. Bar-Tal, D. Jacobson, & A. Klieman (Eds.), *Security concerns: Insights from the Israeli experience* (pp. 167-180). Greenwich, CT: JAI.

Pratkanis, A. R., Breckler, S. J., & Greenwald, A. G. (Eds.). (1989). *Attitude structure and function.* Hillsdale, NJ: Lawrence Erlbaum.

Preston, P. (1978). *The coming of the Spanish Civil War: Reform reaction and revolution in the Second Republic, 1931-1936.* London: Macmillan.

Prifti, P. R. (1978). *Socialist Albania since 1944: Domestic and foreign developments.* Cambridge: MIT Press.

Pruitt, D. G. (1965). Definition of the situation as a determinant of international action. In H. G. Kelman (Ed.), *International behavior: A social-psychological analysis.* (pp. 391-432). New York: Holt.

Pruitt, D. G., & Rubin, J. Z. (1986). *Social conflict.* New York: Random House.

Pruitt, D. G., & Snyder, R. C. (Eds.). (1969). *Theory and research on the causes of war.* Englewood Cliffs, NJ: Prentice Hall.

Pye, L. W. (1962). *Politics, personality, and nation building: Burma's search for identity.* New Haven, CT: Yale University Press.

Quattrone, G. A., & Tversky, A. (1988). Contrasting rational and psychological analyses of political choice. *American Political Science Review, 82,* 719-736.

Raviv, A., Bar-Tal, D., Raviv, A., & Abin, R. (1993). Measuring epistemic authority: Studies of politicians and professors. *European Journal of Personality, 7,* 119-138.

Renshon, S. A. (Ed.). (1977). *Handbook of political socialization.* New York: Free Press.

Resnick, L. B. (1991). Shared cognition: Thinking as social practice. In L. B. Resnick, J. M. Levine, & S. D. Teasley (Eds.), *Perspectives on socially shared cognition* (pp. 1-20). Washington, DC: American Psychological Association.

Resnick, L. B., Levine, J. M., & Teasley, S. D. (Eds.). (1991). *Perspectives on socially shared cognition.* Washington, DC: American Psychological Association.

Reykowski, J. (1982). Social motivation. *Annual Review of Psychology, 33,* 123-154.

Reykowski, J. (Ed.). (1995). *Ordinary images of democracy.* Warszawa, Poland: Wydawnictwo Instytutu Psychologi. (Polish)

Reykowski, J. (1996). The levels of political thinking and solution of social coordination tasks. *Czasopismo Psychologiczne, 2,* 7-30. (Polish)

Reykowski, J. (1997). Patriotism and the collective system of meanings. In D. Bar-Tal & E. Staub (Eds.), *Patriotism in the lives of individuals and nations* (pp. 108-128). Chicago: Nelson-Hall.

Rijsman, J., & Stroebe, W. (1989). The two social psychologies or whatever happened to the crisis? *European Journal of Social Psychology, 19,* 339-344.

Ring, K. (1967). Experimental social psychology: Some sober questions about some frivolous values. *Journal of Experimental Social Psychology, 3* 113-123.

Roberts, J. M. (1964). The self-management of cultures. In W. H. Goodenough (Ed.), *Explorations in cultural anthropology* (pp. 433-454). New York: McGraw-Hill.

Roccas, S. (1996). *The effect of group and individual characteristics and their interaction on identification with groups.* Doctoral dissertation submitted to the Hebrew University, Jerusalem.

Rommetveit, R. (1974). *On message structure: A framework for the study of language and communication.* New York: John Wiley.

Rose, R. (1985). National pride in cross-national perspective. *International Social Science Journal, 37,* 85-96.

Rosenfeld, S. (1980, September, 10). Tranquil and divided in face of a torrent of hatred. *Ma'ariv.* (Hebrew)

Rothenberg, P. S. (Ed.). (1988). *Racism and sexism.* New York: St. Martin's.

Sampson, E. E. (1977). Psychology and the American ideal. *Journal of Personality and Social Psychology, 35,* 767-782.

Samuel, R. (Ed.). (1989). *Patriotism: The making and unmaking of British national identity* (Vol. 3). London: Routledge.

Sanna, L. J., & Parks, C. D. (1997). Group research trends in social and organizational psychology: Whatever happened to intragroup research. *Psychological Science, 8,* 161-267.

Savada, A. M. (Ed.). (1994). *North Korea: A country study.* Washington, DC: Library of Congress, Federal Research Division.

Schaller, M., & Conway, L. G., III (in press). From cognition to culture: The origins of stereotypes that really matter. In G. Moskowitz (Ed.), *Cognitive social psychology: On the tenure and future of social cognition.* Mahwah, NJ: Lawrence Erlbaum.

Schneider, D. J. (1991). Social cognition. *Annual Review of Psychology, 42,* 527-561.

Schneider, W. (1984). Public opinion. In J. S. Nye, Jr. (Ed.), *The making of America's Soviet policy* (pp. 11-35). New Haven, CT: Yale University Press.

Schwartz, B. (1991). Mourning and the making of a sacred symbol: Durkheim and the Lincoln assassination. *Social Forces, 70,* 343-364.

Schweid, E. (1985). *The land of Israel: National home or land of destiny.* Rutherford, NJ: Fairleigh Dickinson University Press.

Sellers, J. B. (1950). *Slavery in Alabama.* Tuscaloosa, AL: University of Alabama Press.

Shafer, B. C. (1972). *Faces of nationalism: New realities and old myths.* New York: Harcourt Brace Jovanovich.

Shalev, H. (1997, September 12). Natanyahu does not have solution to terror. *Yedioth Ahronoth.* (Hebrew)

Shamir, J., & Shamir, M. (1993). *The dynamics of Israeli public opinion on peace and the territories* (Research Report No. 1). Tel Aviv: Tel Aviv University, Tami Steinmetz Center for Peace Research.

Shawcross, W. (1974). *Crime and compromise; Janos Kadar and the politics of Hungary since revolution.* London: Weidenfeld & Nicolson.

Sheehan, B. W. (1972). Indian-White relations in early America: A review essay. In H. M. Bahr, B. A. Chadwick, & R. C. Day (Eds.), *Native Americans today: Sociological perspectives* (pp. 7-23). New York: Harper & Row.

Sherif, M. (1936). *The psychology of social norms.* New York: Harper.

Sherif, M. (1951). A preliminary experimental study of inter-group relations. In J. H. Rohner & M. Sherif (Eds.), *Social psychology at the crossroads* (pp. 388-424). New York: Harper.

Sherif, M., & Cantril, H. (1947). *The psychology of ego-involvements.* New York: John Wiley.

Sherif, M., & Sherif, C. W. (1964). *Reference groups.* New York: Harper & Row.

Sherman, S. J., Judd, C. M., & Park, B. (1989). Social cognition. *Annual Review of Psychology, 40,* 281-326.

Shils, E. (1972). *The constitution of society.* Chicago: University of Chicago Press.

Shimoni, G. (1995). *The Zionist ideology.* Boston, MA: Brandeis University Press.

Shweder, R. A., & LeVine, R. A. (Eds.). (1984). *Culture theory.* Cambridge, UK: Cambridge University Press.

Sidanius, J., & Pratto, F. (1999). *Social dominance: An intergroup theory of social hierarchy and oppression.* New York: Cambridge University Press.

Siegal, M. (1991). A clash of conversational work: Interpreting cognitive development through communication. In L. B. Resnick, J. M. Levine, & S. D. Teasley (Eds.), *Perspectives on socially shared cognition* (pp. 23-40). Washington, DC: American Psychological Association.

Simmel, G. (1955). *Conflict.* Glencoe, IL: Free Press.

Simon, H. A. (1976). Discussion: Cognition and social behavior. In J. S. Carroll & J. W. Payne (Eds.), *Cognition and social behavior* (pp. 253-286). Hillsdale, NJ: Lawrence Erlbaum.

Simonson, I. (1992). The influence of anticipating regret and responsibility on purchase decisions. *Journal of Consumer Research, 19,* 105-118.

Simonson, I., & Tversky, A. (1992). Choice in context: Tradeoff contrast and extreme aversion. *Journal of Marketing Research, 29,* 281-295.

Smelser, N. J. (1962). *Theory of collective behavior.* New York: Free Press.

Smircich, L. (1983). Organizations as shared meanings. In L. R. Pondy, P. Y. Frost, G. Morgan, & T. C. Dandridge (Eds.), *Organizational symbolism* (pp. 55-65). Greenwich, CT: JAI.

Smith, H. (1976). *The Russians.* New York: Quadrangle.

Smith, M. B. (1968). Personality in politics: A conceptual map with application to the problem of political rationality. In O. Gareau (Ed.), *Political research and political theory* (pp. 77-101). Cambridge, MA: Harvard University Press.

Smith, M. B. (1972). Is experimental social psychology advancing? *Journal of Experimental Social Psychology, 8,* 86-96.

Smith, M. B., Bruner, J. S., & White, R. W. (1956). *Opinions and personality.* New York: John Wiley.

Smith, R. J. (1978). The future of an illusion: American social psychology. *Personality and Social Psychology, 4,* 173-176.

Smith, R. J. (1983). *Japanese society.* Cambridge, UK: Cambridge University Press.

Smith, T. W. (1983). The polls: American attitudes toward the Soviet Union and communism. *Public Opinion Quarterly, 47,* 277-292.

Smock, C. D. (1955). The influence of psychological stress on the "Intolerance of Ambiguity." *Journal of Abnormal and Social Psychology, 50,* 177-182.

Smoke, R. (1975). National security affairs. In F. I. Greenstein & N. W. Polsby (Eds.), *Handbook of political science: International politics* (Vol. 8, pp. 247-362). Reading, MA: Addison-Wesley.

Smoke, R. (1984). *National security and the nuclear dilemma: An introduction to the American experience.* New York: Random House.

Smooha, S. (1978). *Israel: Pluralism and conflict.* Berkeley: University of California Press.

Sniderman, P. M. (1975). *Personality and democratic politics.* Berkeley: University of California Press.

Snyder, L. L. (1976). *Varieties of nationalism: A comparative study.* Hinsdale, IL: Dryden.

Snyder, M. (1979). Self-monitoring processes. In L. Berkowitz (Ed.), *Advances in experimental social psychology* (Vol. 12, pp. 86-131). New York: Academic Press.

South Africa 1977. (1978). Pretoria, South Africa.

Sperber, D. (1985). Anthropology and psychology: Towards an epidemiology of representations. *Man, 20,* 73-89.

Sperber, D. (1996). *Explaining culture: A naturalistic approach.* Oxford: Blackwell.

Srull, T. K., & Wyer, R. S., Jr. (Eds.). (1988). *Advances in social cognition* (Vol. 1). Hillsdale, NJ: Lawrence Erlbaum.

Stampp, K. M. (1956). *The peculiar institution: Slavery in the ante-bellum South.* New York: Vintage.

Stangor, C., & Schaller, M. (1996). Stereotypes as individual and collective representations. In C. N. Macrae, C. Stangor, & M. Hewstone (Eds.), *Stereotypes and stereotyping* (pp. 3-37). New York: Guilford.

Staub, E. (1989). *The roots of evil: The psychological and cultural origins of genocide.* New York: Cambridge University Press.

Stein, H. F. (1978). Judaism and the group-fantasy of martydom: The psychodynamic paradox of survival through persecution. *Journal of Psychohistory, 6,* 151-210.

Stein, H. F. (1985). Psychological complementarity in Soviet-American relations. *Political Psychology, 6,* 249-261.

Stern, P. C. (1995). Why do people sacrifice for their nations? *Political Psychology, 16,* 117-235.

Stone, R. A. (1982). *Social change in Israel.* New York: Praeger.

Stryker, S. (1989). The two psychologies: Additional thoughts. *Social Forces, 68,* 45-54.

Sullivan, J. L., Fried, A., & Dietz, M. G. (1992). Patriotism, politics, and the presidential elections of 1988. *American Journal of Political Science, 36,* 200-234.

Sumner, W. G. (1906). *Folkways,* New York: Mentor Book.

Swidler, A., & Arditi, J. (1994). The new sociology of knowledge. *Annual Review of Sociology, 20,* 305-329.

Tajfel, H. (1978). Social categorization, social identity, and social comparison. In
    H. Tajfel (Ed.), *Differentiation between social groups* (pp. 61-76). London: Aca-
    demic Press.
Tajfel, H. (1981). *Human groups and social categories: Studies in social psychology.*
    Cambridge, UK: Cambridge University Press.
Tajfel, H. (1982). *Social identity and intergroup relations.* Cambridge, UK: Cam-
    bridge University Press.
Tajfel, H. (1984). Intergroup relations, social myths, and social justice in social psy-
    chology. In H. Tajfel (Ed.), *The social dimension: European developments in social
    psychology* (Vol. 2, pp. 695-715). Cambridge, UK: Cambridge University Press.
Tajfel, H., & Turner, J. C. (1979). An integrative theory of intergroup conflict. In
    W. G. Austin & S. Worchel (Eds.), *The social psychology of intergroup relations*
    (pp. 33-47). Monterey, CA: Brooks/Cole.
Tajfel, H., & Turner, J. C. (1986). The social identity theory of intergroup relations. In
    S. Worchel & W. G. Austin (Eds.), *Psychology of intergroup relations* (pp.7-24).
    Monterey, CA: Brooks/Cole.
Tannenbaum, E. R. (1972). *Fascism in Italy: Society and culture, 1922-1945.* New
    York: Basic Books.
Tannenbaum, F. (1945). On certain characteristics of American democracy. *Political
    Science Quarterly, 60,* 343-350.
Tarde, G. (1969). *On communication and social influence: Selected papers.* Chicago:
    University of Chicago Press.
Taylor, S. W. (1998). The social being in social psychology. In D. T. Gilbert, S. T.
    Fiske, & G. Lindzey (Eds.), *The handbook of social psychology* (4th ed., Vol. 1,
    pp. 58-95). Boston, MA: McGraw-Hill.
Terry, D. J., Hogg, M. A., & Duck, J. M. (1999). Group membership, social identity,
    and attitudes. In D. Abrams & M. A. Hogg (Eds.), *Social identity and social cogni-
    tion* (pp. 280-314). Oxford, UK: Blackwell.
Tetlock, P. E. (1989). Structure and function in political belief systems. In A. R.
    Pratkanis, S. J. Breckler, & A. G. Greenwald (Eds.), *Attitude structure and func-
    tion* (pp. 129-152). Hillsdale, NJ: Lawrence Erlbaum.
Thomas, W. I., & Znaniecki, F. (1918). *The Polish peasant in Europe and America*
    (Vol. 1). Boston: Badger.
Tsunoda, R., de Bary, T., & Kenne, D. (1958). *Sources of Japanese tradition.* New
    York: Columbia University Press.
Turner, J. C. (1982). Towards a cognitive redefinition of the social group. In H. Tajfel
    (Ed.), *Social identity and intergroup relations* (pp. 15-40). Cambridge, UK: Cam-
    bridge University Press.
Turner, J. C. (1991). *Social influence.* Pacific Grove, CA: Brooks/Cole.
Turner, J. C. (1999). Some current issues in research on social identity and self-
    categorization theories. In N. Ellemers, R. Spears, & B. Dosje (Eds.), *Social iden-
    tity* (pp. 6-34). Oxford, UK: Blackwell.
Turner, J. C., Hogg, M. A., Oakes, P. J., Reicher, S. D., & Wetherell, M. S. (1987).
    Rediscovering the social group: A self-categorizing theory. Oxford, UK:
    Blackwell.

Tversky, A., & Kahneman, D. (1991). Loss aversion riskless choice: A reference-dependent model. *Quarterly Journal of Economics, 106,* 1040-1061.

Urian, D. (1997). *The Arab in Israeli drama and theatre.* Amsterdam: Harwood.

van der Stoel, M. (1988). Breaking the laager: Two track Western policy toward South Africa. In G. F. Treverton (Ed.), *Europe, America, and South Africa* (pp. 49-76). New York: Council on Foreign Relations.

van Zyl Slabbert, F. (1989). *The system and the struggle: Reform, revolt, and reaction in South Africa.* Johannesburg, South Africa: Jonathan Ball.

Vertzberger, Y. (1991). *The world in their minds.* Palo Alto, CA: Stanford University Press.

Vital, D. (1982). *Zionism: The formative years.* Oxford, UK: Clarendon Press.

Volkan, V. D. (1996). Bosnia-Herzegovina: Ancient fuel of a modern inferno. *Mind and Human Interaction, 7,* 110-127.

Volkan, V. D., & Itzkowitz, N. (1993). "Istanbul, not Constantinople": The Western world's view of "the Turks." *Mind and Human Interaction, 4,* 129-140.

Vygotsky, L. S. (1962). *Thought and language.* Cambridge: MIT Press.

Waever, O., Buzan, B., Kelstrup, M., & Lemaitre, P. (1993). *Identity, migration, and the new security agenda in Europe.* London: Pinter.

Walsh, J. P., & Fahey, L. (1986). The role of negotiated belief structures in strategy making. *Journal of Management, 12,* 325-338.

Walsh, J. P., Henderson, C. M., & Deighton, J. (1988). Negotiated belief structures and decision performance: An empirical investigation. *Organizational Behavior and Human Decision Processes, 42,* 194-216.

Weber, M. (1958). *The Protestant ethic and the spirit of capitalism.* New York: Scribner. (originally published 1904)

Wegner, D. M. (1987). Transactive memory: A contemporary analysis of the group mind. In B. Mullen & G. R. Goethals (Eds.), *Theories of group behavior* (pp. 185-208). New York: Springer-Verlag.

Weick, K. E., & Gilfillan, D. P. (1971). Fate of arbitrary traditions in a laboratory microculture. *Journal of Personality and Social Psychology, 17,* 179-191.

Weimer, W. B. (1979). *Psychology and the conceptual foundations of science.* Hillsdale, NJ: Lawence Erlbaum.

Welch, W. (1970). *American images of Soviet foreign policy.* New Haven, CT: Yale University Press.

Weller, S. C. (1987). Shared knowledge, intracultural variation, and knowledge aggregation. *American Behavioral Scientist, 31,* 178-193.

White, R. H. (1984). *Fearful warriors: A psychological profile of U.S.-Soviet relations.* New York: Free Press.

White, R. W. (1959). Motivation reconsidered: The concept of competence. *Psychological Review, 66,* 297-333.

White, S. (1974). *Political culture and Soviet politics.* London: Macmillan.

White, S., Gill, G., & Slider, D. (1993). *The politics of transition: Shaping a post-Soviet future.* Cambridge, UK: Cambridge University Press.

Wichert, S. (1994). *Northern Ireland since 1945.* London: Longman.

Williams, R. M. (1970). *American society* (3rd ed.). New York: Knopf.

Wilson, J. Q., & Hernstein, R. J. (1985). *Crime and human nature.* New York: Simon & Schuster.

Wilson, M., & Canter, D. (1993). Shared concepts in group decision making: A model for decisions based on qualitative data. *British Journal of Social Psychology, 32,* 159-172.

Winograd, T. (1972). Understanding natural language. *Cognitive Psychology, 3,* 1-191.

Wistrich, R. (1985). *Hitler's apocalypse: Jews and the Nazi legacy.* London: Weidenfeld & Nicolson.

Wittenbrink, B., & Henly, J. R. (1996). Creating social reality: Informational social influence and the content of stereotypic beliefs. *Personality and Social Psychology Bulletin, 22,* 598-610.

Wood, F. G. (1970). *Black scare: The racist response to emancipation and reconstruction.* Berkeley: University of California Press.

Worchel, S. (1999). *Written in blood: Ethic identity and the struggle for human harmony.* New York: Worth.

Wundt, W. (1916). *Elements of folk psychology.* London: Allen & Unwin.

Wyer, R. S., Jr., & Srull, T. K. (1980). The processing of social stimulus information: A conceptual integration. In R. Hastie, T. M. Ostrom, E. B. Ebbesen, R. S. Wyer, R. S. Hamilton, & D. E. Carston (Eds.), *Person memory: The cognitive basis of social perception* (pp. 227-300). Hillsdale, NJ: Lawrence Erlbaum.

Wyer, R. S., & Srull, T. K. (Eds.). (1984). *Handbook of social cognition* (Vols. 1-3), Hillsdale, NJ: Lawrence Erlbaum.

Wyer, R. S., Jr., & Srull, T. K. (1986). Human cognition in its social context. *Psychological Review, 93,* 322-359.

Wyer, R. S., Jr., & Srull, T. K. (Eds.). (1994). *Handbook of social cognition* (2nd ed., Vols. 1-2). Hillsdale, NJ: Lawrence Erlbaum.

Yaar, E., Hermann, T., & Nadler, A. (1995). *The Israeli-Palestinian process: The view of the Israeli public.* Tel Aviv: Tel Aviv University, The Tami Steinmetz Center for Peace Research.

Yang, S. C. (1994). *The North and South Korean political systems: A comparative analysis.* Boulder, CO: Westview.

Yaniv, A. (1993). A question of survival: The military and politics under siege. In A. Yaniv (Ed.), *National security and democracy in Israel* (pp. 81-103). Boulder, CO: Lynne Rienner.

Yankelovich, D., & Smoke, R. (1988). America's "new thinking." *Foreign Affairs, 67,* 1-17.

Zelinsky, W. (1988). *Nation into state: The shifting symbolic foundations of American nationalism.* Chapel Hill: University of North Carolina Press.

Zerubavel, Y. (1995). *Recovered roots: Collective memory and the making of Israeli national tradition.* Chicago: University of Chicago Press.

Zohar, N. (1972). *An image of the Arab in readers.* Unpublished M.A. thesis submitted to the Hebrew University, Jerusalem. (Hebrew)

Name Index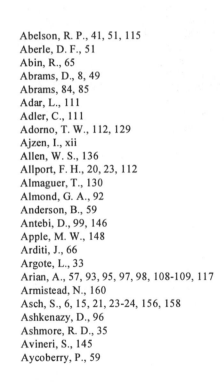

197

Subject Index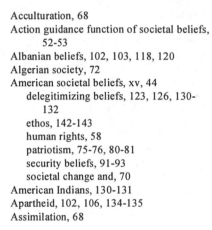

About the Author

Daniel Bar-Tal is Professor of Psychology at the School of Education, Tel Aviv University. He is also President of the International Society of Political Psychology for 1999-2000. His research interests are in political and social psychology, especially societal beliefs regarding conflict, delegitimization, security, patriotism, and the siege mentality. He is the author of *Group Beliefs* (1990) and is coeditor of *Social Psychology of Intergroup Relations* (1988), *Stereotyping and Prejudice* (1989), *Patriotism in the Lives of Individuals and Nations* (1997), *Security Concerns: Insights From the Israeli Experience* (1998), and *How Children Understand War and Peace* (1999).